Cybersecurity in Smart Homes

SCIENCES

Networks and Communications, Field Director – Guy Pujolle

Network Security, Subject Head – Rida Khatoun

Cybersecurity in Smart Homes

Architectures, Solutions and Technologies

Coordinated by
Rida Khatoun

WILEY

First published 2022 in Great Britain and the United States by ISTE Ltd and John Wiley & Sons, Inc.

ISTE Ltd
27-37 St George's Road
London SW19 4EU
UK

www.iste.co.uk

John Wiley & Sons, Inc.
111 River Street
Hoboken, NJ 07030
USA

www.wiley.com

Library of Congress Control Number: 2022931518

British Library Cataloguing-in-Publication Data
A CIP record for this book is available from the British Library
ISBN 978-1-78945-086-6

ERC code:
PE6 Computer Science and Informatics
 PE6_2 Computer systems, parallel/distributed systems, sensor networks, embedded systems, cyber-physical systems
PE7 Systems and Communication Engineering
 PE7_8 Networks (communication networks, sensor networks, networks of robots, etc.)

Contents

Chapter 2. Smart Home Device Security: A Survey of Smart Home Authentication Methods with a Focus on Mutual Authentication and Key Management Practices

Chapter 7. sTiki: A Mutual Authentication Protocol for Constrained Sensor Devices   245

Corinna SCHMITT, Severin SIFFERT and Burkhard STILLER

1

Home Automation Solutions for SecureWSN

Corinna SCHMITT[1] and Marvin WEBER[2]

[1]*Research Institute CODE, Universität der Bundeswehr München,
Neubiberg, Germany*
[2]*MNM-Team, Ludwig Maximilians Universität München, Munich, Germany*

Today, many different devices are connected and form small networks that are an integral part of the Internet of Things (IoT) (Rose *et al.* 2015; ITU 2016). Such networks are typically designed for individual solutions to serve a particular purpose. In the private sector, the most common application of such networks are seen in smart home scenarios. Constrained devices (Bormann *et al.* 2020) are used to monitor environmental data in order to trigger actions depending on analysis results. Well-known examples are closing/opening windows and shades or activating/deactivating lights and fans. In literature such scenarios are counted to the IoT subarea of cyber-physical systems (CPS) and due to a close impact to the residents of homes a secure environments is essential.

SecureWSNs (Schmitt 2020) are a powerful framework supporting different hardware and operating systems in the data collection process. Furthermore, they provide many services to residents in order for them to monitor environmental data (e.g. temperature, brightness, and humidity) within their home. To control network access, a fine-grained access management solution is integrated alongside resource-specific security protocols for required communication of components. Until now the system only supports monitoring of environmental data and lacks integration and controlling of actors establishing a comfortable zone to live at home fulfilling the concept of a CPS (Pahl 2014). As involved components usually work wirelessly, it

Cybersecurity in Smart Homes,
coordinated by Rida KHATOUN. © ISTE Ltd 2022.

is necessary to have full control of the network itself. Therefore, a secure solution to integrate actors (e.g. fans or lights) communicating over different standards (e.g. Bluetooth or ZigBee (Schmitt 2019)) into the deployed network is necessary. Furthermore, only authorized users should have the opportunity to configure the devices accordingly.

This chapter summarizes the current situation, concerns and requests of smart home users, which are categorized and discussed to establish the design requirements for a SecureWSN establishing a prototyped CPS. Consequently, a SecureWSN is presented in detail with special focus on: (a) secure integration of two actors using different communication standards; and (b) handling the configuration of them while respecting privacy concerns (Porambage *et al.* 2016) of residents. In order to allow only network owners to integrate actors into the system, and configure them, a credentials check is performed on the gateway component CoMaDa. If this check is passed successfully, the network owner is able to integrate the actors into the CPS. Furthermore, configuration details can be specified. Here, thresholds can be set when an actor (e.g. fan or lamp) should be activated or deactivated. Such thresholds can be modified during runtime in order to react to requirements (i.e. still too warm) immediately and flexible. In order to check if the actor works appropriately, two graphical user interfaces are available. The evaluation provided in this chapter is a proof of operation. Overall, it has to be kept in mind that home automation solutions might introduce risks and threats to an existing system, but this is overcome here by: (i) integration of several security checks for verification of ownership; and (ii) providing the user with a detailed and step-wise introduction for setting the system up. Besides these, the home owner receives (iii) physical security for the home by putting lights on when not at home or automatically cooling down the interior if it is too hot or vice versa, as well as monitoring the total smart environment.

1.1. Introduction

Smart homes have been gaining increasing attention and have become more widespread by promising to deliver more cost-effective, energy efficient heating, enhanced security solutions, or autonomic adoption to personal preferences. Another driver is the ability to control the lights, media center and many other appliances without a switch but a smart voice assistant instead. Devices that enable these features are becoming more and more affordable, new product categories are yet to be developed and whole new product ranges to be explored. One such example is the "Ring Always Home Cam", an indoor drone, released by Amazon in September 2020 (Bünte 2020). This device monitors home security by patrolling the property room by room, notifying absent residents about potential security threats.

Home automation (HA) can be seen as being part of a smart home, allowing it to perform actions autonomously to fulfill specified goals such as keeping the temperature at a certain level, closing the windows when it rains, or dropping the shades when the sun shines. However, most of the commercially available product solutions leverage several drawbacks such as the requirement to use the vendor-provided cloud for controlling and automating devices or the incompatibility of different manufacturer appliances or protocols. The enforced cloud-connection, in particular, may deter those who are privacy conscious given the nature of the data collected and how it is used by the vendors is not known (Bernheim Brush *et al.* 2011; Dague 2017).

In order to enable monitoring and collection of environmental data, multiple sensors (also known as *nodes*) are combined to form a wireless sensor network (WSN). These WSNs are mostly built of constrained devices, meaning those with limited processing, storage and power resources. A SecureWSN (Schmitt 2020) is a framework consisting of three components: (1) The WSN component, which collects environmental data; (2) the CoMaDa[1] component, which configures and manages the deployed WSN and handles receiving data; and (3) WebMaDa[2], which provides the backend infrastructure of the framework and a web-based framework for mobile access. It makes it possible to create and maintain a WSN in a secure manner, enabling data gathering of multiple nodes within a network, featuring secure data transmission and additionally providing rich functionality for aggregating, monitoring, and visualizing the sensors data. WebMaDa follows the idea of a cloud-based approach but, due to its configuration in the WSN network, the owner has complete control of their network and settings without any involvement from the WebMaDa administrator, including the "right to be forgotten" if requested. Thus, WebMaDa is more secure than a classic cloud service provider. Additionally, if a user does not want to use or integrate a cloud connection, and does not rely on the remote service offered by WebMaDa, the system is also fully functional without the WebMaDa integration. Different node hardware running various supported operating systems (OSs) can be used to feed the system with environmental data, including temperature, humidity, noise or brightness measurements (Schmitt *et al.* 2013; Schmitt 2020).

The remainder of this chapter[3] is structured as follows: section 1.2 presents all required background knowledge for the home automation solution, HAIFA. This ranges from the characteristics of a SecureWSN where the solution is integrated, common communication standards and machine-to-machine protocols, the monitor-analyse-plan-execute-knowledge (MAPE-K) model that is applied, as well as hardware and libraries used. Section 1.3 presents insights into the design decisions for

---

1. Configuration, management and data handling framework.

2. Web-based management and data handling framework.

3. This chapter is based on the Bachelor Thesis (Weber 2020) submitted by Marvin Weber at the Ludwig Maximilians Universität München, Germany in 2020 and included in the SecureWSNs project (Schmitt 2020).

the realized home automation solution HAIFA for a SecureWSN. Here, functional and architectural requirements are specified, the envisioned architecture introduced and further decisions justified. Section 1.4 discusses the actual implementation of HAIFA, broken down into the requisite parts. In section 1.5 the implementation is evaluated before drawing conclusions.

1.2. Background

This section introduces the background information required to understand the design decisions made in section 1.3. First, the SecureWSN framework that the HAIFA is integrated into is explained. Second, important home automation concepts are introduced, including protocols for publish/subscribe mechanisms (i.e. MQTT and CoAP), the fundamental MAPE-K model for triggering interaction between sensors and actuators, and related hardware and projects.

1.2.1. *SecureWSN*

Figure 1.1 illustrates the different components and their involvement in building the SecureWSN framework to monitor environments in smart homes/buildings with constrained devices (Schmitt 2020). The collecting network is a WSN built of different types of constrained devices that use different operating systems – TinyOS, Contiki and RIOT OS (TinyOS 2021; Contiki-NG 2020; RIOT OS 2021) – and can be accessed via two components. These components are graphical user interfaces (GUI) called CoMaDa and WebMaDa, which offer the user an effective platform following the click mentality to configure and monitor the deployed network (Schmitt 2019).

For the developed home automation solution HAIFA, the WSN component is assumed to be a black box and only delivers environmental data such as temperature or humidity. These values are used as input for HAIFA to trigger actuators (e.g. a fan or lamp). Thus, in the following, only CoMaDa and WebMaDa are described in more detail, as these are the locations where the implementation of HAIFA is placed.

1.2.1.1. *CoMaDa characteristics*

The implementation of CoMaDa follows a modular approach meaning its functionality can be easily extended with new features using modules. In fact, some of its core features are provided by modules, including one used together with nodes that run the specific operating system, providing the configuration and deployment interface for them and making it possible to program the actual hardware. General configuration and monitoring is enabled through modules, including one that makes it possible to access and execute commands via a secure shell (SSH) connection and another that deploys an administration frontend by acting as a small web server. This frontend makes it possible to configure the nodes and to monitor and visualize their data and topology with diagrams. Only essential details of the design decisions taken for HAIFA are presented in section 1.3, answering the following two questions: How do modules work in general? How can these modules interact with one another? For further information, the reader is referred to Schmitt *et al.* (2013) and Schmitt (2020).

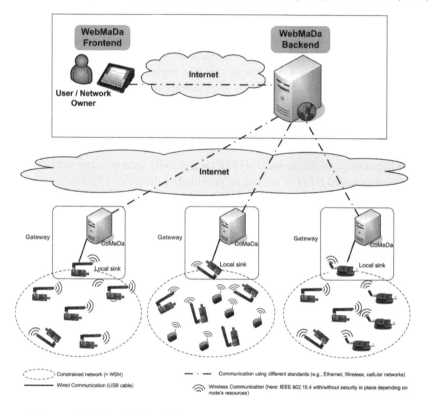

Figure 1.1. *The relationship between all components of a SecureWSN (Schmitt 2019). For a color version of this figure, see www.iste.co.uk/khatoun/cybersecurity.zip*

The *message bus* is a globally available notification system that allows any module to publish messages on it. Additionally, it enables subscription to certain message types that may be published on the bus. Custom-defined handlers are called by the message bus system when a new message is received, i.e. when any other participant of the bus published it. Example events are the `NewNodeMessage`, which is published whenever a new node is added to the WSN, or the `WSNModuleAddedEvent`, which is fired as soon as a new module is attached to CoMaDa. This system allows two different parts to react to specific events of the other one without having to know of or depend on each other.

The *WSN-Modules* support feature-extensions in CoMaDa. Each WSN-Module must extend the `WSNModule` class providing access to the actual WSN (i.e. the virtual representation of it) including its data (e.g. sensor values or the node topology) and to different services provided by other WSN-Modules as well. Several life-cycle methods are implemented (initialization, shutdown and post-shutdown) allowing the WSN-Module to execute necessary steps before actually running or shutting-down itself. Within the initialization of a life-cycle method a WSN-Module may register other WSN-Modules as dependencies, together with a callback handler. This dependency informs CoMaDa to call the registered handler as soon as the dependent WSN-Module is ready to use. Additionally, the handler gets access to the actual initialized WSN-Module allowing it to use available services. Each WSN-Module implements a run-method containing the actual work of it running on a separate thread.

The hypertext transfer protocol (HTTP) is generally used to serve websites on the Internet and so called *HTTP-Controllers*, provided by the `WSNHTTPServerModule` (HTTP-Module), enable CoMaDa to act as a web server, allowing it to serve a website. This website represents a GUI for the user to interact with the deployed network (e.g. granting access privileges or viewing received measurements). Furthermore, any other module may depend on it to add its own HTTP-Controller to the HTTP-Module. Each controller is responsible for one namespace, i.e. one specific uniform resource locator (URL). This namespace is defined by the WSN-Module which attaches the controller to the HTTP-Module. A HomeAutomationHttpController, for instance, could handle requests sent to the `/homeautomation/*` URL, including all sub-URLs (such as `/homeautomation/doSomething`). Controllers may interact with their module (i.e. the one that added them to the HTTP-Module). Other functionalities, like adding a new entry to the main menu of the administration frontend is also available. Additionally, the HTTP-Module is used by the `TinyOSHelperModule`, including configuration and deployment interfaces for the deployed nodes.

The *administration frontend* is written as an AngularJS JavaScript application (AngularJS 2021). The main purpose of the respective library is to add dynamic behavior to websites rather than just serving a static site built with basic Hypertext Markup Language (HTML). For that, AngularJS leverages the use of widgets, which support two-way data binding and are composed of an HTML template and a JavaScript component, also referred to as the model. This means the HTML-template may use variables of the model maintained in the JavaScript component and updates the template (i.e. the actual view/website) whenever data in the model changes. Additionally, the JavaScript component may also implement enhanced features such as handling clicks on a button of the template or sending HTTP-Requests to a backend, such as the one provided by the HTTP-Controllers of the HTTP-Module. The CoMaDa frontend itself is divided into several widgets with individual responsibility for the frontend. Those widgets can be added through the HTTP-Module, allowing any WSN-Module to add new widgets to the frontend.

Allowing flexible interchangeability of concrete implementations, the *dependency injection* pattern is used in some parts of CoMaDa. As a result, which implementation should be used can be decided during runtime. For this, classes that obtain dependencies by injection require abstract interfaces that provide methods for all required services. The actual injected objects for these dependencies can be anything, as long as they implement the required interfaces. The Google Guice framework (see the Guice Dependency Injection Framework in GitHub (2020a)) is used to configure and perform the dependency injection in CoMaDa.

The *WSN-Framework* is a component within CoMaDa that creates the actual WSNApp and attaches desired WSNModules to it. It is only one single class that contains the main Java method and additionally uses the Guice framework and a special configuration file to specify which WSN-Modules and implementations are required. The WSNApp is the concrete application managing the (virtual representation of the) WSN and comprises all attached modules and the global message bus, as well as all drivers and protocols required for the communication with the different nodes of the WSN.

From this point, the terms WSNFramework, WSNApp and CoMaDa may be used to refer to the entire CoMaDa component (formally representing a framework) in general.

1.2.1.2. *WebMaDa characteristics*

As CoMaDa is designed to configure the nodes, it was decided that only network owners have access to it. This decision contradicts the general request from users to also have access to the network while being physically apart from it. Thus, WebMaDa, the third component of SecureWSNs was developed over time in order to address this request for remote access. As illustrated in Figure 1.1, each CoMaDa instance is connected to one global WebMaDa server to continuously upload the sensor data of the WSN via CoMaDa (respectively the gateway built out of the last node in the WSN and the CoMaDa component). In turn, WebMaDa can manage multiple WSNs as they are distinguishable due to unique IDs stored in a configuration file in CoMaDa (Schmitt 2019).

WebMaDa's backend is written in PHP, while the frontend uses Smarty (a PHP render engine), the Bootstrap CSS, and the jQuery JavaScript-framework. The backend has access to a MySQL database (see Figure 1.2), which is used to store data of each WSN and additional data like network's credentials or information of registered users. The frontend GUI illustrates the monitored data in different ways and allows pulling data out of reporting interval. For network owners an option to filtering data or to adjust privileges in fine-grained manner is also integrated (Schmitt *et al.* 2016a; Schmitt 2019).

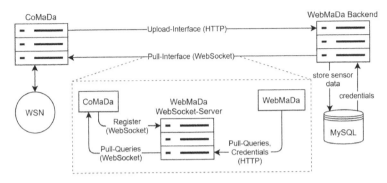

Figure 1.2. *CoMaDa and WebMaDa bi-directional communication (Weber 2020)*

In order to allow communication between CoMaDa and WebMaDa (e.g. for uploading data or pulling data), respective interfaces are integrated (Schmitt *et al.* 2016a; Schmitt 2019).

– The *Upload-Interface* shown in the upper part of Figure 1.2 enables CoMaDa to send data directly to WebMaDa by making HTTP-Requests to the upload interface/endpoint (i.e. a specific URL) of WebMaDa.

– The *Pull-Interface* solves the problem of CoMaDa not having a public (static) IP-address or domain. The WebSocket server (WSS) is used to establish a connection from WebMaDa to CoMaDa (see bottom part of Figure 1.2). The latter one registers itself at the WSS (whose domain is also public) – again by providing the credentials – and opens a WebSocket. Pull requests are sent from WebMaDa to its WSS using the open WebSocket to forward the query to CoMaDa.

The two aforementioned interfaces are managed and used by a module called the WSNWebModule. WebMaDa in turn handles uploads in a PHP script executed on requests to the Upload-Interface. It also uses the WSS using HTTP-requests for communication via another backend script, sending pull requests to CoMaDa. Although the interfaces serve a special purpose by default, they can be used to transmit any type of data making them interesting for the envisioned HAIFA communication flow, with some extensions.

1.2.2. *Communication standards*

As illustrated by a number of publications, several communication standards surround the IoT which foster the principle of machine-to-machine communication (e.g. IEEE 802.15.4, ZigBee, LoRa or NBIoT[4]) (Karl and Willig 2007; ZigBee Alliance 2012; Schmitt 2019; LoRa Alliance n.d.). As the intended home automation

---

4. https://www.gsma.com/iot/narrow-band-internet-of-things-nb-iot/, last accessed February 1, 2022.

solution requires a physical connection between several devices, this section introduces common protocols for a connection between actuators and gateways, as assumed in home automation.

1.2.2.1. *ZigBee*

ZigBee (ZigBee Alliance 2012) is a common communication standard for constrained networks targeting efficient resource consumption and short-range communication. It builds on IEEE 802.15.4 which represents the physical (PHY) layer and the medium access control (MAC) layer. The PHY layer is responsible for the actual data transmission over the physical radio channel (technical realization); the MAC layer enables reliable communication in a wireless network; this includes creating a personal area network (PAN) and assigning unique addresses (PANIDs) to devices that have joined the PAN.

The IEEE 802.15.4 standard defines two types of device (Institute of Electrical and Electronics Engineers 2020): (1) A *full function device* (FFD) is capable of operating as the (PAN) coordinator and is essential for starting and maintaining the network (2) A *reduced function device* (RFD) in comparison does not satisfy requirements to operate as a coordinator and is therefore intended for simple applications (e.g. light switches or passive sensors). Together, these two devices build a network, which can either follow a star topology or a peer-to-peer topology. In the first case, communication is only established between the PAN coordinator and joined devices. In the latter case, communication can be established between all devices within the range – except for communication between two RFDs.

The ZigBee standard (ZigBee Alliance 2012) extends IEEE 802.15.4 by two upper layers: the network layer (NWK) and the application layer (APL). The NWK layer coordinates routing between devices and organizes tree and mesh networks, while the APL layer provides the application framework hosting the application objects (i.e. the actual application) on ZigBee devices. As a result of this specification, ZigBee formally divides devices into three classes and therefore differs from IEEE 802.15.4: (1) the *ZigBee coordinator* function as a PAN coordinator and as a ZigBee router; (2) the *ZigBee router* is also a FFD controlling the personal operation space (i.e. in reference to IEEE 802.15.4, they act as a coordinator in their PAN) and is capable of route discovery within the network; and (3) the *ZigBee devices* (also called end devices) that are equivalent to RFDs (e.g. a light switch or fan). Linking the three device classes to a network usually results in a cluster or mesh topology. This means a ZigBee coordinator manages the network and can have connections to ZigBee routers and/or ZigBee devices. Furthermore, several ZigBee routers can be connected to one another and to several ZigBee devices to provide backup routes in case parts of the network break down or a ZigBee gateway gets lost and the PAN functionality must be taken over (Karl and Willig 2007).

ZigBee is most widely used in home automation systems, for example for smart bulbs, smart irrigation systems, smart door locks and many more components. ZigBee works well as a protocol for these devices, since none of them require high bandwidths and only provide a limited amount of energy, as many automation systems (e.g. a door lock or a surveillance camera) rely on the use of a battery. Further use cases of ZigBee have been demonstrated, e.g. the use of ZigBee in cars (Tsai *et al.* 2007), and also industrial and medical health care systems (Wheeler 2007; Lee *et al.* 2009) are increasingly making use of the protocol.

1.2.2.2. *Bluetooth low energy*

Bluetooth Low Energy (BLE), also referred to as Bluetooth Smart, is another standard for wireless personal area networks (WPAN). Compared to classic Bluetooth it was introduced to reduce power consumption in order to be used in constraint devices with limited resources, similar to ZigBee. Of a similar standard of traditional Bluetooth, BLE defines a network stack with several layers of which the two lower ones (the PHY layer and link layer) are implemented by the controller, which typically runs on the actual radio module. The host implements upper layers on the application processor and it may be extended by the application logic of vendors using BLE (Gomez *et al.* 2012; Bluetooth Special Interest Group 2019).

Unlike ZigBee, BLE is a point-to-point protocol, only allowing communication with devices within the direct physical range. Therefore, BLE is often used for smart devices that constantly require a connection to the same device, like smart watches or wireless headsets, which always have to be connected to a smartphone or computer to function properly. However, BLE is also used in other scenarios, like home automation, health care or indoor positioning (Gomez *et al.* 2012; Cabarkapa *et al.* 2015; Bluetooth Special Interest Group 2019).

1.2.2.3. *Publish/subscribe protocols*

Besides the aforementioned two communication standards, special protocols for machine-to-machine communication for publish/subcribe services were established over time. The most popular ones – MQTT and COAP – are briefly described here and a comparison is summarized in Table 1.1[5].

The *message queuing telemetry transport* (MQTT) protocol, defined by the OASIS[6], is a publish/subscribe protocol designed for machine-to-machine communication, especially for devices with limited performance, power supply, or bandwidth. All clients are connected to one MQTT server (also called the broker) and publish messages in topics. Topics are organized in a tree structure with subtopics

---

5. https://www.pickdata.net/news/mqtt-vs-coap-best-iot-protocol, last accessed February 1, 2022.

6. Organization for the Advancement of Structured Information Standards.

(e.g. sensors/kitchen/temperature or actuators/bedroom/light) and can be subscribed to by clients. If a new message is published, the server sends this message to all clients that have subscribed to the topic in which the new message was published. Usually, messages are only sent to clients after they have subscribed to a certain topic; except for messages with the retained flag set to true. The most recent retained message per topic is stored on the server and sent immediately when a new client subscribes to the corresponding topic. MQTT messages can be sent with three different quality of service (QoS) levels: $QoS = 0$, delivers messages once without confirmation, hence, it is suitable for networks with high reliability but also high transmission costs; $QoS = 1$, messages are resent if the sender does not receive an acknowledgment in time, which can lead to multiple deliveries of the message if the acknowledgment gets lost; $QoS = 2$, messages are delivered exactly once, which is ensured by a two step acknowledgment process. QoS level 1 and 2 are used where bandwidth is not limited nor expensive but where delivery must be ensured; level 2 is used when it's particularly important to deliver a message exactly once. MQTT runs over the TCP/IP stack but a separate MQTT specification – MQTT for sensor networks (MQTT-SN) – designed for use with non-TCP networks, like WSNs using the ZigBee protocol, was introduced in 2007. Apart from adjustments for characteristics of WSNs the MQTT-SN specification is very similar to that of MQTT. MQTT supports security mechanisms for authentication of users through a valid username-password combination. However, transport of MQTT is not encrypted by default, thus, passwords are transmitted in cleartext. In order to avoid this security breach, a transport layer security (TLS) encryption can be used; this additionally allows the client to authenticate the server by its certificate. Depending on the MQTT server in use, additional security instruments may be available. For instance, the Mosquitto MQTT broker supports restriction of user access to specific topics (Stanford-Clark and Truong 2013; OASIS 2019; Paessler 2019; Light 2020).

The *constrained application protocol* (CoAP) has also been designed for machine-to-machine communication and follows the representational state transfer (REST) approach with a request/response interaction model, thus, it shares similarities with the well-known HTTP protocol such as use of uniform resource identifiers (URI). CoAP differentiates four different message types: confirmables are messages that must be acknowledged with an acknowledgment message; non-confirmables do not need any confirmation and reset messages can be used to indicate processing of the message was not possible. Although the REST architecture is primarily designed for communication between a client and a server (unicast), CoAP offers additional multicast support which is often required by IoT applications. Unlike HTTP, with TCP CoAP uses a datagram-oriented transport protocol, typically the user datagram protocol (UDP). Additionally, the datagram transport security layer (DTLS) can be used to secure, i.e. encrypt the UDP transport connection (Bormann *et al.* 2012; Shelby *et al.* 2014).

Feature	MQTT	CoAP
Base protocol	TCP	UDP
Model used for communication	Publish-subscribe	Request-response, publish-subscribe
Communication node	M:N	1:1
Power consumption	Higher than CoAP	Lower than MQTT
RESTful	No	Yes
Number of message type used	16	4
Header size	2 Byte	4 Byte
Messaging	Asynchronous	Asynchronous synchronous
Reliability	3 quality of service levels (QoS 0: delivery not guaranteed, QoS 1: delivery confirmation, QoS 2: delivery double confirmation)	Confirmable messages, non-confirmable messages, acknowledgements, retransmissions
Implementation	Easy to implement, hard to add extensions	Few existing libraries and support
Security	Not defined or can use TLS/SSL	DTLS or IPSec
Other	Useful for connections with remote location, no error-handling	Low overhead, Low latency, NAT issues

Table 1.1. *Comparison between MQTT and CoAP*

1.2.3. *The monitor-analyze-plan-execute-knowledge model*

IBM introduced the monitor-analyze-plan-execute-knowledge (MAPE-K) model as a general architecture for autonomic elements, which are (parts of) systems that "manage their internal behavior [...] in accordance with policies that humans [...] have established" to fulfill high-level goals (such as, "keep the temperature in the bedroom at 20 degrees") (Kephart and Chess 2003). Figure 1.3 illustrates the model (i.e. the autonomic element) composed of several elements and the actual MAPE-K cycle, adapted to the developed HAIFA solution and specific components of a SecureWSN. The managed element represents a physical or software resource that is controlled by the autonomic manager. The element can be any target, from a low-level physical component (e.g. processor and storage) to a high-level software component (e.g. complex web server and home automation system). The manager consumes input of sensors (comparable to the SecureWSN nodes) and supplies them to the first phase of the MAPE-K cycle; in the end, this returns instructions for the actuators to manipulate (i.e. control) the managed element (Kephart and Chess 2003; Huebscher and McCann 2008).

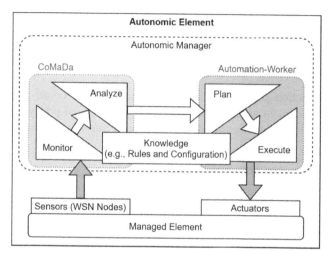

Figure 1.3. *MAPE-K model from IBM (Kephart and Chess 2003). For a color version of this figure, see www.iste.co.uk/khatoun/cybersecurity.zip*

The core of the model proposed by IBM is the actual MAPE-K cycle, which consists of the knowledge that may contain additional context and information – such as the prior mentioned policies – and the main four phases (Kephart and Chess 2003; Pahl *et al.* 2009; Pahl 2014).

1) **Monitor**: responsible for observing data (i.e. sensor measurements) that provide the required information for the remaining phases. Additionally, it processes the raw sensor data and provides comparable and normalized data (i.e. in reasonable and uniform units).

2) **Analyze**: data provided by the monitor may be analyzed, which means, e.g. checking two sensor values against each other or combining multiple sensor values (aggregation).

3) **Plan**: the planning component decides whether an action needs to be taken based on the analyzed data. This is where the knowledge is often required. It provides the configuration in the form of rules, thresholds, etc. and corresponding actions that should be taken if those rules apply or the thresholds are exceeded.

4) **Execute**: all actions that have been planned by the previous phase are requested to be executed by the executor.

Policies describe the goal of an autonomic element. Kephart and Walsh introduced a unified framework with three different types of policies, which are briefly summarized below (Kephart and Walsh 2004).

– **Action policies** simply define actions that should be taken if the element is in a specific state. They follow the form: "If x, then y", where y is a set of actions to be executed when all conditions from a set x are fulfilled.

– **Goal policies** define the desired state and the element has to choose suitable actions to achieve this state autonomously. Goal policies are defined on a higher level than action policies, as the human entity only has to configure what the desired state is, not how to achieve it.

– **Utility function policies** generate a goal policy based on all potential states. This allows the element to change the current objective (goal policy) depending on the current state by evaluating all possible states and returning the best one.

1.2.4. *Hardware and libraries*

As discussed in section 1.2.2.1, each ZigBee network requires a ZigBee coordinator which creates and manages the network. To provide this functionality, various devices ("ZigBee sticks" or adapters) can be used. One of the most popular adapters is the CC2531 from Texas Instruments[7]. Equipped with 256 KB ROM and 8 KB RAM, it is not very powerful but is strong enough to maintain a small ZigBee network and is also very affordable (less than € 10). However, if custom images should be flashed on the adapter, the CC Debugger (around € 35) has to be purchased as well; sets including both the adapter and debugger are available for around € 35. Another well-known adapter is the ConBee II from Dresden Elektronik[8]. Its specifications are comparable to those of the CC2531 but, with a price between € 35–40, it is slightly more expensive, even though no additional device is required for flashing custom images. All mentioned prices are based on the Amazon shopping platform[9].

Several libraries that provide an interface to communicate with ZigBee adapters are available. In the following, a selection of these is briefly described as they appear to be promising for the envisioned HAIFA and can be integrated smoothly into the existing infrastructure.

Zigbee2Mqtt and **Zigpy** natively support the two adapters mentioned, popular in smart home environments. ZigBee2Mqtt is written in JavaScript and runs within a Node.js[10] environment. It supports several different ZigBee adapters to create a ZigBee network and handles the communication with connected devices, respectively

---

7. https://www.ti.com/product/CC2531, last accessed February 1, 2022.

8. https://www.phoscon.de/en/conbee2, last accessed February 1, 2022.

9. https://www.amazon.de/dp/B07T77BFW1 and https://www.amazon.de/dp/B07PZ7ZHG5, last accessed February 1, 2022.

10. Node.js: Server-Side JavaScript Execution.

actuators. The network and its appliances are exposed via MQTT, hence the library also requires a MQTT broker to be used properly. Reading state information of actuators and controlling them is enabled through certain MQTT-topics. The main advantage of this library is the huge support of different ZigBee actuators. According to the documentation (Kanters 2020a), more than 1000 different devices are supported, including light bulbs, power switches, window shades, water sensors and many more. This means that for those devices, features such as adjustable brightness or color temperature can be set through the API, i.e. specific MQTT topics. An alternative library written in Python is Zigpy, which also supports numerous ZigBee adapters. It is also used by the Home Assistant implementation for their ZigBee integration and offers support for communication with various ZigBee devices. However, device-specific functions, such as with Zigbee2Mqtt, are not implemented or supported natively (Keller 2014; Chetroi 2020; Kanters 2020a).

In order for the MQTT protocol to be used by multiple clients, a MQTT broker is required (see section 1.2.2.3) (Light 2017, 2020). To host a broker such as this, various pieces of open source software are available. Two important ones are presented here as main representatives. **Mosquitto** is an implementation of the MQTT protocol, supporting the latest version 5 and implementing nearly all features of the standard. It is developed by the Eclipse foundation and available for all major operating systems including Ubuntu. Support for TLS encryption with certificates is available as well as authentication of clients either via the username-password combination or also via certificates. **RabbitMQ** can be seen as an alternative to Mosquitto (RabbitMQ 2020). The broker originally implemented the advanced message queuing protocol (AMQP) but, in the meanwhile, support for MQTT and other protocols has been added. However, until now, MQTT support is only given for the older MQTT version 3.1.1. The software is available for all important platforms, too, and like Mosquitto, various authentication mechanisms are offered. Since the CoMaDa framework is written in Java, a corresponding Java MQTT client would be necessary to connect to a MQTT broker. Such a client is the open source implementation from HiveMQ, the **HiveMQ MQTT Client** (GitHub 2020b). The client supports MQTT version 5 and provides an API with various methods to subscribe to topics or publish messages within them. Credentials may be provided by username-password combinations, alternative certificate-based authentication is supported as well.

1.3. Design decisions

This section presents the design decisions for the implementation and integration of the HAIFA, based on the background information given in section 1.2. First, the identified requirements are specified, followed by a brief description of the HAIFA architecture. Finally, integration into the mobile interface WebMaDa is explained, which enables the system to be controlled remotely.

1.3.1. *Requirements*

The envisioned HA solution HAIFA is expected to be integrated into the existing infrastructure of a SecureWSN. Thus, the infrastructure was analyzed in detail and necessary requirements (R) for the final design and architecture of HAIFA were specified. These requirements can be categorized into (i) functional and (ii) non-functional requirements. The second category also describe parts of the functional requirements (respectively requirements resulting from them) on a lower, more technical and implementation-related level.

1.3.1.1. *Functional requirements*

A HA by definition requires actuators in the system in order to change states in the local environment, based on decisions influenced by measurements or given thresholds. Changing a state can be done in two ways: either by changing the state of the actuator itself (i.e. switching a light bulb on or off) or changing the state of any device by the actuator (i.e. turning a power switch connected to a fan on or off). As these two simple examples show, actuators are available from many different vendors and they may use different protocols for communication with the bridge. The envisioned **HAIFA should support different hardware and protocols (R1)** by acting as a bridge for more than just one manufacturer and, thus, enabling interoperability between different vendors and device types. In general, it should be possible to extend support for other variants as well.

Integration of actuators (R2) is essential for the system to work and be useful, thus, all actuators connected to the HAIFA should be controllable and manageable by the user through the HAIFA. An actuator should be unregistered by default, which means no interaction with it is possible. By registering an actuator and assigning a name to it, it will be possible to control it and use it according to certain rules. This additional registration step ensures that the WSN-Owner is definitely aware of attaching a new actuator to the system. Only registered actuators should be controllable remotely through WebMaDa. Controlling an actuator means executing supported actions or commands on it, such as turning a light on or off, changing the brightness of the light or toggling the on-off state of a power switch.

A **rule-based configuration (R3)** may be provided and managed by the WSN-Owner (respectively the residents of the home in general) to define the desired behavior of the actual automation. The owner should be able to create rules that define conditions and actions. Conditions are composed of any sensor's value, a comparator, and a threshold; for instance: "if the temperature of node 3 is below 23 degrees". Additionally, rules should be pause-/unpauseable and time frames may be assigned to them to define certain time slots in which the rule is allowed to perform actions, e.g. "On Mondays from 8 am to 9 pm and on Fridays from 3.15 pm to 4 pm". The actions should be performed when all conditions are satisfied and they can be one of the available commands offered by any registered actuator. Furthermore, conditions as well as actions are not limited to one single node or actuator. Thus, it should be possible to add an entire set of conditions based on different sensor values as well as actions performed on different actuators to one single rule. Changes to rules (including editing, pausing/un-pausing or deleting them) as well as the history (i.e. timestamps) of the last checks and executions of them should be logged. These logs should be made available to the WSN-Owner through a user interface.

There are several use cases conceivable where **remote access to adjust rules and thresholds (R4)**, add new rules or control actuators is useful or required. Examples are adjusting the thresholds of a rule controlling the heater in a room or ensuring lights are turned off. Therefore, it should be possible to control registered actuators and mange rules remotely. WebMaDa should be used as the remote endpoint since it already comprises the data and its visualization of the deployed WSN, as well as a user and permission management system.

1.3.1.2. *Non-functional requirements*

Besides the functional requirements given in section 1.3.1.1, four more requirements were identified that are essential to ensure that the system is reliable and can function properly. These requirements are briefly described here.

In order to permanently save registered actuators (especially their assigned name), configured rules and their corresponding logs **storage (R5)** are required. Available storage options (such as databases, file storage, etc.) may vary from system to system, thus, the storage should be represented by an abstract interface while the actual implementation of it is interchangeable. WebMaDa is required to store data (namely available actuators, rules and the logs) as well. However, as it is a closed system responsible for multiple CoMaDa instances, interchangeability is not required here. Thus, the existing database used by the WebMaDa backend should also be used for the new HA data.

Since CoMaDa runs on devices with limited resources, the HAIFA must not consume too much storage. Therefore, stored **logs (R6)** on a CoMaDa server should be **cleaned up regularly**, keeping only the most recent ones. WebMaDa, on the other hand, is not that limited in terms of resources. Hence, no cleanup is required there, which means the history for the entire lifetime of a WSN can be looked up.

Actions, defined in **rules (R7)**, are executed when the corresponding conditions are satisfied. This requires some sort of periodic/regular check to determine whether the conditions are fulfilled or not.

In order to make the integration of configuration into the administration frontend (and WebMaDa) easier, all components within the HAIFA should be able to **convert**

themselves into a JSON representation and backwards (R8)[11]. This is required because JavaScript on a frontend can only handle JSON data objects. Moreover, Java has also integrated support of JSON data types. The JSON notation can also easily be used to store the state of actuators and the configuration of rules in the database, respectively the storage.

1.3.2. *HAIFA architecture*

Taking into account all eight of the above requirements results in the HAIFA architecture being realized, as illustrated in Figure 1.4. As HAIFA is required to be integrated into the existing infrastructure of a SecureWSN, and may be further extended by actuators in the future, the focus is on simple extension opportunities. Thus, HAIFA has been divided into several components and sub-parts, each of which has its own clear domain of responsibility, as outlined in section 1.3.2.1. More details about the flexible and expandable approach realized are given in section 1.3.2.2.

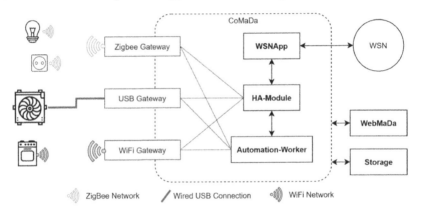

Figure 1.4. *High level architecture of the HAIFA model. For a color version of this figure, see www.iste.co.uk/khatoun/cybersecurity.zip*

1.3.2.1. *Components and structure of the HA module*

The HAIFA is comprised of several components with clear responsibilities, as shown in Figure 1.4. The core module for HAIFA is the home automation module (`HA-Module`) as it is responsible for the core task realized by the MAPE-K cycle and triggers the actuators based on the decisions taken. Thus, it needs to work together with the `Automation-Worker` to observe applied rules and the WSNApp, which

---

11. JavaScript Object Notation.

is responsible for getting the data from the collection points in the deployed WSN. In the following, we describe these parts from a design perspective and, in section 1.4, from an implementation perspective.

The **home automation module (HA-Module)** is the main entry point of the entire HAIFA, orchestrating communication with any other part of the WSNFramework, respectively CoMaDa and especially the WSN itself, and ensuring a properly executed start of the HAIFA. According to Schmitt *et al.* (2013), it will act as a WSN-Module and be attached to the WSNApp (i.e. CoMaDa) during the bootstrap process of the framework. Besides handling communication and data flow between the different modules, the WSNApp and all other components of the HAIFA, it is responsible for the startup of those other components and initializing any required dependencies. This includes loading all stored rules and registered actuators, booting the HTTP controller for the administration frontend, registering handlers for certain messages on the global message bus and, finally, starting the Automation-Worker. The sequence diagram in Figure 1.5 shows this startup procedure: initially, a client – usually the WSNFramework, which is responsible for the initial assemble and boot process to create the desired CoMaDa instance – starts the HAIFA by creating a new HA-Module. Next, the module leverages the storage to get registered actuators and stored rules and starts the above-mentioned components. The client may attach new gateways at any time. The HA functionality will be integrated into CoMaDa by HAIFA. This HAIFA will be one WSN-Module, thus, in the latter part of this chapter, the term HA-Module refers to the specific "entry" component, while the term HAIFA is used to refer to the entire system (i.e. the entire WSN-Module) in general.

Actuators are the devices with which the actual automation is physically performed. It may be any device, such as light bulbs or power switches. Technically, each actuator is represented by one single Java object which may be used by any other component of the HAIFA. All available actuators are held and provided by the core HA-Module. Each actuator supports the execution of at least one command. The HAIFA provides abstract interfaces for generic actuator types like lights or switches, while gateways provide their actual implementation, which may vary depending on the gateway.

Commands represent low-level, elementary actions which may be supported by actuators. In this case, low-level and elementary means that commands are not specific per actuator. Instead, each command describes a generic action that might be supported by multiple actuators and cannot be further simplified. Example commands are turn on or turn off, both of which are applicable for multiple devices. To allow additional customization commands may require one ore more arguments such as set brightness (value) where value would be an argument specifying the desired brightness to be set. The last command is, of course, not as generic as the two previous ones but still not only suitable for a single device.

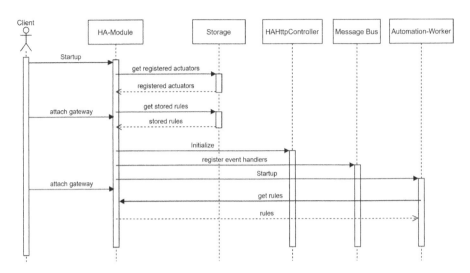

Figure 1.5. *HAIFA startup sequence*

The logic and functionality of how to (physically) control and manage actuators is not integrated into the core of the HA-Module because this approach would lack a clear separation of concerns and complicates two main objectives: concurrent support of multiple device, vendor and protocol types, as well as extending support for new actuators. Both would probably require code changes and logic adjustments in a component that should not be responsible for managing physical devices, since the HA-Module must be seen as the organizing part of the entire system, delegating low-level tasks to sub-components. **Gateways** are used to overcome this issue. A gateway is the connection between virtual representations of actuators, their corresponding physical device, and the HA-Module, respectively the entire HAIFA. They handle communication between those parts, also notifying the HA-Module whenever new devices have been added (by the WSN-Owner). As indicated in the sequence diagram in Figure 1.5, gateways can be attached to the module at any time (after it has loaded the registered actuators from the storage to recognize them). A gateway may act as the physical endpoint for connected actuators, e.g. by directly acting as or using a ZigBee coordinator (see section 1.2.2.1) and, thus, as the coordinator of a network with multiple actuators. However, gateways may also use additional (external) services to provide their functionality. Figure 1.6 shows how a client (again, this could be the WSNFramework) can create a new gateway and add actuators to it. The gateway in turn attaches itself to the HA-Module (retrieved by the client having access to it) and announces each new actuator. These are also added by the client, i.e. in this case mostly the WSN-Owner, who connects the physical devices to the gateway. The client may retrieve all actuators from the HA-Module and execute supported commands on them which are forwarded to the physical device by the gateway. This also shows that other components never interact with any gateway directly, as the HA-Module provides access to all available actuators. This abstraction allows all components to ignore the physical communication and connection since they work with implementations of abstract interfaces – actuators and commands – provided by the gateways.

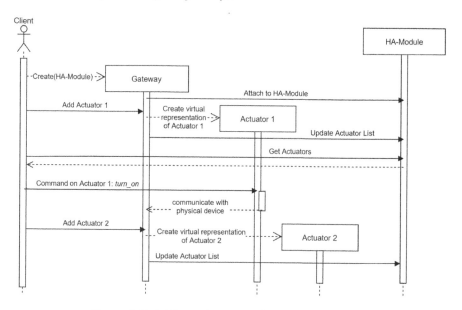

Figure 1.6. *Adding gateways and actuators to HAIFA*

Figure 1.7. *Overview of HAIFA hardware. For a color version of this figure, see www.iste.co.uk/khatoun/cybersecurity.zip*

In order to enable actual automation the WSN-Owner may create so-called rules following detailed instructions step-wise pointing out guidelines related to security issues that might occur. To ensure that only the WSN-Owner adds or modifies rules, credential checks are continuously performed and the AAA (authentication, authorization and accounting) principle from security fundamentals is applied (Boyd and Mathuria 2010). Generally, many different types of rules may be supported. They abstract the execution of actions, i.e. commands on actuators, combined with some sort of condition. While this HAIFA prototype only implements condition rules (see section 1.3.1.1) other types of checking the need for execution than conditions on WSN nodes, such as keeping a node's sensor value on a certain level, are thinkable as well. The abstraction is ensured by forcing rules to implement a certain interface and, thus, providing two services: one to check whether actions have to be taken (i.e. all conditions are fulfilled) and another to perform those actions on the actuators. The HA-Module provides the current list of active rules which are added, removed or changed by other components, such as the HTTP controller or through a remote WebMaDa instance via the WSNWebModule.

While actuators, commands and rules can be seen as the configuration part of the automation, the automation part is not yet provided by any component. It will be undertaken by the Automation-Worker, whose main task is to regularly check for all rules, whether any of them are required to perform actions based on the current values of the nodes in the WSN. If so, it uses the second service of the corresponding rules to do so. Additionally, providing access to all actuators and WSN nodes to the rules ensures their proper functionality and allows them to first decide if all conditions are satisfied and then to execute the necessary commands on the actuators. Finally, the Automation-Worker creates log entries for every check and every execution of the rules via the HA-Module. Figure 1.8 shows a sequence diagram of one iteration of the automation cycle and its interaction with the HA-Module and the configured rules. At first, the worker retrieves current setup rules, nodes and actuators and then checks if actions are required and, if so, lets the rules perform them. Both are enabled by providing access to the nodes and actuators. Additionally, the worker logs the results using the HA-Module, depending on whether an action was required and changes to actuators were actually made (for example, turning on a light that is already turned on would not result in changes).

As explained in section 1.2.1.1, modules may register additional **HTTP controllers**. The HA-Module should also provide such a controller to integrate itself into the administration frontend. It may be used to manage the automation rules, register or unregister actuators, execute commands on registered actuators, and provide access to the logs of the rules. All available endpoints for the user (WSN-Owner) to access and manage the HAIFA and how they interact with it are shown in Figure 1.9, including the HAHttpController for local (i.e. from within the network CoMaDa is deployed in) as well as the WSNWebModule for remote access via WebMaDa.

The WSNWebModule (see section 1.2.1.2) already exists and is responsible for the communication between CoMaDa and WebMaDa (upload and pull interfaces). To avoid duplication of code and features within the WSNFramework, this module should be used for required HAIFA communication which includes uploading registered actuators, rules and the rule logs to WebMaDa. Additionally, WebMaDa must be able to modify and add new rules and execute commands on actuators. Figure 1.9 illustrates how the `WSNWebModule` acts as a middleware for data transmission between WebMaDa and the `HA-Module`, respectively the HAIFA in general.

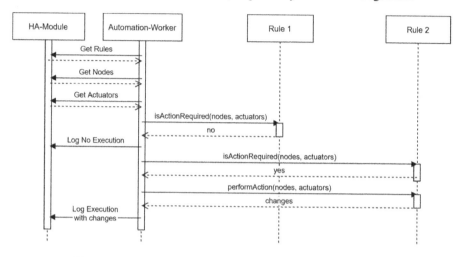

Figure 1.8. *One iteration of the* `Automation-Worker` *cycle*

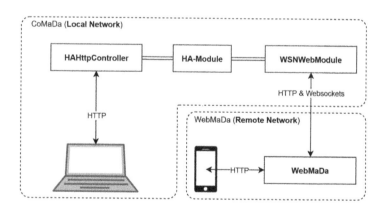

Figure 1.9. *HAIFA configuration and management endpoints*

In section 1.3.1.2 the need for a database/storage solution was explained. The original CoMaDa system has already been extended by an external (PostgreSQL) database enhancing logging possibilities and local storage of data (Ott 2017). In order to ensure interchangeability of the database system, the `HA-Module` only requires an abstract interface that defines required methods for operating as the `IHAStorage` (i.e. the storage interface used by the `HA-Module`). However, the reference implemented storage will be integrated into the existing database. This avoids multiple concurrently running database management systems in the background and data of all CoMaDa modules will remain in one single source of truth.

1.3.2.2. *Expandability support*

One of the main goals is to easily allow extending features for components introduced in section 1.3.2.1, or even exchange complete implementations of single components like replacing the PostgreSQL storage with a MySQL database for instance. Therefore, expandability in particular is supported and endorsed for the following three items for HAIFA.

– **Rules**: the abstract rule interface with services to check for necessary actions and execute them ensures that different rule implementations are supported and can easily be integrated into the system. In addition, only the management frontend endpoints (administration frontend in CoMaDa and WebMaDa) would have to be adjusted to create new rule types such as these. The `Automation-Worker` on the other side would not require any adjustments.

– **Commands**: adding new commands might become necessary when new devices with new functionalities are integrated into the HAIFA. Since the actuators (gateway implementations) take care of how to execute a command, new ones only have to be integrated into a globally available list of commands.

– **Actuators**: new types of actuators can easily be supported by introducing a new abstract interface for it. The gateway implementations need to provide actual implementations of them to make use of the new type.

Aside from these three items, gateways are the most important part in terms of flexibility and multi-device and multi-protocol support (especially interoperability of different automation device vendors). As they are only attached to the actual `HA-Module`, it is easy to implement new gateways or extend the support and features of existing ones. The only requirement is to satisfy the interface in terms of actuators and commands, more precisely, to keep the list of connected actuators up to date and to provide them as implementations of the abstract definitions to the `HA-Module`. All other components only interact with the devices through the consistent interface, never having to interact with gateways and vice versa.

1.3.2.3. *HAIFA ZigBee Gateway*

The realized HAIFA follows the concept of the gateway approach. This decision will mean HAIFA is prepared for the future, as support of different technologies becomes possible as long as they can be integrated into the infrastructure, respecting the defined requirements R1–R8. The following paragraphs present decisions taken for the final ZigBee gateway for HAIFA.

In order to get the most out of the single implemented gateway, the decision is mainly based on the general availability of devices. The Smart Homes Report 2018 shows that, in the UK, the Philips Hue[12] and Hive (Hive Home n.d.) together share 60% of the smart lighting market (YouGov 2018); both vendors use the ZigBee protocol for inter-device communication, common other vendors like IKEA or Osram rely on ZigBee as well.

Furthermore, ZigBee is better suited to HA scenarios due to the native possibility of using a mesh network topology. Since devices within an apartment may be distributed across several rooms, some of them may lack direct connection to the coordinator device (the bridge). Hence, other appliances can act as ZigBee routers to enable communication with the network for such devices, too. Thus, HAIFA uses ZigBee instead of Bluetooth Low Energy. Furthermore, the existing infrastructure of the SecureWSN is already using ZigBee.

We have decided to use the Texas Instruments CC2531 coordinator based on the simple fact that it is the most affordable solution. Initial costs for the adapter and debugger are approximately the same as for the ConBee II; if more adapters are bought in the future, however, the debugger does not need to be purchased again and the actual adapter is much cheaper. The CC2531 adapter and the debugger are shown in Figure 1.7, on the right. Appropriate hardware has to be used to test the implemented HAIFA and the ZigBee gateway. We decided to use two light bulbs because of their widespread use in consumer home automation. Additionally, one power switch is used as this type of actuator provides great flexibility in terms of controllable devices. All devices used are shown in Figure 1.7, on the left.

In order to communicate through the CC2531 adapter, one of the two libraries presented in section 1.2.4 should be used. Both cannot be integrated into CoMaDa directly as Zigbee2Mqtt is written in JavaScript and communicates via MQTT, while Zigpy is written in Python. The decision to use the Zigbee2Mqtt library is based on two reasons: (1) simple integration and (2) device support. Even though both libraries cannot be integrated directly into CoMaDa, it seems to be easier to integrate a MQTT client into CoMaDa to connect it with the library. In addition, Zigpy would also need some sort of integration bridge into CoMaDa. This would probably end up like a "Zigpy-to-Mqtt" component or similar, written in Python and also requiring CoMaDa

---

12. The authors are aware of the fact that attacks on the Philips Hue were successful, resulting in a takeover of the smart home's WLAN. But in the reported attacks this was done using the WLAN IEEE 802.11 and not ZigBee. Furthermore, it must be kept in mind that Philips Hue was used for prototyping only here and the bulb was configured in the way either use ZigBee or WLAN. Any other intelligent light bulb can be used as long as a specific gateway within the SecureWSN is programmed and integrated, making the total system independent of the vendor's gateway or application given the freedom of own security support and specification of boundaries.

to act as MQTT client. Zigbee2Mqtt natively supports many home automation devices including those shown in Figure 1.7. Zigpy lacks such an integration and would require adding support for each device manually.

The Zigbee2Mqtt library already supports MQTT. However, it would be possible to fork the existing repository and add an integration for the CoAP protocol. There are two reasons why this is not done. First, the MQTT approach is better suited to the CoMaDa concept. For now, only the HAIFA would use the MQTT client to access and control actuators. But there are potential scenarios where other WSN-Modules (or CoMaDa itself) may use this integration as well. For instance, it would be possible to integrate ZigBee devices (especially various sensors) as nodes into the WSN requiring a new driver to access devices via the Zigbee2Mqtt library. While CoAP does have a multicast support, MQTT and its topic system would work very well in such a scenario. Every interested module could just subscribe to specific topics of interest (such as values of connected sensors) or publish messages to control any device within the ZigBee network. The CoAP integration would require more logic to support this multi-usage. Second, it would mean additional effort to implement CoAP into the library while the MQTT solution already exists and works flawlessly. Hence, HAIFA will use MQTT instead of CoAP.

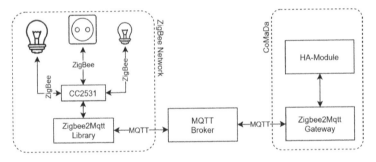

Figure 1.10. *HAIFA ZigBee gateway with communication flows*

Figure 1.10 illustrates the composed **HAIFA ZigBee gateway**. On the right side is the actual CoMaDa framework, where the **Zigbee2Mqtt gateway** communicates over an (external) MQTT broker with the corresponding library. The CC2531 adapter is used to maintain the ZigBee network, shown on the left side. This also demonstrates a not yet mentioned advantage of the architecture: since the library is a standalone application and not integrated into CoMaDa, both are locally independent. Hence, the ZigBee network may be set up in a completely different location than CoMaDa, such as in a garage while the CoMaDa server runs inside the house. The only requirement is that both are connected to the Internet if the MQTT broker is exposed to it or, if not, both are connected to the same network. The realized setup integrates both the MQTT broker and the library into the CoMaDa instance. The Zigbee2Mqtt gateway implements the abstract actuator types (e.g. light bulb and power switch) defined by the HAIFA. But instead of providing one implementation per supported physical device, actual supported commands should be dynamically added to the virtual device objects. This only requires a configuration file to be provided with each supported physical device, its actuator type and all of its supported commands. Mosquitto is used as the MQTT broker due to the simple fact that it supports MQTT v5 and is only built to act as MQTT broker, hence, it has no overhead by supporting other protocols like RabbitMQ does. Client-wise, the HiveMQ MQTT Java client allows the Zigbee2Mqtt gateway to connect to the broker.

1.3.2.4. HAIFA database design

The PostreSQL database will be used by HAIFA to store registered actuators, rules and rule logs. The `HA-Module` will coordinate communication with the storage. The resulting relational database schema is rather simple and shown in Figure 1.11. $ha\_actuators(identifier, name)$ will simply store all registered actuators together with the name assigned to them. $ha\_rules(id, ruletype, rule, paused)$ will be filled with rules. The id is unique per rule, $conditionRule$ is the only available $rule\_type$ for now, $rule$ is the JSON representation of the rule and $paused$ stores whether a rule is paused or not. Finally, all $log - entries$ with associated $log\_timestamp$, the corresponding $rule\_id$ and a log_type will be held by $ha\_rule\_logs(id, rule\_id, log\_type, log\_timestamp, previous\_rule\_json)$. All available log types and a short description of them are listed in Table 1.2. Only when updating or deleting rules is the $previous\_rule\_json$ saved along with the log entry, in order to keep track of the changes made to a rule.

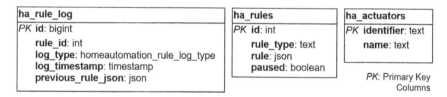

Figure 1.11. *Database schema of the HAIFA CoMaDa part*

1.3.2.5. HAIFA MAPE-K cycle design

The key functionality of the HAIFA is its automation capability, utilized by the MAPE-K model (see section 1.2.3). The knowledge consists of the rules set by the WSN-Owner, and define the desired behavior of HAIFA. Referring to the MAPE-K policies, those rules would be action policies as they define actions (command executions on actuators) that should be taken if the chosen conditions (node value thresholds) are met. As illustrated in Figure 1.3, CoMaDa already provides the monitor and analyze part of the MAPE-K cycle. This means the `WSNApp` exposes the virtual representation of the WSN including most recent node values. The `Automation-Worker` makes use of this by periodically fetching the data to proceed to the planning part of the cycle. CoMaDa also already provides data in consistent units and additionally supports aggregation directly within aggregation nodes. The interval of the periodic checks may be adjusted by the WSN-Owner. The two missing parts – plan and execute – are more or less combined within the `Automation-Worker`. During the periodic checks all rules are traversed and executed if their conditions are all fulfilled. Thus, instead of actually planning the execution, the worker directly executes actions of satisfied rules. The rules are provided via the knowledge which is always held and retrievable through the main module component, i.e. the `HA-Module`.

Log type	Description
`checkedWithoutExecution`	The rule was checked, but no action was required (not all conditions were met).
`executedWithChanges`	The rule was checked and executed, at least one actuator changed its state.
`executedWithoutChanges`	The rule was checked and executed, but no actuator changed its state (e.g. a light was tried to turn on that already was turned on).
`ruleUpdated`	The WSN-Owner updated the rule, e.g. added or removed conditions, commands and time frames.
`ruleDeleted`	The rule has been deleted by the WSN-Owner.

Table 1.2. *Rule automation for available log types*

Figure 1.3 gives an overview of how received values from deployed nodes in the WSN are used to feed the MAPE-K cycle, resulting in actions performed by the actuators to adjust certain parameters of the managed element, i.e. the home (e.g. the temperature and the brightness). It might seem that periodic monitoring could also be replaced by constantly monitoring sensor values by subscribing to the corresponding event that is fired by the `WSNApp` whenever new sensor values are received by the framework, in order to improve the reactivity of the HAIFA to changing environmental parameters. We decided against this approach for two reasons: first, this would probably lead to a very high frequency of checking and executing rules depending on the amount of connected nodes and how frequently they push new sensor values; second, even though it is possible to include values of multiple node sensors into one rule, updates of sensor values are received one by one. Thus, on receiving an update of a node used in such a rule, other required values might not have received an update simultaneously. In this case the latest values pushed before could be used for all "missing" nodes, but to simplify the general process this has been omitted.

1.3.3. *WebMaDa integration*

In order to address the general user request of mobility, WebMaDa should be integrated into the HAIFA for configuring rules and executing actions on actuators. This requires some sort of communication between WebMaDa and CoMaDa, which is the single source of truth in terms of connected actuators and rules. The solution used for this information exchange and the database design that will be used to store required data on the WebMaDa server, which is described next.

The upload and pull interfaces (see section 1.2.1.2) both cover necessary communication channels required by the new HAIFA: "uploading" registered actuators (i.e. their name, type and supported commands), rules and rule logs, as well as sending "(pull-)requests" to execute commands or update rules back to CoMaDa.

Currently, each available kind of message (e.g. C_SENSOR: upload new measured sensor value to WebMaDa; or PULL: send new pull-request to CoMaDa) are sent in their separate upload/pull message. Received messages are processed by message-specific handlers on both sides. However, to keep the required changes inside of the existing implementation as small as possible, a new message type will not be implemented, along with a new handler for each possible "home automation event". Instead, only one new message type – a home automation message – is used to bundle all available events and types of information that need to be transferred between the two SecureWSN parts. This approach also makes it possible to support old versions of CoMaDa which do not yet include the new HAIFA, along with other required adjustments. Due to the modular structure and concept of CoMaDa this is an essential requirement.

Additionally, adjustments are required for the **WebSocket Server**, since it currently only creates messages of type PULL.

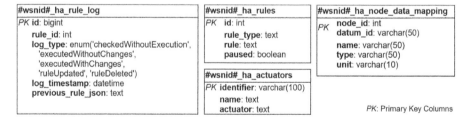

Figure 1.12. *Database schema of the HAIFA WebMaDa part*

WebMaDa's database scheme is similar to CoMaDa's database scheme but has two key differences integrated, as illustrated in Figure 1.12. New is an **Actuators Table**. CoMaDa always has access to the state and information of actuators through their virtual representation. Since WebMaDa lacks this access, actuator data has to be uploaded to it as well, including name and, especially, supported commands. The text column `actuator` in the `#wsnid#_ha_actuators` table is used to store the latest JSON representation of the actuator uploaded by CoMaDa. Furthermore, a **Node Data Mapping** table exists as each node in the deployed WSN exposes several sensors and provides their data. These datums are used within the rule conditions, hence, to create and update rules via WebMaDa it is also necessary to know the correct mapping of sensor/datum name to the corresponding unit. WebMaDa indeed is already aware of these mappings as they are stored in the reports (i.e. values of the nodes) uploaded by CoMaDa. But to decouple the HAIFA from the rest of the WebMaDa features, a separate table will be used and kept up-to-date by CoMaDa (through periodic uploads). The respective table `#wsnid#_ha_node_data_mapping(node_id, datum_id, name, type, unit)` will store name, type and unit for each node-datum combination available in the WSN. As per definition, each table is unique per virtual WSN, `#wsnid#` will be replaced by the actual id of the related WSN.

In order to keep validation and overall logic of rule creation within CoMaDa, WebMaDa does not directly create rules. Instead, a request to create a new rule is sent to CoMaDa which in turn creates the rule if allowed and possible, followed by uploading it to WebMaDa again. From then on, it will be shown to the WSN-Owner there, too. **Executing commands on actuators** is also realized by requesting CoMaDa to do so. Furthermore, CoMaDa always updates **rules**, **actuators**, **rule logs** and **node-datum mappings** as soon as they have been changed by uploading them to WebMaDa.

1.4. Implementation

The realized prototyped HA solution HAIFA requires several implementation parts to build the final `HAIFA-module`: (1) the `HAIFA-module` needs to be integrated in CoMaDa; (2) a ZigBee gateway; and (3) a connection establishment between CoMaDa and WebMaDa.

1.4.1. *CoMaDa integration*

In this section, all abstract interfaces for actuators, rules, conditions and gateways, as well as core classes such as the `HA-Module`, the `Automation-Worker`, and the storage implementation are specified. The following definitions of terms are used: the term `HAIFA(-Module)` always refers to the entire `WSN-Module` implementation of CoMaDa and the term `HA-Module` refers to the core component as defined in section 1.3.2.1.

1.4.1.1. *Interfaces and core classes*

Figure 1.13 illustrates all interfaces used within the HAIFA-Module. Only the integration with the WSNWebModule for WebMaDa communication is not shown (see section 1.4.3). The central endpoint of the HAIFA-Module is the actual implementation of the abstract WSNModule class, namely the HA-Module organizing the communication and the setup of all other components. As shown in Figure 1.13, all main parts of the HAIFA-Module are represented by interfaces, thus, actual implementations can be exchanged with less effort. Section 1.4.1.2 describes the implementation of the HA-Module, all other interfaces and their reference implementation are explained throughout sections 1.4.1.3 to 1.4.1.10.

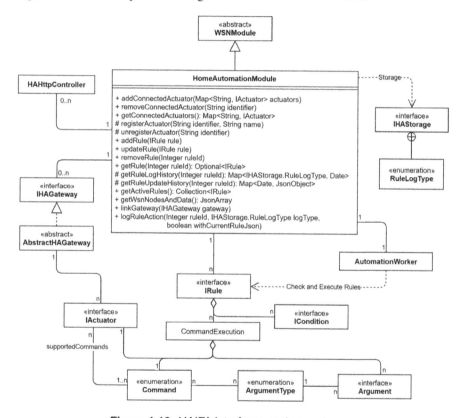

Figure 1.13. *HAIFA interfaces and core classes*

The code of the HAIFA-Module is separated into several packages each with its own domain of responsibility. Besides the base package de.tum.in.net.WSN DataFramework.Modules.HomeAutomation, which includes the HA-Module and the HAHttpController, the following five packages are used: (1) the `HomeAutomation.Actuator`, including generic actuator implementations and interfaces for supported actuator types like `ILight` and `ISwitch` for light bulbs and power switches; (2) the `HomeAutomation.Actuator.Cmd` including the command and argument implementations used to control actuators; (3) the `HomeAutomation.Automation` including implementations and interfaces of conditions, rules and the `Automation-Worker`; (4) the `HomeAutomation.Database` holding the storage interface and reference PostgreSQL database implementation; and (5) the `HomeAutomation.Gateway`. This last package comprises the interface and abstract implementation with basic default functionality of a gateway. In principle, the actual gateway implementations can also be put in their own sub-package, as was done for the reference gateway (called `HomeAutomation.Gateway.Zigbee2Mqtt`).

```
1   @Override
2   protected void _init() {
3       // ...
4       this._moduleDependent(
5           WSNHTTPServerModule.class, "setupHttpController", null
6       );
7       this.initializeStoredRules();
8       this.haStorage.cleanupRuleLog(this.rules);
9       // ...
10  }
11
12  @Override
13  protected void _run() {
14          // ...
15          AutomationWorker worker = new AutomationWorker(this,
16                  this.app().wsn());
17          worker.setCheckInterval(this.workerCheckInterval);
18          this.automationWorkerThread = new Thread(worker);
19          this.automationWorkerThread.start();
20          // ...
21  }
22
23  @Override
24  protected void _shutdown() {
25          this.automationWorkerThread.interrupt();
26          // ...
27  }
```

Listing 1.1. *HA-Module life-cycle methods*

1.4.1.2. *HA module*

The `HomeAutomationModule` is regarded as the entry point of the entire HAIFA, thus, it is deriving the abstract `WSNModule` class and implementing required methods. These are primarily the life-cycle methods `_init()`, `_run()`, and _shutdown(), partially shown in Listing 1.1. During initialization (see _init() in lines 2–10) stored rules are "initialized" which means they are loaded from the storage and parsed into real Java object representations. Also, the rule log is cleaned up (see line 8) to limit the disk space used by the storage as required in section 1.3.2.1 and further described in section 1.4.1.7. The _run() method creates a new thread for the Automation-Worker and starts its execution (lines 15–19) while _shutdown() terminates the worker again by interrupting it (see line 25). Lines 15–16 ensure that the Automation-Worker will have access to the HA-Module and the virtual WSN representation, as both are given to the constructor of the worker. All important public methods from the module are shown in the class diagram in Figure 1.13. They are either self-explanatory or explained in detail in sections 1.4.1.3 to 1.4.1.10, where dependent components are using them.

```
1   public void onWsnSensorUpdate (SensorUpdateMessage __) {
2     // Ensure method is allowed to be executed
3     long now = new Date ().getTime ();
4     if (now - this.lastWsnSensorUpdate
5       < NODE_LIST_UPDATE_PAUSE_MILLISECONDS) {
6       return ;
7     }
8     this.lastWsnSensorUpdate = now;
9     Thread updateThread = new Thread (() -> {
10      try {
11        Thread.sleep (NODE_LIST_UPDATE_DEFER_MILLISECONDS);
12        logger.info ("Processing node list and
13        node sensors/ data ...");
14        // Publish update message -> trigger WebMaDa Upload
15        HomeAutomationUpdateMessage msg =
16          new HomeAutomationUpdateMessage (
17        HomeAutomationUpdateMessage.Type.NODE_LIST_UPDATE,
18        this.getWsnNodesAndData()
19        );
20        this.app ().getMessageBus ().publish (msg);
21      } catch (InterruptedException e) { /* ... */ }
22    });
23    updateThread.setDaemon (true);
24    updateThread.start ();
25  }
```

Listing 1.2. *HA-Module – node-datum mapping update handler*

In section 1.3.3, the need for a node-sensor mapping was explained, including all available nodes from the WSN and their sensors (i.e. "datums") with corresponding units. Several options to achieve this are available. For example, uploading the current mapping once on CoMaDa's initial bootstrap, however, nodes may be added afterwards or have not been announced yet. Therefore, the HA-Module registers an event handler (shown in Listing 1.2) for the SensorUpdateMessage published whenever new node sensors (data types) are available. Unfortunately, this message is published whenever a node sends its template and also for each datum separately. Thus, multiple update messages are sent for every node at a constant interval depending on how the node has been programmed (how often templates are published). In order to prevent too frequent updates this handler is only allowed to be executed every NODE_LIST_UPDATE_PAUSE_MILLISECONDS ms (realized in lines 2–8 of Listing 1.2). Additionally, to ensure all sensors are included in the update it is deferred for NODE_LIST_UPDATE_DEFER_MILLISECONDS ms (see line 11) as usually the first update message of multiple (new) SensorUpdateMessages triggers the handler, but all of them should be included into the mapping, of course. This has been implemented by running the update on its own thread (updateThread) which sleeps for the desired amount of ms before actually publishing the updated mappings. Further handling and use of creating and publishing corresponding HomeAutomationUpdateMessages is clarified in section 1.4.4. The mentioned mappings are created by the getWsnNodesAndData() method, shown in Listing 1.3. It creates a JSON array containing an object for each available node (nodeInfo in line 4). Each node object contains an array with all sensors of the node, including the name, type, unit and current value of the sensor (see lines 6–17). The node and sensor data is provided by the WSNApp service (see line 3).

```
1    public JsonArray getWsnNodesAndData() {
2      JsonArrayBuilder nodes = Json.createArrayBuilder();
3      for (Node node : this.app().wsn().nodes().values()) {
4        JsonObjectBuilder nodeInfo = Json.createObjectBuilder();
5        nodeInfo.add("id", node.getNodeID().asInt());
6        // get available node data (i.e. the sensors of the node)
7        // and for each sensor/ datum get meta data + current value
8        JsonObjectBuilder nodeData = Json.createObjectBuilder();
9        for (Node.Datum datum : node.data()) {
10         JsonObjectBuilder datumMap = Json.createObjectBuilder();
11         datumMap.add("id", datum.getID().toString());
12         datumMap.add("name", datum.getName());
13         datumMap.add("type", datum.getType());
14         datumMap.add("value", datum.getValue().toString());
15         datumMap.add("unit", datum.getUnit() == null ? "" :
16             datum.getUnit());
17         nodeData.add(datum.getID().toString(), datumMap);
18       }
19       nodeInfo.add("data", nodeData);
20       nodes.add(nodeInfo);
21     }
22     return nodes.build();
23   }
```

Listing 1.3. *HA-Module - create node-datum mappings*

1.4.1.3. *Actuator, commands and arguments*

In order to provide a uniform interface of accessing and controlling actuators (IActuator), interfaces for available actuator types (ILight and ISwitch), as well as an abstract base implementation of a generic actuator (Actuator) are provided by HAIFA (see Figure 1.14). Each actuator is of one specific ActuatorType and supports one or more Commands. All available commands are represented by an enumeration (enum) which holds information of how many additional arguments are required, along with their respective descriptions and a reference to the enum type of the required argument. The NumberArgument is implementing the Argument interface and its loadFromString(String value) method is used to create the argument. Therefore, they are provided as strings by the administration frontend or WebMaDa. Actuator implementations of gateways may then use provided arguments to execute commands properly. Those implementations shall of course be aware of the required argument types per command. ArgumentTypes hold a reference to their implementing class. Thus, the right class from which the argument has to be created can be easily obtained by getting required arguments from a command and then getting the implementing class from the argument type (enum). A CommandExecution bundles all information required to execute a specific command on an actuator. It is used for instance by rules to determine the actions. An execution consists of exactly one actuator (more precisely: its identifier), the Command to execute, and a list of arguments which are required by the command. The Automation-Worker will then "unwrap" the CommandExecution and execute all contained commands.

1.4.1.4. *Rules and conditions*

Rules may be of various types, taking different data sources into account to determine whether its actions should be executed or not. The only requirement is to implement the IRule interface, which ensures compatibility with the Automation-Worker. Structure and relations of the rule and condition interfaces and classes are shown in Figure 1.15.

The methods checkForActionRequired(...) and performAction (...) both receive all available nodes and actuators by the Automation-Worker. They are used to check if the rule "wants" to execute its actions and to execute them if so. The latter returns a CompletableFuture <Boolean>, which should resolve to a boolean in the future being true if any actuators' state changed or else false. The abstract implementation Rule takes care of generic tasks like handling the TimeFrameCondition or implementing a number of other methods not shown in the class diagram. These other methods include tasks such as setting the name, pausing/unpausing the rule and getter methods for the respective data.

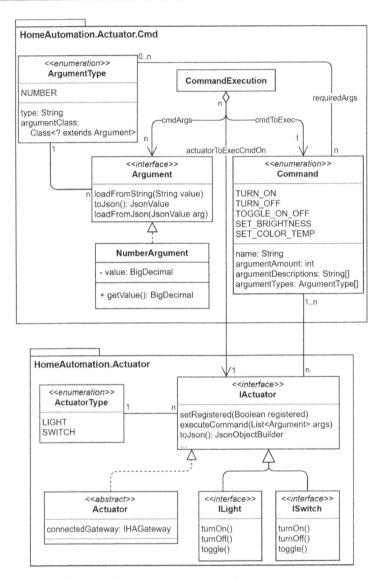

Figure 1.14. *Actuators, commands, and arguments*

Conditions are described by the `ICondition` interface whose most important method is `isFulfilled()`, which informs us whether the condition is fulfilled or not. Two conditions are available in HAIFA, as illustrated in Figure 1.15, which are (1) the `NodeThresholdCondition` and (2) the `TimeFrameCondition`. The first condition allows us to verify that a specific sensor value is given. Therefore, it saves the identifier of a node together with one of its sensors, an

ICondition.Comparator (e.g. smaller, equal, or greater) and a threshold. It is considered to be fulfilled when the given sensor value compared to the threshold according to the comparator yields true. For example, with nodeID=1, datumID=2, comparator='>', threshold=3.4: "The condition is true, if the value of node 1's sensor 2 is greater than 3.4". The second condition contains a list of TimeFrames, each of which describes a valid weekday and a start and end time. This condition is considered to be fulfilled when at least one included time-frame matches the current weekday and time. It should be kept in mind that each IRule may have an optional time frame condition defining valid time slots for the corresponding rule in which it may be executed.

At the moment HAIFA includes one example rule, the ConditionRule. It consists of at least one Command-Execution and an arbitrary amount of IConditions, which all have to be fulfilled in order to execute the rules' actions (i.e. its command executions).

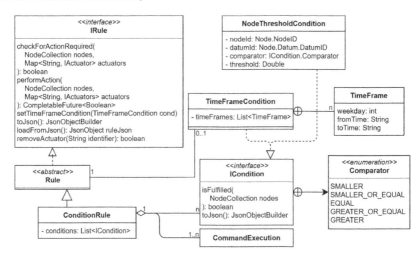

Figure 1.15. *Rules and conditions*

1.4.1.5. *HAIFA's gateway interface*

Gateways encapsulate the connection to different physical actuator devices, thus, a uniform interface is required to attach them to the HAIFA, specifically the HA-Module (see Figure 1.6). Listing 1.4 shows this interface and its four required methods. This results from the limited number of tasks for gateways, which mainly consist of adding and removing actuators to and from the HA-Module. Actuators, on the other side, have an internal reference to the gateway that they were created by and are controlled through their own interface. During the creation of a new gateway by a client, the HA-Module must be assigned to the gateway (setHAModule(...)). The gateway will then attach itself and connected actuators to the module using methods provided by the `HomeAutomationModule` illustrated in Figure 1.13 (`linkGateway(...)`, `addConnectedActuator(...)`, and `removeConnectedActuator(...)`). The implementation of the reference ZigBee gateway is described in section 1.4.2.

```
1  public interface IHAGateway {
2    Map<String, IActuator> getAllConnectedActuators();
3    void setHAModule(HomeAutomationModule module);
4    void setupHttpController(WSNHTTPServerModule httpModule)
5        throws InstantiationException;
6    MessageBus getMessageBus();
7  }
```

Listing 1.4. *The gateway interface*

1.4.1.6. *HAIFA's automation-worker*

Although the `Automation-Worker` is one of the core components of HAIFA, its underlying code is rather simple, as shown in Listing 1.5. The `HomeAutomationModule` creates a new instance of the `Automation-Worker` and supplies access to the WSN and `HA-Module` during its initialization (see lines 7–11). By creating a new thread from the `Automation-Worker` "as `Runable`" and starting it (see Listing 1.1), the execution of the `run()` method is started. The method itself then periodically executes the `execute()` method, realized by letting the thread sleep for the desired amount of seconds (see lines 15–20). The sleep period can be set by an additional method not shown in the listing, through the `HA-Module`.

The execution-method performs the actual work, but is also not very complex. First, all available nodes, actuators, and automation rules are retrieved from the WSN, respectively the `HA-Module` (lines 24–26). Second, all of the rules are checked to determine whether they are paused, and if not, if they are required to take action. Execution is only performed if both checks turn out to be true. Rules provide this check and execution logic through their interface. The worker does not need to know how to verify the need for execution nor how to do it. This abstraction allows the code of the `Automation-Worker` to be very simple, as it is only responsible for triggering all rules to check and execute their actions regularly, and giving them access to all nodes and actuators (see line 33 and 34).

One additional task is to log the outcome of the checks, as shown in lines 33–49 in Listing 1.5. Depending on whether a rule is executed or not, and if yes, whether any actuator changed its state or not, the corresponding log-type (see Table 1.2) is used to log an action for the rule using the method provided by the `HomeAutomationModule` shown in Figure 1.13 (`logRuleAction(...)`). The JSON representation is never logged by the worker (hence, the third parameter of the log method is always false) as the `Automation-Worker` does not change the configuration of the rule.

```
 1   public class AutomationWorker implements Runnable {
 2
 3     private int checkInterval = 1000 * 5; // 30 seconds by default
 4     private final HomeAutomationModule haModule;
 5     private final WSN wsn;
 6
 7     public AutomationWorker(HomeAutomationModule haModule,
 8           WSN wsn) {
 9       this.haModule = haModule;
10       this.wsn = wsn;
11     }
12
13     @Override
14     public void run() {
15       try {
16         while (true) {
17           this.execute();
18           Thread.sleep(checkInterval);
19         }
20       } catch (InterruptedException e) { /* ... */ }
21     }
22
23     private void execute() {
24       NodeCollection nodes = this.wsn.nodes();
25       Map<String, IActuator> actuators =
26           this.haModule.getConnectedActuators();
27
28       this.haModule.getActiveRules().forEach(rule -> {
29         if (rule.isPaused()) {
30           return;
31         }
32
33         if (rule.checkForActionRequired(nodes, actuators)) {
34           rule.performAction(nodes, actuators)
35             .thenAccept((changed) -> {
36               this.haModule.logRuleAction(
37                 rule.getId(),
38                 changed
39                 ? IHAStorage.RuleLogType.EXECUTED_WITH_CHANGES
40                 : IHAStorage.RuleLogType.EXECUTED_WITHOUT_CHANGES,
41                 false
42               );
43             });
44         } else {
45           this.haModule.logRuleAction(
46             rule.getId(),
47                 IHAStorage.RuleLogType.CHECKED_WITHOUT_EXECUTION,
48                 false
49           );
50         }
51       });
52     }
```

Listing 1.5. *Implementation of the* `Automation-Worker`

```
1    public interface IHAStorage {
2      int RULE_LOG_KEEP_UPDATE_ENTRIES_AMOUNT = 50;
3      Map<String , String> getActuators ();
4      void setActuator (String identifier , String name);
5      void removeActuator (String identifier);
6      Map<Integer , IRule> getRules ();
7      IRule getRule (Integer ruleId);
8      Integer addRule (IRule rule);
9      void updateRule (IRule rule);
10     void removeRule (Integer ruleId);
11     void logRuleAction (RuleLogType logType , Integer ruleId ,
12        Timestamp logTimestamp , boolean withCurrentRuleJson);
13     void cleanupRuleLog ();
14     Map<RuleLogType , Date> getRuleExecutionLogHistory
15            (Integer ruleId);
16     Map<Date , JsonObject> getLastRuleUpdates
17            (Integer ruleId , int amount);
18     enum RuleLogType {
19       //...
20     }
21   }
```

Listing 1.6. *The storage interface*

1.4.1.7. *HAIFA's storage interface*

The storage interface provides functionality to store and retrieve rules, actuators, and logs. It is used by HAIFA to ensure data persistence, even if the CoMaDa application restarts or the hardware crashes. Listing 1.6 includes used interface methods that are mostly self-explanatory and, thus, only four of them are described in detail here. The getActuators method returns a map of actuator identifiers (strings) to their registered name of all actuators that have been stored (i.e. registered actuators). setActuator and removeActuator are the equivalent methods used to register and unregister (i.e. store and delete) actuators. The addRules method is responsible for adding new rules, updateRule handles the updating of existing rules, and removeRule removes rules. In order to get an overview of existing rules, the getRules and getRule methods are called, returning all available rules mapped to their corresponding ID, and respectively one single rule by its ID. Addressing the logging request for HAIFA, the logRuleAction method was created. It logs a specific rule action (logType), and all of them are defined in IHAStorage.RuleLogType enum, reflecting the types defined in Table 1.2. If $withCurrentRuleJson = true$, the JSON-representation of the rule in its current state will be logged, along with the timestamp and type. This is only done when changing or deleting a rule and not if an execution is logged, since no changes are applied to the rule setup in this case. The cleanupRuleLog method ensures that the storage does not require too much space, by removing old log entries according to the requirement in section 1.3.1.2. Only the latest log entry is kept, except for update-entries where the amount of entries to keep is defined in the RULE_LOG_KEEP_UPDATE_ENTRIES_AMOUNT constant. Additionally, logs from rules that have been deleted are removed entirely, except for the last log-entry added due to the deletion. Sometimes it makes sense to know the history of a rule. This is handled by the `getRuleExecutionLogHistory` method, which returns all the log types shown in Table 1.2, along with the last timestamp that this type has been logged for this rule. Changes to the rule configuration may be retrieved through the `getLastRuleUpdates` method.

```
1   @Override
2   public Map<Integer, IRule> getRules() {
3     Map<Integer, IRule> result = new HashMap<>();
4     try {
5       PreparedStatement stm = this.getConnection().prepareStatement(
6               "SELECT id, rule_type, rule, paused FROM ha_rules"
7       );
8       ResultSet queryResult = stm.executeQuery();
9       while (queryResult.next()) {
10        String ruleType = queryResult.getString("rule_type");
11        String ruleJson = queryResult.getString("rule");
12        try {
13          IRule rule = (IRule) Class.forName(ruleType)
14                .getDeclaredConstructor().newInstance();
15          rule.loadFromJson(
16            Json.createReader(new StringReader(ruleJson)).readObject()
17          );
18          rule.setPaused(queryResult.getBoolean("paused"));
19          result.put(rule.getId(), rule);
20        } catch (Exception e) { /* ... */ }
21      }
22    } catch (SQLException e) { /* ... */ }
23    return result;
24  }
```

Listing 1.7. *The PostgreSQL storage implementation - fetch all rules*

The provided solution in HAIFA's prototype is the `PostgresStorage` class implementing the IHA-Storage interface. It utilizes the PostgreSQL database already available on the currently used CoMaDa VMs. The schema of the database tables is introduced in section 1.3.2.4 and since most of the statements required for the different methods are more or less similar, the exemplary `getRules()` implementation is shown in Listing 1.7. A short SQL statement fetches all stored rules from the database (see lines 5–8). For each rule the *id*, *rule type*, *rule*, and *paused* columns are retrieved. The *rule* column stores the latest JSON representation of the rule, while the *rule_type* column holds the name of the class implementing the related rule type. Thus, it can be used to create an instance of the right rule class (see lines 13–14). Even though only `ConditionRules` are supported for now, this ensures the compatibility of other rule types with the storage system in the future. This compatibility is also ensured by how the rule is loaded, namely by a method provided by its related class (`loadFromJson(...)`). Lines 15–18 show how the rule object loads itself from the JSON representation retrieved from the database. Thus, each available rule type takes care of how to parse the JSON, load, and create required data (e.g. conditions and executions). The connection to the PostgreSQL database is realized through the same library initially used to access the database from CoMaDa in (Ott 2017). Within the PostgresStorage class, this connection object is provided by the getConnection() method, returning the active connection or establishing it if it has not yet happened (see line 5).

1.4.1.8. *Administration frontend*

Adding the possibility of dynamically adjusting the configuration (i.e. registering actuators, managing rules, and viewing logs) is essential for the HAIFA to be really useful. Two mechanisms are provided for that: First, the CoMaDa administration frontend is extended by management features for the HAIFA. Second, WebMaDa can be used to manage rules and execute commands on actuators.

In section 1.2.1.1 the WSNHTTPServerModule was introduced, providing access to HTTP-Controllers, allowing the creation of sites within the frontend[13]. The HAHttpController extends the WSNHTTPController and serves a configuration page for the HAIFA (see Figure 1.16). The controller itself is registered by the HA-Module under the namespace "homeautomation", as shown in Listing 1.8, and provides endpoints (i.e. HTTP URLs that can be accessed by the AngularJS frontend under the /homeautomation/* path) to fetch available nodes, rules, logs, and update rules, for example. Schmitt *et al.* (2013) describe how these endpoints (each represented by a single method in the HAHttpController) and paths function, in detail. The setupHttpController() method is called by the WSNApp as a result of registering the HTTP-Module as a dependent module for the HA-Module (see section 1.2.1.1), as shown in line 4 of Listing 1.1.

The frontend part, on the other side, is integrated into the existing AngluarJS frontend by providing several new widgets, which are used to build up the main configuration page. Schmitt *et al.* (2016b) and Strasser (2016) extensively explain how widgets and AngularJS work and how they are integrated into the existing frontend. This is briefly summarized in section 1.2.1.1.

```
1    //...
2          httpModule.registerController(
3                "homeautomation", HAHttpController.class, this
4          ).getServerModule()
5                .registerLink(new String[]{"Home Automation"},
6                      "/homeautomation");
7          //...
8    }
```

Listing 1.8. *HAHttpController's registration of the* HA-Module

---

13. In this section, "Administration Frontend" is referred to as "Frontend" for simplicity.

Figure 1.16. *HAIFA's administration frontend in CoMaDa*

As illustrated in Figure 1.16, actuators are listed at the top, and can be registered with a name and also unregistered again. All available commands are shown for registered actuators, including the possibility to actually execute them and provide potential necessary arguments. Next, all available nodes and their sensors are shown, followed by rules and the possibility to add new ones, edit, or delete existing ones. Figure 1.17 depicts the history provided by each rule, even allowing any previous state (i.e. settings/configuration) of a rule before it has been changed to be shown. The red bordered "rule creation" component (also reused for "rule edits") made up of three different (reusable) widgets is shown in Figure 1.18. The blue, green, and purple bordered widgets represent lists for conditions, time frames and commands, and are also used for displaying rules in the overview (see Figure 1.16). They can also be leveraged by new rule types in the future.

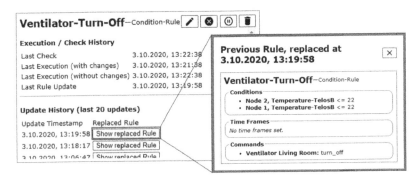

Figure 1.17. *Rule log visualization of the administration interface*

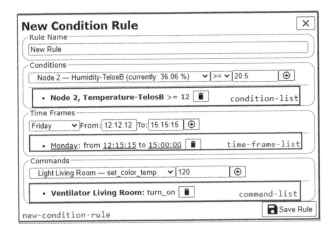

Figure 1.18. *Rule creation - AngularJS widget and sub-widgets. For a color version of this figure, see www.iste.co.uk/khatoun/cybersecurity.zip*

One example scenario, namely executing a command on an actuator, of how the frontend interacts with the HAHttpController is shown in Listings 1.9 and 1.10. However, the focus is not on explaining how this specific feature works, but rather how the communication between both endpoints works in general. In the second listing a GET-request is sent from the frontend (in the browser) to the HTTP-Controller endpoint. As shown, GET-parameters in the URL are added to supply the identifier, command, and arguments. In turn, the HTTP-Controller executes the method matching the given URL (/homeautomation/executedevicecommand will be handled by executedevicecommandAction()) and has access to the given GET- and POST-parameters via the req.arguments object. It uses the HA-Module to obtain the targeted actuator and execute the command on it. Responses to the frontend containing arbitrary data can also be added by setting the res.body value accordingly.

```
1   public  void  executedevicecommandAction (HTTPRequest req ,
2                   HTTPResponse res) {
3     String identifier = req.arguments.get("deviceIdentifier").
4       toString();
5     String command = req.arguments.get("command").toString();
6     Command cmd = Command.getValueByName(command);
7
8     IActuator act = this.haModule.getConnectedActuators().
9       get(identifier);
10    try {
11      if (cmd.getArgumentsAmount() == 0) {
12        act.executeCommand(cmd);
13      } else {
14        JsonArray args = Json.createReader(
15          new StringReader ( req . arguments . get (" arguments ").
16        toString ())).readArray();
17        act.executeCommand(cmd,
18            cmd.parseCommandArgumentsFromJsonArray(args));
19      }
20    } catch (Exception e) {
21      res.body = "error".getBytes();
22    }
23
24    res.body = "success".getBytes();
25  }
```

Listing 1.9. *HAHttpController - execute command on actuator*

```
1   scope.executeActuatorCommand = (identifier ,command,argAmount) => {
2     let argumentData = '';
3     if (argAmount > 0) {
4       // get arguments ....
5       argumentData = "arguments =..." /* ... */;
6     }
7     $http.get(
8       '/homeautomation / executedevicecommand ? deviceIdentifier=
9       ${identifier}&command=${command}&${argumentData}'
10    ).then(() => { /* Fetch updated actuator state ... */ });
11  }
```

Listing 1.10. *AngularJS frontend sending requests*
to the HAHttpController

1.4.1.9. *Bootstrapping within the WSNFramework*

Due to the flexible approach of the HAIFA in terms of which gateways are in use and which actual implementations of certain interfaces (such as the storage) should be used, the module has to be setup properly during the launch of CoMaDa. Two mechanisms are used for this process: first, the Java-main method within the

WSNFramework class where the WSNApp is created and all desired modules are attached; second, the Google Guice Framework (see section 1.2.1.1), which allows the definition of the implementations that should be used for interfaces, and additionally, can inject them as instantiated objects in the constructor or any class variable of an object that is created by the Guice Framework.

The HA-Module will be created by the WSNFramework, which is also where all of the gateways are created (with the help of Guice) and attached to the module (see Listing 1.11). All other "flexible" components and requirements, such as the storage, are injected through the Guice framework. Therefore, the bindings have to be setup correctly so that Guice is able to provide/inject the right instantiated objects for defined interfaces. Listing 1.12 shows how an instance of the PostgresStorage is bound to the IHAStorage interface (*appProperties* holds all values read from a configuration file provided by the WSN-Owner), while Listing 1.13 shows how this binding is injected into the constructor of the HA-Module (triggered by the @Inject annotation).

```
1   // ...
2   HomeAutomationModule haMod = injector.getInstance
3        (HomeAutomationModule.class);
4   haMod.linkGateway(injector.getInstance(Zigbee2MqttGateway.class));
5   app.addModule(haMod);
```

Listing 1.11. *Instantiation of the* HA-Module *and gateway attachments*

```
1   IHAStorage haStorage = new PostgresStorage(
2        this.appProperties.getProperty("db.host"),
3        this.appProperties.getProperty("db.database"),
4        this.appProperties.getProperty("db.user"),
5        this.appProperties.getProperty("db.password")
6   );
7   bind(IHAStorage.class).toInstance(haStorage);
```

Listing 1.12. *Guice binding of object instances to interfaces*

```
1   @Inject
2   public HomeAutomationModule(Properties appProperties,
3        IHAStorage storage) {
4        // ...
5        this.haStorage = storage;
6   }
```

Listing 1.13. *Injection of the storage by Guice into the* HA-Module *constructor*

```
1   public  void  foo () {
2           logger.info ("Info  message");
3           logger.warn ("Warning !");
4           try { /*  ...  */ } catch (Exception  e) {
5                   logger.fatal ("Fatal! Following  exception
6                           occured:", e);
7           }
8   }
```

Listing 1.14. *Usage of an Apache Log4j 2 Logger*

Figure 1.19. *Logging output of CoMaDa (white messages = WebMaDa responses). For a color version of this figure, see www.iste.co.uk/khatoun/cybersecurity.zip*

1.4.1.10. *Logging*

Logging is an important concept and technique, which can be used to retrace the behavior of a program after an error has occurred, or to just check if everything worked and was executed as planned. The HAIFA implementation makes use of the Apache Log4j 2 library (Logging Services 2020). This library is used for logging in Java applications and has already been integrated into the WSNFramework. The user can provide a configuration file which defines where log messages should be stored or outputted to (e.g. output to the console, into a file, and database), and what minimum level is required by the message to be handled.

Logging has been integrated everywhere where it makes sense in the HAIFA, where keeping the balance between necessary and too much information. Listing 1.14 shows, how a logger can generally be "retrieved" and how log messages of different levels are actually logged. The exemplary logging output in Figure 1.19 results from adding a new gateway to the HA-Module, cleaning up the rule log, and one rule-check cycle where the actions of both available rules are not executed, due to unfulfilled conditions. Log messages like this, stored in a log-file, may help the WSN-Owner to solve problems by checking if rules were correctly checked and gateways were added properly, for example. However, it is up to the WSN-Owner to configure the log config-file according to their needs by adjusting the required log-levels and setting outputs the messages should be sent to. The documentation of Log4j (Logging Services 2020) might help to find the appropriate settings.

1.4.2. HAIFA's ZigBee Gateway

Gateways are used to connect physical actuators with the HAIFA. The architecture of the reference ZigBee Gateway was introduced in section 1.3.2.3, including the usage of the Zigbee2Mqtt library. The upcoming sections describe how this library is installed on the CoMaDa VM/server and how the connection with the ZigBee adapter is established, and are followed by a presentation of the CoMaDa side gateway implementation.

1.4.2.1. Installation and setup of the environment

Zigbee2Mqtt (also called "*bridge*" in this chapter) is written in JavaScript and, thus, requires the Node.js environment to be executed. Additionally, a MQTT broker is required and is used by the bridge and the gateway to communicate with each other. Mosquitto (see section 1.2.4), is used as the broker. For installation details refer to Light (2020). While the Mosquitto MQTT broker runs immediately after the installation is exposed to the default MQTT port 1883 (OASIS 2019) in the local network, the bridge has to be started manually (see section 1.4.2.3). Traffic sent between the different MQTT communication participants (broker and clients, i.e. bridge and gateway) is additionally encrypted using TLS with a self generated certificate and secured by requiring a valid username-password-combination.

To allow easy starting, stopping, and monitoring of the bridge, it will be registered as a *systemd service* (systemd 2020) named **Zigbee2mqtt.service**. This allows the WSN-Owner to manage the service with the following commands:

– `systemctl start Zigbee2mqtt.service` to start the service;

– `systemctl stop Zigbee2mqtt.service` to stop the service; and

– `journalctl - u Zigbee2mqtt.service -f` to view the logs of the service.

The HTTP-Controller of the gateway, presented in section 1.4.2.4, will also use this service to start and stop the bridge. This allows the WSN-Owner to do so via the administration frontend.

1.4.2.2. Connection of the ZigBee adapter to Zigbee2Mqtt

The ZigBee adapter has to be connected to the bridge. In order to flash a custom image for Zigbee2Mqtt on it, the CC Debugger from Texas Instruments is used (Kanters 2020a, 2020b). After successfully flashing the image the adapter can connect to the server entity of the CoMaDa server. The access to it is then provided through a file handle by Ubuntu. Figure 1.20 shows this file handle along with another handle reflecting the sink[14] of the WSN. The bottom part of the figure shows the configuration file of the bridge, including the path to the file handle of the ZigBee adapter allowing the bridge to communicate with it.

1.4.2.3. *Configuring and controlling the Zigbee2Mqtt bridge*

The configuration of the bridge is realized through the configuration file presented in Figure 1.20. For instance, setting the first option (`permit_join`) to true or false allows new devices to join the network or not. For the sake of security this should be set to false as soon as all required devices have been added to the network. The *mqtt* section defines the hostname (*server*) and credentials of the MQTT broker, as well as the base topic, which is used by the bridge. In this example the MQTT broker additionally requires authentication and provides TLS encryption, thus, the corresponding certificate has to be known (path defined in the ca config-string) by the bridge to verify the integrity of the server.

However, every change to the configuration file requires a restart of the bridge, thus, the second option available for configuration changes is more convenient: the bridge exposes all of the configuration settings in certain MQTT topics and listens in on other topics, allowing those parameters (with an exception of the MQTT host settings of course) to be changed. The `permit_join` setting can be adjusted by publishing a message with either *true* or *false* to the `zigbee2mqtt/bridge/config/permit_join` topic, for example.

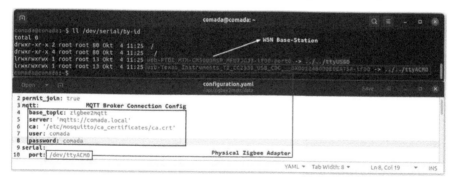

Figure 1.20. *Devices connected to the CoMaDa server and Zigbee2Mqtt configuration file. For a color version of this figure, see www.iste.co.uk/khatoun/cybersecurity.zip*

14. A sink is defined as the last node in a WSN establishing the communication from wireless to wired infrastructure, and can usually only forward packages. Sometimes it is also called a base station (Karl and Willig 2007).

All connected devices along with their current internal data-state ($\hat{=}$ the current status, e.g. their ON-OFF-*state* and their *brightness*) are also exposed within the tree structure, an example of which is shown in Figure 1.21. Publishing messages into the underlying set topic of a corresponding actuator allows a specific value of the actuator to be changed, e.g. setting the brightness and turning it on/off. CoMaDa's gateway implementation will also use these MQTT topics and messages to read and manipulate the state of actuators.

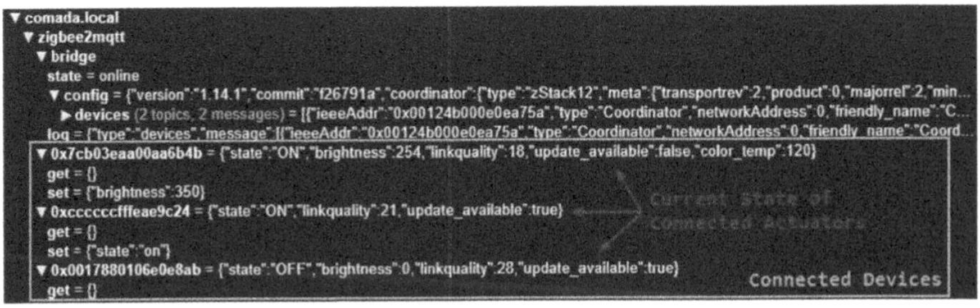

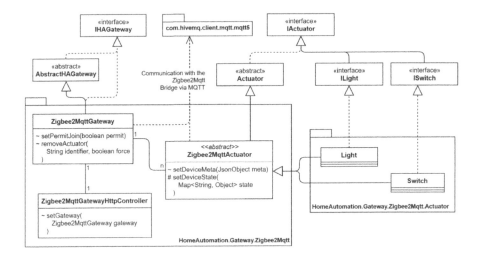

Figure 1.21. *Zigbee2Mqtt's topic tree. For a color version of this figure, see www.iste.co.uk/khatoun/cybersecurity.zip*

Figure 1.22. *Zigbee2Mqtt's gateway class diagram*

1.4.2.4. *Gateway implementation*

All classes of the ZigBee-Gateway, along with the implemented interfaces, are shown in Figure 1.22. The implementation can be divided into three building blocks, the actual Gateway, Actuators, and a separate HTTP-Controller for the gateway.

The `Zigbee2MqttGateway` implements the `IHAGateway` interface and is, thus, the main entry point and organizing part of the gateway. Using the MQTT-client library from HiveMQ (see section 1.2.4), it subscribes to certain topics of the ZigBee bridge, such as the current device list. Its main task is to keep track of this list and create or destroy the virtual actuator objects representing the physical devices. It also has to attach and "detach" them to and from the `HA-Module`.

```
 1  {
 2    "IKEA": {
 3      "E1603/E1702": {
 4        "class": "de.tum.in.net.WSNDataFramework.Modules.
 5           HomeAutomation.Gateway.Zigbee2Mqtt.Actuator.Switch",
 6        "supportedCommands": ["turn_on", "turn_off", "toggle_on_off"]
 7      }
 8    },
 9    "OSRAM": {
10      "AB32840": {
11        "class": "de.tum.in.net.WSNDataFramework.Modules.
12           HomeAutomation.Gateway.Zigbee2Mqtt.Actuator.Light",
13        "supportedCommands": ["turn_on", "turn_off", "toggle_on_off",
14          "set_brightness", "set_color_temp"]
15      }
16    },
17    "Philips": {
18      "8718699673147": {
19        "class": "de.tum.in.net.WSNDataFramework.Modules.
20           HomeAutomation.Gateway.Zigbee2Mqtt.Actuator.Light",
21        "supportedCommands": ["turn_on", "turn_off", "toggle_on_off",
22          "set_brightness"]
23      }
24    }
25  }
```

Listing 1.15. *Configuration file with actuator-command-mappings*

Therefore, the gateway has to map newly added devices to their actual actuator type and identify the commands they support. A simple configuration file shown in Listing 1.15, provided by the WSN-Owner, contains this mapping for the three devices used. The file contains one JSON-object with all of the used vendors as keys, which again all have supported device-models as keys. The device-objects include the class that should be used to represent the device and a list of all supported commands. The example shows that this approach allows different supported commands for two actuators of type *light*, without having to consider it in actuator implementations or use two distinct classes. Listing 1.16 shows a shortened version of how the gateway creates correct instances for every newly connected device. The `deviceList` variable contains all of these new devices (line 1), and for all of them, the `deviceMeta` information is used to get the correct `actuatorConfig` object (see Listing 1.15, the entire object is exposed through the `vendorModelMapping` class variable). Then, an instance of the defined class can be created and all supported commands are added to the new actuator instance (see lines 18–33). The actuator will be instantiated with references to the gateway and the MQTT-client, and can thus subscribe to topics by itself.

```
1   deviceList.forEach((device -> {
2     JsonObject deviceMeta = (JsonObject) device;
3     String identifier, vendor, model;
4     IActuator actuator;
5
6     //load identifier, vendor and model
7     identifier = deviceMeta.getString("friendly_name");
8     vendor = deviceMeta.getString("vendor");
9     model = deviceMeta.getString("model");
10
11    //vendorModelMapping contains entire configuration json-object
12    JsonObject vendorActuators =
13        this.vendorModelMapping.getJsonObject(vendor);
14    JsonObject actuatorConfig =
15        vendorActuators.getJsonObject(model);
16
17    try {
18      actuator = (IActuator)
19          Class.forName(actuatorConfig.getString("class"))
20        .getDeclaredConstructor(
21            String.class, Zigbee2MqttGateway.class,
22            Mqtt5Client.class, JsonObject.class
23        ).newInstance(identifier, this, this.mqttClient, deviceMeta);
24
25      //add/ set supported commands of actuator instance
26      List<Command> supportedCommands = new ArrayList<>();
27      actuatorConfig.getJsonArray("supportedCommands").
28          forEach(command -> {
29        supportedCommands.add(
30          Command.getValueByName(((JsonString) command).getString())
31        );
32      });
33      actuator.setSupportedCommands(supportedCommands);
34    } catch (Exception e) { /* ... */ }
35
36    this.connectedActuators.put(identifier, actuator);
37  }));
```

Listing 1.16. *Actuator instantiation for ZigBee gateway*

Additionally, the `Zigbee2MqttGateway` can be used to change the `permit_join` parameter of the bridge and request a (force-)removal of a connected device. Force-removals may be necessary if a device has been reset and, thus, is not able to "leave" the network by itself (usually the network coordinator requests a device to leave the network). The HiveMQ MQTT Client is used to connect to the MQTT broker, subscribe to topics, and publish new messages. Listing 1.17 shows an example of how a topic can be subscribed to and how messages can be published. All of the topics used by the Zigbee2Mqtt bridge are listed on the corresponding documentation website (Kanters 2020b).

```
1   // subscribe to message
2   this.mqttClient.subscribeWith()
3           .topicFilter("zigbee2mqtt/bridge/config/devices")
4           .callback(this::onDeviceListUpdate).send();
5
6   // publish message
7   this.mqttClient.publishWith()
8           .topic("zigbee2mqtt/bridge/config/permit_join")
9           .payload("false".getBytes()).send();
```

Listing 1.17. *HiveMQ MQTT Java client usage*

```
1    protected void setDeviceState(Map<String, Object> state) {
2        String jsonPayload = JSONValue.toJSONString(state);
3
4        // gatewayBaseTopic holds the MQTT base topic - "zigbee2mqtt"
5        // identifier is the identifier of the acutator
6        this.mqttClient.publishWith()
7            .topic(this.gatewayBaseTopic + "/" + this.identifier + "/set")
8            .payload(jsonPayload.getBytes())
9            .send();
10   }
```

Listing 1.18. *ZigBee gateway actuator* `setDeviceState(...)` *method*

Actuator classes implement two interfaces, the `IActuator` and one of the type-interfaces, such as the `ILight` and `ISwitch`. In the ZigBee Gateway each actuator extends the generic `Zigbee2MqttActuator`, which provides (among others) the important setDeviceState(`Map<String, Object> state`) method. It can be used to send a request to the bridge to set certain values of the state (by publishing a message in the corresponding topic of the actuator). In Figure 1.21 such a request is shown to set the brightness to the value 350. The different implementations of the actuator types (`Light` and `Switch`, see Figure 1.22) only have to handle command executions for every possible command for that type. For example, a switch would never execute the `set_brightness` command, hence, it must not handle it. A light might execute this command in general, even though some lights probably do not support it. Listing 1.18 shows the very simple method for setting the state. It basically just publishes a JSON-object created from the given map that contains every value that should be adjusted and the corresponding new value. The values are stored as a Java-Object in the map because multiple types are possible: e.g. `String` for ON/OFF and `Integer` for a brightness value.

Command executions in the actuator implementations are realized using a switch statement. The corresponding method for a light is partially shown in Listing 1.19. Depending on the command, the state map is filled with the related value-name (e.g. *brightness* and *color_temp*) and the corresponding new value (see lines 12–21). The value is retrieved from the arguments list, while the type of argument is clear for each command. Finally, the setDeviceState(...) method is used to publish the request to the MQTT broker.

```
1   @Override
2   public void executeCommand (Command command,
3           List<Argument> arguments)
4       throws Exception {
5   if (! this.getSupportedCommands().contains(command)) {
6       throw new Exception("Command not supported by this Actuator!");
7   }
8
9   HashMap<String, Object> state = new HashMap<>();
10  switch (command) {
11      // ...
12      case SET_BRIGHTNESS:
13          state.put("brightness", ((NumberArgument) arguments.get(0)).
14          getValue().intValue());
15          this.setDeviceState(state);
16          break;
17      case SET_COLOR_TEMP:
18          state.put("color_temp", ((NumberArgument) arguments.get(0)).
19          getValue().intValue());
20          this.setDeviceState(state);
21          break;
22      default:
23          throw new Exception("Command not supported by this
24          Actuator-Type!");
25      }
26  }
```

Listing 1.19. *ZigBee gateway actuator – executing commands*

Each gateway may register its separate HTTP-Controller to provide an additional page within the administration frontend. The controller itself works in a similar way to the general one of the HAIFA, described in section 1.4.1.8. It is registered by the HA-Module, invoking the setupHttpController(...) method (see Listing 1.4) on the gateway after it has been linked to the module. The frontend part is implemented using AngularJS widgets providing functionalities to start/stop the bridge, permitting devices to join the network or revoke the permit, and to remove devices from the ZigBee network maintained by the bridge. The visual interface is shown in Figure 1.23. All of the required features are provided via methods by the Zigbee2MqttGateway (accessible from the

`Zigbee2MqttGatewayHttpController`), which will publish corresponding messages to the MQTT broker to perform the requested actions from the user "forwarded" by the HTTP-Controller to the gateway.

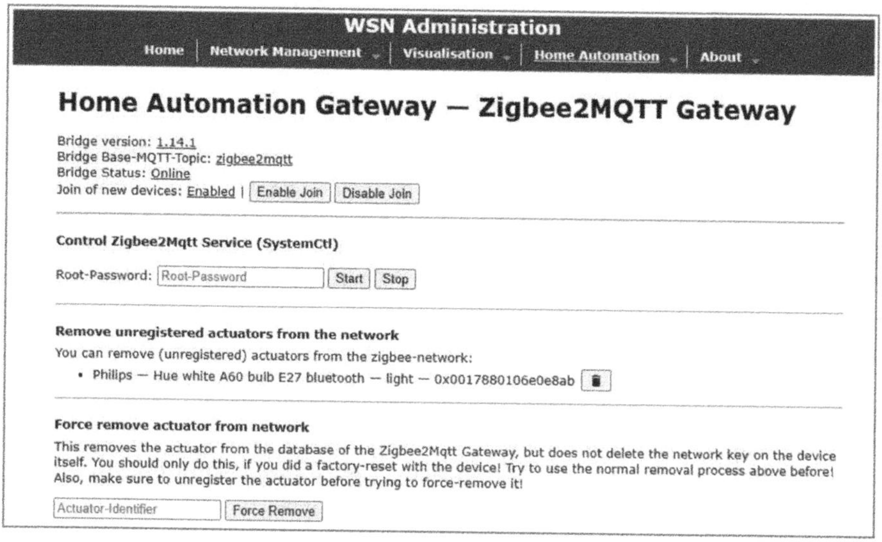

Figure 1.23. *ZigBee's gateway administration frontend*

1.4.3. *WebMaDa integration*

In order to integrate WebMaDa into the HAIFA, several steps are required. The Upload- and Pull- Interface shared between WebMaDa and CoMaDa must be extended to be capable of exchanging other messages than just sensor data and pull requests and, additionally, a new frontend interface must be integrated into WebMaDa, allowing the WSN-Owner to control actuators and manage rules.

Different database tables are created for each virtual WSN in WebMaDa, they are mainly used to store the sensor values for now. To be able to store HAIFA data, they will be extended by the four new tables shown in Figure 1.12. Furthermore, a migration script is added to WebMaDa, creating the missing tables for already existing WSNs. This allows the WSN-Owner to seamlessly enable the HAIFA-Module in CoMaDa, while WebMaDa will create all of the necessary tables for the WSN. However, WebMaDa has to be opened once to trigger the migration before any HAIFA data can be uploaded.

1.4.4. *Uploading HA data to WebMaDa*

The WSNWebModule generally features uploads to WebMaDa. Therefore, it registers message-handlers for messages, which are published on the message bus by other parts of CoMaDa whenever a new data upload is required. Every possible message is processed by a separate handler and, thus, has its own message event that is published. Some examples are the NewNodeMessage or SensorUpdateMessage. However, to keep the impact and changes of the HAIFA to the WSNWebModule as small as possible, only one new message type is introduced: the HOME_AUTOMATION_MESSAGE. Its upload is triggered by the publication of the HomeAutomationUpdateMessage (see Listing 1.20) on the message bus. This class includes an enum (see lines 14–16) with all actual available message types uploaded to WebMaDa by the HAIFA. As soon as any of the related events occurs, e.g. a new rule is added, or a new actuator is registered, the corresponding part in the HA-Module creates a new HomeAutomationUpdateMessage with the correct HA message type (in the example the RULE_LIST_UPDATE or ACTUATOR_LIST_UPDATE type) and publishes it on the bus (shown in lines 16–20 of Listing 1.2). The WSNWebModule listens to this event and uploads the message to WebMaDa (see Listing 1.21). The @Handler annotation registers the method as the handler for published messages, with a class type given by the first argument of the method. It then delegates the data-upload to the designated uploader.

```
1  public class HomeAutomationUpdateMessage implements IMessage {
2    private final Type type;
3    private final JsonValue msg;
4
5    public HomeAutomationUpdateMessage(Type type, JsonValue msg) {
6      this.type = type;
7      this.msg = msg;
8    }
9
10   public HomeAutomationMessageFacade getMsg() {
11     return new HomeAutomationMessageFacade(this.type, this.msg);
12   }
13
14   public enum Type {
15     ACTUATOR_LIST_UPDATE, ACTUATOR_UPDATE, ADD_RULE_LOG,
16     NODE_LIST_UPDATE, RULE_LIST_UPDATE
17   }
18 }
```

Listing 1.20. *Message class for HA updates*

```
1   @Handler
2   public void uploadHomeAutomationMessage(HomeAutomationUpdateMessage
3   message) {
4     HomeAutomationMessageFacade content = message.getMsg();
5     UploadMessage toUpload =
6       this.homeAutomationUploader.formMessage(content);
7     this.homeAutomationUploader.upload(toUpload, this.httpConn);
8   }
```

Listing 1.21. *Handler for uploading messages to WebMaDa*

```
1    class HomeAutomationHandler extends AbstractHandler {
2      const MSG_TYPE_ACTUATOR_LIST_UPDATE = 'ACTUATOR_LIST_UPDATE';
3      const MSG_TYPE_ACTUATOR_UPDATE = 'ACTUATOR_UPDATE';
4      const MSG_TYPE_ADD_RULE_LOG = 'ADD_RULE_LOG';
5      const MSG_TYPE_NODE_LIST_UPDATE = 'NODE_LIST_UPDATE';
6      const MSG_TYPE_RULE_LIST_UPDATE = 'RULE_LIST_UPDATE';
7
8      public function handle($message, &$uploadPdo) {
9        $msgContent = json_decode($message['content']
10           ['msgContent'], true);
11       $msgType = $message['content']['msgType'];
12
13       switch ($msgType) {
14         case self::MSG_TYPE_ADD_RULE_LOG:
15           $this->handleAddRuleLog($msgContent, $uploadPdo);
16           break;
17         // handling of all other message types...
18       }
19     }
20   }
21
22   private function handleAddRuleLog(array $logEntry, PDO &$pdo):
23       void {
24     try {
25       $handle = $pdo->prepare('CALL HomeAutomation_AddRuleLog(?,?,?,
26         ?,?)');
27       $handle->bindValue(1, $_SESSION['wsnId']);
28       $handle->bindValue(2, (int) $logEntry['ruleId']);
29       $handle->bindValue(3, $logEntry['logType']);
30       $handle->bindValue(4, $logEntry['logTimestamp']);
31       $handle->bindValue(5, json_encode($logEntry
32         ['previousRuleJson']));
33       $handle->execute();
34       $handle->closeCursor();
35     } catch (PDOException $e) { /** ... */ }
36     $this->sendResponse(S_SUCCESS, 'Inserted log entry!');
37   }
```

Listing 1.22. *WebMaDa's upload handler for HA messages*

WebMaDa on the other side processes uploads through corresponding handlers for each message type. Thus, a new message handler for the HOME_AUTOMATION_MESSAGE has to be added. Each handler implements the handle() method, which is invoked whenever a new message for this handler is received by WebMaDa. The HomeAutomationHandler processes incoming messages based on the "internal" HA message type (see Listing 1.22). The excerpt in the listing includes the handling of adding a new rule log entry, however, other messages are processed in a fairly similar way. SQL procedures are available for every access to the database, the one used for adding rule logs is shown in Listing 1.23. The required data (including *WSN-ID*, *rule ID*, *log-type*, *log timestamp*, and JSON-representation of the rule) are handed over as arguments (see line 1–6), while the actual insertion into the database is realized by a simple INSERT-statement shown in line 13–15. The handler in Listing 1.22 calls the SQL procedure with respective values from the received message to insert the new rule log into the database (see lines 25–34). The $pdo object provides access to the MySQL database of WebMaDa. Within the handler the correct method for further processing is determined within the switch in lines 13–18, and all message types are defined in PHP constants in lines 2–6.

```
1   CREATE PROCEDURE 'HomeAutomation_AddRuleLog'
2       (IN 'p_wsnid' VARCHAR(30),
3   IN 'p_ruleid' INT(11),
4   IN 'p_log_type' TEXT,
5   IN 'p_log_timestamp' DATETIME,
6   IN 'p_previous_rule_json' TEXT)
7   BEGIN
8
9   SET @p_ruleid = p_ruleid;
10  SET @p_log_type = p_log_type;
11  SET @p_log_timestamp = p_log_timestamp;
12  SET @p_previous_rule_json = p_previous_rule_json;
13  SET @s = CONCAT('INSERT INTO ', p_wsnid, '_ha_rule_log
14      (rule_id, log_type, log_timestamp, previous_rule_json)
15      VALUES (?, ?, ?, ?)');
16
17  PREPARE stmt FROM @s;
18
19  EXECUTE stmt USING @p_ruleid, @p_log_type,
20      @p_log_timestamp, @p_previous_rule_json;
21
22  DEALLOCATE PREPARE stmt;
23  END $$
```

Listing 1.23. *SQL procedure inserting new rule logs into the database*

1.4.5. *Sending HA messages from WebMaDa to CoMaDa*

Pull requests are sent through the WSS from WebMaDa to CoMaDa, as explained in section 1.2.1.2. For HA messages this can be achieved with the backend/homeAutomationRequest.php script, callable from any frontend part to send a request to CoMaDa through the WSS. Listing 1.24 shows how the script refers the request to the WSS, adding the type homeAutomationMessage to it in line 2 to let the WSS know which type of request to forward to CoMaDa. The curl-functions of PHP are used in lines 8–13 to first initialize the curl-request, configure it, and finally send the curl-request, i.e. a HTTP-Request to the WSS. The response is echoed (i.e. outputted) by the script so that the frontend can access the response and show appropriate success or error messages. Section 1.4.6 explains how the JavaScript frontend sends requests to this backend script.

```
1   $curlRequestData = $_POST;
2   $curlRequestData['messageType'] = 'homeAutomationMessage';
3   $curlRequestData['wsn'] = $wsnId;
4   $curlRequestData['haMessage'] = json_encode([
5       'action' => $_POST['haAction'],
6       'payload' => $_POST['haPayload']
7   ]);
8   $ch = curl_init(Config::$webSocketServerEndpoint);
9   curl_setopt($ch, CURLOPT_POST, 1);
10  curl_setopt($ch, CURLOPT_POSTFIELDS,
11      http_build_query($curlRequestData));
12  // ...
13  $response = curl_exec($ch);
14  echo $response;
```

Listing 1.24. *WebMaDa - send HA request to the WSS*

Up until now, only messages of type PULL were created and processed by the WSS. Hence, from now on WebMaDa additionally sends the message-type to the WSS to let it know which message type (e.g. PULL or the new HOME_AUTOMATION_MESSAGE) it has to forward to CoMaDa (see line 2 of Listing 1.24). In order to definitely ensure compatibility with the existing version of WebMaDa or the WSS, the message type PULL is assumed if no type is given (see lines 4–8 of Listing 1.25). This does not change the previous behavior and thus enables backwards compatibility. Other than that, the WSS mainly works in the same way as before. Listing 1.25 shows how different message types are differentiated and processed. Pull-queries are handled exactly as before with only one difference: the handling has been outsourced into a separate method, along with a new method for HA messages; a switch-statement determines the right method to use (see lines 10–18). HA messages are forwarded to CoMaDa using the new HOME_AUTOMATION_MESSAGE type and include the payload retrieved from the

WebMaDa frontend (see section 1.4.6 and Listing 1.24). Detailed explanations of how the WSS builds requests and sends them to CoMaDa are given in (Schmitt *et al.* 2016a).

```
1    @Override
2    protected void doPost(HttpServletRequest req,
3      HttpServletResponse resp) throws IOException {
4        // get message type (pull query or home automation)
5        String messageType = "pullQuery"; // default
6        if (req.getParameter("messageType") != null) {
7            messageType = req.getParameter("messageType");
8        }
9        // ...
10       switch (messageType) {
11         case "pullQuery":
12           this.handlePullQueryMessage(req, resp);
13           break;
14         case "homeAutomationMessage":
15           this.handleHomeAutomationMessage(req, resp);
16           break;
17         // ...
18       }
19   }
20
21   private void handleHomeAutomationMessage(HttpServletRequest req,
22     HttpServletResponse resp) throws IOException {
23       String wsnId = req.getParameter("wsn");
24       String homeAutomationMsgContent=req.getParameter("haMessage");
25       ClientInformation clientInformation = sessions.get(wsnId);
26       if (clientInformation != null) {
27           Session session = clientInformation.getSession();
28           String socketMsg = buildJsonData(
29               WebSocketMessageType.HOME_AUTOMATION_MESSAGE,
30               Collections.singletonMap("content",
31               homeAutomationMsgContent)
32           );
33           session.getBasicRemote().sendText(socketMsg);
34           resp.getWriter().write("success");
35       } else { /* ... */ }
36   }
```

Listing 1.25. *WSS - Handle HA/PULL requests received from WebMaDa*

On CoMaDa's side, the WSNWebModule is again responsible for handling incoming PULL-requests. Depending on the message type, the processing of received messages is delegated to a related handler. Thus, a new handler for the HOME_AUTOMATION_MESSAGE message is added to the web module to process incoming HA messages from WebMaDa: the HomeAutomationMessageHandler shown in Listing 1.26. Due to an injection of the HA-Module (see line 13), the handler has access to it and can utilize its methods to perform the required actions. All action types are represented by a static constant (see lines 4–11), a switch in the handle() method calls the correct method for the given action (see lines 17–32). In the example, the handler for setting the paused-status of a rule is shown. It can simply retrieve the rule object from the HA-Module and update it accordingly.

```
1   public class HomeAutomationMessageHandler implements
2       IClientHandler {
3
4     private static final String
5       ACTION_TYPE_DELETE_RULE = "DELETE_RULE";
6     private static final String
7       ACTION_TYPE_EXECUTE_COMMAND = "EXECUTE_COMMAND";
8     private static final String
9       ACTION_TYPE_RULE_SET_PAUSED_STATUS = "RULE_SET_PAUSED_STATUS";
10    private static final String
11      ACTION_TYPE_SAVE_RULE = "SAVE_RULE";
12
13    @Inject private HomeAutomationModule haModule;
14
15    @Override
16    public void handle(JsonObject message) {
17      JsonObject content = Json.createReader(
18        new StringReader(message.getString("content"))
19      ).readObject();
20
21      String action = content.getString("action");
22      JsonObject payload = Json
23            .createReader(new StringReader(content.
24              getString("payload")))
25            .readObject();
26
27      switch (action) {
28        case ACTION_TYPE_RULE_SET_PAUSED_STATUS:
29          this.handleRuleSetPausedStatus(payload);
30          break;
31        // handling of other message types ...
32      }
33    }
34
35    private void handleRuleSetPausedStatus(JsonObject payload) {
36      Optional<IRule> rule = this.haModule.getRule(payload.
37          getInt("ruleId"));
38      if (rule.isPresent()) {
39        rule.get().setPaused(payload.getBoolean("paused"));
40        this.haModule.updateRule(rule.get());
41      }
42    }
43  }
```

Listing 1.26. *CoMaDa – handle incoming requests from WebMaDa*

Four actions are available: deleting, updating the paused-status and creating new rules, as well as executing commands on actuators. These actions are all realized – similar to the exemplary handler for setting the paused-status – using the `HA-Module` triggering uploading updated data to WebMaDa again, e.g. when a request to update a rule was received and performed accordingly. This approach also puts the entire logic and responsibility of managing the model (i.e. rules and registered actuators) on the CoMaDa HAIFA part, since WebMaDa only requests to perform certain actions. Therefore, no synchronization or similar has to be maintained between CoMaDa and WebMaDa, as only CoMaDa is allowed to change the actual model.

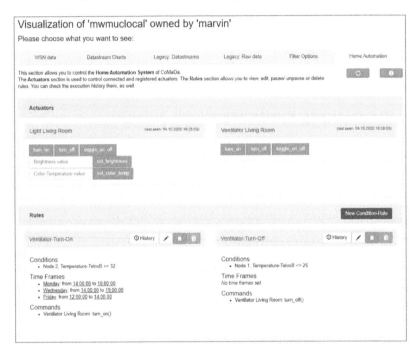

Figure 1.24. *WebMaDa's HAIFA administration frontend. For a color version of this figure, see www.iste.co.uk/khatoun/cybersecurity.zip*

1.4.6. *WebMaDa's frontend*

The HAIFA WebMaDa frontend is integrated into the existing Visualization page in a new tab *Home Automation*, and is only visible for the WSN-Owner. It is implemented using the Smarty template engine added to WebMaDa in Schmitt *et al.* (2016a) and utilizes the jQuery JavaScript framework for sending HTTP-Requests to the backend scripts and enabling dynamic features of the frontend, such as dialogs and interactive forms. Figure 1.24 shows the entire page, which follows a similar structure as the CoMaDa equivalent shown in Figure 1.16. It allows commands to be executed on actuators and automation rules to be managed, for which the edit dialog is shown in Figure 1.25. Bu using JavaScript and jQuery, the frontend is capable of sending requests via the WebMaDa backend script to the WSS (see Listing 1.24), which forwards them to CoMaDa (see Listing 1.25), where they are finally handled (see Listing 1.26). As shown in Listing 1.27, such a request is sent using the ajax service exposed by jQuery. This service allows HTTP-Requests of all different types (e.g. GET and POST) to be sent, arbitrary JSON encoded data to be attached to it (see lines 5–10), and success or errors to be handled in separate functions (see line 11 and 12). In this example, the rule ID, new paused status, and WSN-ID are sent to the backend script, along with the requested action type: HA_ACTION_RULE_SET_PAUSED_STATUS (see lines 2–6 of Listing 1.26 for all action types). The main PHP script – /home-automation.php – loads and renders the Smarty template. It gives the template access to required data such as registered actuators and rules by fetching them from the database through MySQL procedures. These procedures are similar to the one shown in Listing 1.23, except they return data selected from the database based on the given *WSN-ID*.

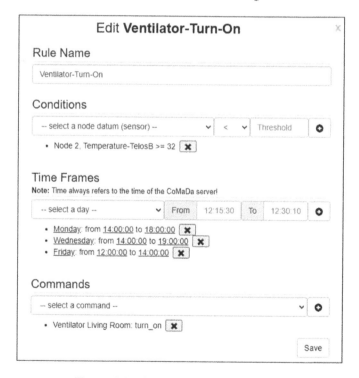

Figure 1.25. *WebMaDa's HAIFA rule edit*

```
1    function  setRulePauseStatus(ruleId,  paused)  {
2      $.ajax({
3        type:  'POST',
4        url:  'backend/homeAutomationRequest.php',
5        data:  {
6          haPayload:  JSON.stringify({  ruleId,  paused:  !! paused  }),
7          haAction:  HA_ACTION_RULE_SET_PAUSED_STATUS,
8          wsn:  (new  URLSearchParams(window.location.search)).get('wsn'),
9          csrf:  getCsrfValue()
10       },
11       success:  ()  =>  {  /* ... */  },
12       error:  ()  =>  {  /* ... */  },
13       dataType:  "html"
14     });
15   }
```

Listing 1.27. *WebMaDa frontend sending HA-requests to the WSS*

1.5. Evaluation of HAIFA

The correctness of the designed workflow and interfaces is proven by proof-of-concept presented throughout this chapter. For the realized HA solution HAIFA, the following three objectives were defined:

– O1: Actuator and Node Hardware interoperability needed to be ensured;

– O2: Automation should be based on the SecureWSN's sensors data;

– O3: Configuration and Management integration into the SecureWSN components CoMaDa and WebMaDa are required.

These three objectives result in four requirements for HAIFA: (R1) HAIFA shall facilitate the easy integration of different types of actuators in terms of hardware, vendor, and/or protocol meeting O1. (R2) WSN-Owners will be able to configure automation of the actuators based on rules, while the sensor values of nodes are used to define certain thresholds, triggering the rules to be performed. In addition to thresholds, time frames may be defined, allowing rules to only be executed during the specified times slots. Hence, R2 relates to O2. (R3) derives implicitly from the request to integrate HAIFA into an existing SecureWSN and, thus, HAIFA needs to be compatible to all supported platforms using CoMaDa. Hence, R3 relates to O1. The last requirement (R4) requests that actuators be registered in CoMaDa, then controlled by executing commands on them from either CoMaDa's or WebMaDa's interfaces. The management of rules should be possible from both systems and the information history of when a rule has been last checked or executed should be displayed. R4 related to O3. The upcoming section proves that HAIFA fullfills the requirements R1-R4 and O1-O3 accordingly.

1.5.1. *Actuator interoperability (R1)*

The gateway approach was selected for HAIFA to support the integration of many different actuator devices, and therefore the ZigBee gateway was implemented and configured accordingly, as described in section 1.4.2. Its functionality is tested by executing various commands on connected actuators. Figure 1.16 shows that connected actuators are attached correctly to the `HA-Module` by the gateway after they have been setup and integrated into the configuration file, according to the gateways design specifications. The gateway's functionality is verified in section 1.5.2, where the rule automation, including executing commands on actuators, is evaluated. In order to extend the support by protocols other than ZigBee, a new gateway can be implemented in a similar manner. All required interfaces are clearly defined and the ZigBee gateway serves as a blue print for the implementation.

1.5.2. *Rule-based automation (R2)*

Figure 1.26 illustrates the testbed used for testing the fulfillment of R2 – the rule based automation. Node 1 is placed in front of a fan (or vent), and Node 2 is outside of its range. The vent is plugged into the Ikea ZigBee power switch, and an Osram ZigBee light bulb is placed next to it. Node 2 is powered by batteries, Node 1 by an USB power adapter and, thus, its operating temperature in the room is much higher (approx. 30°C) than Node 2 (approx. 22°C). This is caused by the heat of the power adapter.

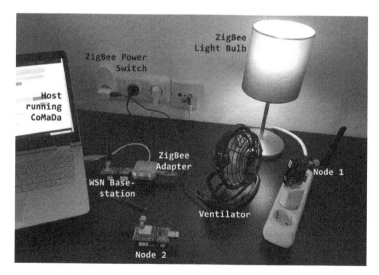

Figure 1.26. *Testbed for rule evaluation. For a color version of this figure, see www.iste.co.uk/khatoun/cybersecurity.zip*

Figure 1.27. *Testing the rule configuration*

The goal of the performed test is the verification of multiple layers of the realized rule system of HAIFA. Three items are investigated: (1) correct interaction when using multiple different sensor values in condition thresholds, (2) performing commands on more than one actuator, and (3) the correct interoperability of more than one rule together. During the testing period it should be ensured that the temperature of Node 1 stays in the range of 25°C to 26°C. A fan is used to control the situation and it is turned on and off if a rule is matched. For testing multiple conditions in one rule the temperature of Node 1 should only be kept in the desired range if the temperature of Node 2 is above 19°C. To cool the device below 19°C, the device is placed into a fridge. The light bulb should be turned on whenever the fan is turned off and vice versa. Two rules are created to maintain the explained scenario and their configuration is depicted in Figure 1.27. Rule 1 – *Vent-On-Light-Off* – means the fan is turned on and the light off if the temperature of Node 1 is above 26°C and the temperature of Node 2 is above 19°C. Furthermore, the rule should only be executed within a specified time frame (here 10:00 a.m. to 3:50 p.m.). With Rule 1 the correct function of multiple conditions and time frames can be proved. Rule 2 – *Vent-Off-Light-On* – causes the fan to shut down and the light to turn on if the temperature of Node 1 is below 25°C.

The detailed process of the testing is summarized in Table 1.3, along with an expectation regarding the actions taken by the HAIFA and the expected impact on the temperature of Node 1. During the test, the temperature of both nodes is monitored using the visualization features of WebMaDa and CoMaDa, as illustrated in Figure 1.28. The graph of Node 1 clearly dropped down to 25°C at 3:30 p.m. when the rules have been activated, remaining between 25°C and 26°C for 10 minutes, until Node 2 was put in the fridge. From this point in time, the temperature of Node 2 dropped far below 19°C and for Node 1 it increased to approx 30°C again without decreasing. The zigzag pattern of Node 1 demonstrates how both rules were alternately executed and kept the temperature within the desired range together. Even after Node 2 was taken out of the fridge at 3:50 p.m. and exceeded 19°C at around 3:53 p.m. again (reflected in the graph at 3:50 p.m., where the temperature of Node 2 approaches approx. 22°C again), the fan was not turned on again due to the expired time frame of the respective rule. During the entire test the light was always powered when the vent was not enabled and vice versa.

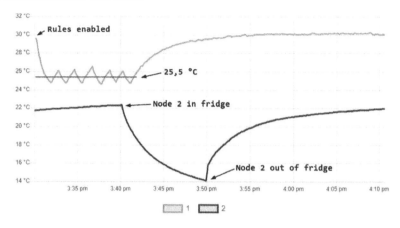

Figure 1.28. *Node visualization of temperature measurements. For a color version of this figure, see www.iste.co.uk/ khatoun/cybersecurity.zip*

Time	Action	Expectation
3:30 p.m.	Rules un-paused	Vent is turned on due to the high operating temp. of Node 1 above 26°C and temp. of Node 2 being above 19°C. Both configured rules should ensure to keep the temperature of Node 1 between 25°C and 26°C by alternately switching the vent on and off.
3:40 p.m.	Node 2 put in fridge	As the temp. of Node 2 falls below 19°C rule Vent- On-Light-Off will stop enabling the vent and, thus, the temp. of Node 1 will increase up to approx. 30°C again.
3:50 p.m.	Node 2 put out of fridge	The temp. of Node 2 increases over 19°C again, but still the vent is not enabled due to the expired time slot. Hence, the temp. of Node 1 will not decrease again.
4:10 p.m.	End of monitoring	–

Table 1.3. *Automation test procedure*

1.5.3. *Node hardware interoperability (R3)*

This integration test verified the proper implementation of the following features as the expectations from Table 1.3 were fully fulfilled: (i) rules are checked and executed properly if all conditions are met, (ii) multiple given conditions need to be satisfied in order to execute the commands, as defined in the related rule, (iii) time-frames define valid slots in which rules are executed, outside of the respective windows no execution takes place, and (iv) commands are executed properly on the corresponding devices (and also on multiple actuators). Thus, the rule automation system has been successfully evaluated and R2 for HAIFA is fulfilled.

The design and implementation of the HAIFA does not have any direct dependency on the actual node implementations, nor has it been changed or adjusted in any way. Instead, the HAIFA uses the virtual representation of the WSN provided by the WSNApp. This abstract layer is implemented by the corresponding driver for the OS, and respectively, the driver and required protocol handlers must provide necessary data to the WSNApp to be able to maintain the virtual WSN. Therefore, as long as any driver correctly integrates itself into the framework, the underlying node hardware or OS does not matter at all.

However, to practically verify this statement a test has been implemented on a CoMaDa system running a network of OpenMote B nodes under RIOT OS and a network with TelosB nodes under TinyOS. No problems were recognized while creating rules and setting thresholds on the node sensor values of these OpenMote nodes. This test verified the node hardware interoperability.

1.5.4. *CoMaDa and WebMaDa management (R4)*

The proper integration of both administration frontends has been tested in several ways. First, commands on actuators have been executed using both endpoints, including commands that require arguments such as setting the brightness. Second, rule management (creation, adjustment, and removal) has been performed on both sides. In fact, the rule setup has been created twice: once using the CoMaDa frontend and a second time within WebMaDa. Furthermore, the upload of rule-logs to WebMaDa has been checked manually by inspecting the database of WebMaDa and visually by visiting the rule log on the WebMaDa frontend. Since all of these tests have worked flawlessly, the management integration of CoMaDa and WebMaDa has been implemented correctly.

1.6. Summary and conclusions

A powerful Home Automation Framework has been designed and integrated into a SecureWSN framework, as presented in this chapter. It integrated itself seamlessly into the existing application and the modular concept of CoMaDa allowed the module to be added to the existing setups of the SecureWSN easily. Smart home devices, i.e. actuators, can be controlled through the framework while the interoperability of different manufacturers and communications standards is ensured by the flexible gateway approach. A gateway is the core entity for communication with physical devices. They are attached to the HA-Module, and are thus made available to all of the other components of the HAIFA. To demonstrate the functionality of the overall architecture a reference ZigBee gateway has been implemented using a ZigBee adapter, along with a third party library to control ZigBee enabled smart home actuators, such as power switches and light bulbs. The actual automation is configured using a rule-based system, where the conditions on certain sensor values have to be fulfilled in order to perform the desired actions on connected actuators. The sensor values are provided by existing entities of the SecureWSN project. All of the different node hardware and OS combinations supported by CoMaDa are compatible with the presented HAIFA. Configuration management and monitoring of rule execution is available throughout both user endpoints of the SecureWSN framework: CoMaDa for the local deployment, setup, and (initial) configuration, as well as for registering actuator devices in the system, and WebMaDa for remote rule management and command executions on actuators from anywhere in the world. Clear APIs have been designed and applied to the implementation in this thesis (reflected in the several interfaces and abstract classes), which allow easy interchangeability and extension of existing or new components of the HAIFA, also including the modular gateways. The final evaluation demonstrated the correct functionality and cooperation of all newly designed and implemented features of the module and the HAIFA in general.

Overall it was shown how actuators can be integrated in a smart home solution, independent of vendor specific gateways or applications, also giving the owner the freedom to integrate their own specifications, work-flows, and implementations. This may introduce risks and threats to the system, but here it is overcome by: (i) integration of several security checks for ownership verification, (ii) providing a detailed and step-wise user guide allowing people who are not tech-savvy to work with it as well, and (iii) logging all changes. Further, (iv) HAIFA also offers home owners physical security. For example, the home owner can make it appear to the outside world that they are present, even though this is not true, and thus deter burglars. Elsewhere, heating, ventilation, and air conditioning (HVAC) systems can be automated on given boundaries, establishing feel-good environments.

1.7. Acknowledgements

This research and implementation is part of a project that has received funding from the European Union's Horizon 2020 research and innovation programme under grant agreement No 830927, named CONCORDIA. Thanks to the Munich Network Management (MNM) Team and the LRZ (Leibniz Supercomputing Center) for the support of WebMaDa in the Computing Cloud.

1.8. References

AngularJS (n.d.). AngularJS Client-Side JavaScript Framework [Online]. Available at: https://angularjs.org/ [Accessed 9 February 2022].

Bernheim Brush, A., Lee, B., Mahajan, R., Agarwal, S., Saroiu, S., Dixon, C. (2011). Home automation in the wild: Challenges and opportunities. *SIGCHI Conference on Human Factors in Computing Systems*, Association for Computing Machinery, New York, 2115–2124.

Bluetooth Special Interest Group (2019). Bluetooth Core Specification v5.2 [Online]. Available at: https://www.bluetooth.com/specifications/bluetooth-core-specification/ [Accessed 9 February 2022].

Bormann, C., Castellani, A.P., Shelby, Z. (2012). CoAP: An application protocol for billions of tiny internet nodes. *IEEE Internet Computing*, 16(2), 62–67.

Bormann, C., Ersue, M., Keranen, A. (2020). Terminology for constrained-node networks [Online]. Available at: https://tools.ietf.org/html/draft-bormann-lwig-7228bis-06 [Accessed 9 February 2022].

Boyd, C. and Mathuria, A. (2010). *Protocols for Authentication and Key Establishment*. Springer, Heidelberg, Germany.

Bünte, O. (2020). Ring Always Home Cam: Amazons autonome Indoor-Drohne soll Innenräume überwachen [Online]. Available at: http://www.tinyurl.com/1vfdqizq [Accessed 9 February 2022].

Cabarkapa, D., Grujic, I., Pavlovic, P. (2015). Comparative analysis of the Bluetooth low-energy indoor positioning systems. *12th International Conference on Telecommunication in Modern Satellite, Cable and Broadcasting Services (TEL SIKS)*, IEEE, New York, 76–79.

Chetroi, A. (2020). Zigpy [Online]. Available at: https://github.com/zigpy/zigpy [Accessed 9 February 2022].

Contiki-NG (2020). Contiki-NG [Online]. Available at: https://github.com/contiki-ng/contiki-ng [Accessed 9 February 2022].

Dague, S. (2017). Why can't we have the internet of nice things? A home automation primer [Online]. Available at: https://opensource.com/article/17/7/home-automation-primer [Accessed 9 February 2022].

GitHub (2020a). Guice Dependency Injection Framwork [Online]. Available at: https://github.com/google/guice [Accessed 9 February 2022].

GitHub (2020b). HiveMQ MQTT Client [Online]. Available at: https://github.com/hivemq/hivemq-mqtt-client [Accessed 9 February 2022].

Gomez, C., Oller, J., Paradells, J. (2012). Overview and evaluation of Bluetooth low energy: An emerging low-power wireless technology. *Sensors*, 12(9), 11734–11753.

Hive Home (n.d.). Build your home with smart home technology [Online]. Available at: https://www.hivehome.com/ [Accessed 9 February 2022].

Huebscher, M.C. and McCann, J.A. (2008). A survey of autonomic computing degrees, models, and applications. *ACM Computing Surveys*, 40(3), 1–28.

Institute of Electrical and Electronics Engineers (2020). IEEE Standard for low-rate wireless networks. Technical report IEEE Std 802.15.4-2020 (Revision of IEEE Std 802.15.4-2015), Institute of Electrical and Electronics Engineers, New York.

ITU (2016). Overview of the internet of things. Technical report ITU-T Y.2060, renumbered as ITU-T Y.4000, International Telecommunication Union [Online]. Available at: https://www. itu.int/rec/dologin_pub.asp?lang=e&id=T-RECY.2060-201206-I!!PDF-E&type=items [Accessed 9 February 2022].

Kanters, K. (2020a). Zigbee2Mqtt Bridge [Online]. Available at: https://github.com/Koenkk/ zigbee2mqtt [Accessed 9 February 2022].

Kanters, K. (2020b). Zigbee2Mqtt Bridge Documentation [Online]. Available at: https://www. zigbee2mqtt.io/ [Accessed 9 February 2022].

Karl, H. and Willig, A. (2007). *Protocols and Architectures for Wireless Sensor Networks*. John Wiley & Sons, Hoboken, NJ, USA.

Keller, M. (2014). Design and implementation of a mobile app to access and manage wireless sensor networks. Master's Thesis, University of Zurich, Department of Informatics, Communication Systems Group, Zurich, Switzerland.

Kephart, J.O. and Chess, D.M. (2003). The vision of autonomic computing. *Computer*, 36(1), 41–50.

Kephart, J.O. and Walsh, W.E. (2004). An artificial intelligence perspective on autonomic computing policies. *5th IEEE International Workshop on Policies for Distributed Systems and Networks (POLICY)*, IEEE, New York, 3–12.

Lee, H.J., Lee, S.H., Ha, K.-S., Jang, H.C., Chung, W.-Y., Kim, J.Y., Chang, Y.-S., Yoo, D.H. (2009). Ubiquitous healthcare service using Zigbee and mobile phone for elderly patients. *International Journal of Medical Informatics*, 78(3), 193–198.

Light, R.A. (2017). Mosquitto: Server and client implementation of the MQTT protocol. *Journal of Open Source Software*, 2(13), 265.

Light, R.A. (2020). Mosquitto documentation – Mosquitto.Conf Man Page [Online]. Available at: https://mosquitto.org/man/mosquitto-conf-5.html [Accessed 9 February 2022].

Logging Services (2020). Apache Log4j 2 [Online]. Available at: http://logging.apache.org/ log4j/2.x/ [Accessed 9 February 2022].

LoRa Alliance (n.d.). LoRa Alliance [Online]. Available at: https://www.lora-alliance.org/ [Accessed 9 February, 2022].

OASIS (2019). MQTT Version 5.0 – OASIS Standard. Technical report, OASIS [Online]. Available at: https://docs.oasis-open.org/mqtt/mqtt/v5.0/os/mqtt-v5.0-os.html [Accessed 9 February 2022].

Ott, C. (2017). Database solution for offline graphical visualization of sensor data. PhD Thesis, University of Zurich, Department of Informatics, Communication Systems Group, Zurich, Switzerland.

Paessler (2019). IT Explained: MQTT [Online]. Available at: https://www.paessler.com/it-explained/mqtt [Accessed 9 February 2022].

Pahl, M.-O. (2014). Distributed smart space orchestration. PhD Thesis, Technische Universität München, Munich, Germany.

Pahl, M.-O., Müller, A., Carle, G., Niedermeier, C., Schuster, M. (2009). Knowledge-based middleware for future home networks. *2nd IFIP Wireless Days (WD)*, IEEE, New York, 1–6.

Porambage, P., Ylianttila, M., Schmitt, C., Kumar, P., Gurtov, A., Vasilakos, A. (2016). The quest for privacy in the internet of things. *Computer Society*, 3, 34–43.

RabbitMQ (2020). RabbitMQ Documentation [Online]. Available at: https://www.rabbitmq.com/documentation.html [Accessed 9 February 2022].

RIOT OS (n.d.). RIOT [Online]. Available at: http://riot-os.org/ [Accessed 9 February 2022].

Rose, K., Eldridge, S., Chapin, L. (2015). The internet of things: An overview – Understanding the issues and challenges of a more connected world [Online]. Available at: https://www.internetsociety.org/wp-content/uploads/2017/08/ISOC-IoT-Overview-20151221-en.pdf [Accessed 9 February 2022].

Schmitt, C. (2019). Trust & security in IoT: Monitoring with constrained devices. Habilitation, University of Zurich, Zurich, Switzerland.

Schmitt, C. (2020). SecureWSN: A framework to monitor environments with constrained devices [Online]. Available at: https://corinna-schmitt.de/securewsn.html [Accessed 9 February 2022].

Schmitt, C., Freitag, A., Carle, G. (2013). CoMaDa: An adaptive framework with graphical support for configuration, management, and data handling tasks for wireless sensor networks. *9th International Conference on Network and Service Management (CNSM)*. IEEE, New York, 211–218.

Schmitt, C., Anliker, C., Stiller, B. (2016a). Pull support for IoT applications using mobile access framework WebMaDa. *3rd World Forum on Internet of Things (WF-IoT)*, IEEE, New York, 377–382.

Schmitt, C., Strasser, T., Stiller, B. (2016b). Third-party-independent data visualization of sensor data in CoMaDa. *12th International Conference on Wireless and Mobile Computing, Networking and Communications (WiMob)*, IEEE, New York, 1–8.

Shelby, Z., Hartke, K., Bormann, C. (2014). The constrained application protocol (CoAP). Technical report 7252, IETF, Fremont, CA, USA.

Stanford-Clark, A. and Truong, H.L. (2013). MQTT for sensor networks (MQTT – SN) protocol specification [Online]. Available at: https://www.oasis-open.org/committees/download.php/66091/MQTT-SN_spec_v1.2.pdf [Accessed 9 February 2022].

Strasser, T. (2016). Offline method for graphical visualization of sensor data [Online]. Available at: https://doi.org/10.1109/WiMOB.2016.7763238.

systemd (2020). systemd [Online]. Available at: https://systemd.io/ [Accessed 9 February 2022].

TinyOS (n.d.). TinyOS [Online]. Available at: http://tinyos.net/ [Accessed 9 February 2022].

Tsai, H.-M., Tonguz, O.K., Saraydar, C., Talty, T., Ames, M., Macdonald, A. (2007). Zigbee-based intra-car wireless sensor networks: A case study. *IEEE Wireless Communications*, 14(6), 67–77.

Weber, M. (2020). Home automation service integration in SecureWSN. Bachelor Thesis, Ludwig-Maximilians-Universität München, Munich, Germany.

Wheeler, A. (2007). Commercial applications of wireless sensor networks using ZigBee. *IEEE Communications Magazine*, 45(4), 70–77.

YouGov (2018). Smart Homes 2018 Report [Online]. Available at: http://www.tinyurl.com/1spnqhrq [Accessed 9 February 2022].

ZigBee Alliance (2012). ZigBee specification. Technical report 53474r20, ZigBee Standards Organization [Online]. Available at: http://www.zigbee.org/download/standards-zigbee-specification/ [Accessed 9 February 2022].

2

Smart Home Device Security: A Survey of Smart Home Authentication Methods with a Focus on Mutual Authentication and Key Management Practices

Robinson RAJU and Melody MOH

Department of Computer Science, San Jose State University, USA

2.1. Introduction

The last decade (2000–2010) saw the remarkable inflection point where the number of inanimate things connected to the Internet overshot the world's population. This happened in 2008 when the number of devices connected to the Internet became greater than the world's population of around 6.7 billion people (Moh and Raju 2018). In the ensuing decade (2010–2020), the number has not only more than doubled as it crossed 20 billion (Gyarmathy 2020), but the "things" have become smarter.

"IoT" (Internet of Things), "IIoT" (Industrial Internet of Things), "CPS" (Cyber-Physical Systems) are the common terms that are used to describe the ecosystem of these "smart things". IoT is a network of interconnected computing devices with the ability to transfer data over a network without needing human interaction (Moh and Raju 2018). CPSs are a subset of IoT devices that not only

Cybersecurity in Smart Homes,
coordinated by Rida KHATOUN. © ISTE Ltd 2022.

connect to the Internet but also act on the physical environment that they are deployed into. These "smart devices" have become ubiquitous and have pervaded almost every sphere of people's lives. There are now "smart homes" in which devices in the home connect to the Internet and can provide data to the residents, "smart medical appliances" that not only monitor remotely but also administer medicines in a timely fashion, "smart bridges" that have sensors to monitor load, "smart power grids" to detect disruptions and manage the distribution of power, "smart machinery" that has embedded sensors in heavy machinery to increase worker safety and improve automation, and so on (Moh and Raju 2019). As devices become more miniature, the usage of BSNs (Body Sensor Networks), which are wearable computing devices, either implanted or placed on the body, is also on the rise (Raju *et al.* 2018).

According to some estimates, over 100 new devices connect to the Internet every second (Gyarmathy 2020). Of these, smart home devices are seeing the fastest growth due to their ability to make life more automated and convenient. For instance, smart speaker devices like Amazon Echo are in over 30 percent of US households that have a broadband connection as of March 2019 (Gyarmathy 2020).

The explosive growth and the general lack of regulation and standardization have resulted in millions of devices in homes and offices with privacy and security issues. Moreover, people are attracted by the futuristic features that would make their lives more comfortable, and this focus on utility and optimism blinds them to the security and privacy issues. Who would not want to have a baby monitor that can alert them when the baby wakes up, a thermostat that adjusts itself without intervention, or a smart speaker that can switch on lights and other similar devices?

People are then alarmed when a widespread cyber-attack occurs, and their data is stolen, or their privacy violated. For instance, the Dyn DDoS attack in 2016 (Greenstein 2019) that disrupted almost the entire Internet was possible due to attackers getting access to thousands of IoT devices, especially smart home devices. Often, the consumers blame the manufacturers for not making the devices secure enough. However, in most instances, the breach happens due to the consumers not resetting the default passwords to access the device. The sharp increase in home deliveries in 2020 due to the Covid-19 pandemic has given rise to an increase in package thefts (Stickle and Felson 2020). This has led to an increasing number of people purchasing smart home camera systems like the Ring doorbell or Nest camera. At the same time, the smart home camera is one of the most vulnerable devices in the home and was called the "Consumer IoT failure of the year" in 2019 by IoT Analytics (Lueth 2020) due to the sheer number of security breaches with them.

Therefore, the privacy and security of IoT devices at home are of paramount importance. Manufacturers should acknowledge that most consumers do not know how the smart devices work, are not proficient in updating security settings and have no idea of privacy exposure. Researchers have proposed many solutions to increase awareness as early as the purchase stage. Options like adopting a "nutrition label" on boxes that sell smart devices (Emami-Naeini *et al.* 2020) or having a standardized privacy fact-sheet similar to what financial organizations in the US have, have been proposed along with many others. While increasing the awareness of consumers is a path that needs to be taken, manufacturers also need to step up to increase the security posture of the devices. It could be as simple as forcing customers to change default passwords. Another mechanism found in many secure web-based systems is to use mutual authentication/mutual TLS.

The premise of mutual authentication is that only trusted client devices can connect to smart home devices or the network. Two-way authentication is the default mode for protocols like SSH (secure shell). It is, however, optional in TLS (Transport Layer Security). By default, the TLS protocol proves the server's identity to the client using an X.509 certificate, but the client's identity verification is left to the server. Client-side verification may not be possible for servers that serve a lot of anonymous clients. However, in the case of smart home devices, it can be enforced since the clients who need access to the smart devices are minimal and need to be trusted.

This chapter aims to study authentication mechanisms in smart home systems with a focus on mutual authentication as a solution to improve the security posture of smart home devices. It gives an overview of a smart connected home system, security issues and solutions in smart devices, a primer on mutual TLS, key management practices, mutual authentication in smart home systems and its challenges as well as open research items.

2.2. Smart home – introduction and technologies

2.2.1. *Smart home – introduction*

A smart connected home is a residence set up with IoT devices that help with comfort, convenience, entertainment and security (Aldrich 2003; Mantas *et al.* 2011) with regard to the people and things within the home. Figure 2.1 shows some examples of smart home devices. Different terms like smart home, connected home, smart connected home, and so on are used in this context. Originally, "smart home" referred to homes that had automated devices within the home, "connected home" referred to homes connected over IP-based networks, and "smart connected home" referred to homes that had both of these. However, increasingly these terms are being used interchangeably, and in general, "smart home" today refers to "smart connected home".

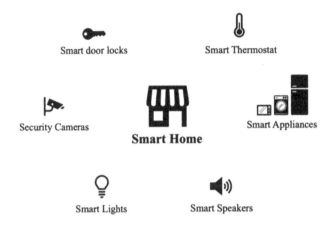

Figure 2.1. *Smart home ecosystem*

Many aspects of the home that had to be managed manually in the past can now be managed using smart devices. This is partly due to the advancement of technology that has given rise to miniature devices that can sense and process more data, and also to the development of machine learning techniques to process and understand large amounts of data quickly.

In this regard, the smart home is going in the same direction as the smart car, with each new model having more sensors to not only help drive the car but also maintain it. Just a couple of decades ago, there were very few sensors in cars, and now there are hundreds. There are sensors in the tires, cameras all around, sensors on the seats, radars, ultrasonic sensors, vision-based sensors, and so on, giving consumers the ability to enjoy features like blind-spot detection, lane assist, automatic braking, pedestrian warnings, automatic high-beam, voice recognition, voice assistance, and even automatic driving (Möller and Haas 2019). In the same way, there could be smart devices in every corner of the home.

Imagine a home that automatically regulates the temperature in each room by learning the usage pattern of the people and pets in the home, a home that detects if the main door or garage door is left open, where the lights, the door, the blinds can be remotely controlled, where voice control can adjust the lights, where the refrigerator tells if is it time for grocery shopping or even does the shopping for the owners, a home that detects water leaks or plumbing issues, a home that warns the residents of fire damage or even an earthquake before it occurs. As more sensors are introduced into the home, and as more homes are connected to the Internet, the possibilities are endless. Homeowners can be safer than ever and avoid costly maintenance issues altogether (Ghaffarianhoseini *et al.* 2016). Routine home maintenance issues like plumbing leaks and non-replacement of air filters cause extensive damage to the home and the HVAC system. Many home buyers find issues in the home that were not discovered during the home inspection process, many unknown even to the previous owners. Having sensors at different parts of the home could avoid many of the hassles of homeownership and make life more enjoyable. Hence the optimism around the connected home technology is well-founded.

2.2.2. Smart home devices – categories

Smart home devices can be categorized into the following groups based on their utility or the area of the home they control. Kang *et al.* grouped them into welfare, entertainment, environment, security, communication and green (Kang *et al.* 2017). Bugeja categorized them into four groups – energy, entertainment, healthcare and security (Bugeja *et al.* 2018). Mantas *et al.* grouped them into four categories – home appliances, lighting and climate control system, home entertainment system, home communication system, and home security system (Mantas *et al.* 2011).

Based on the growth in consumer devices commonly available in the market, we could categorize them into the following – security, heating and cooling, lighting, appliances, and entertainment. Some devices overlap multiple categories, and some devices may not fall into any of these groups. For instance, Google Nest Wifi is a wireless router and also doubles up as a smart speaker (Google Assistant) system. As a router, it could not be categorized into any of the categories above, but it could be put under the entertainment category as a smart speaker. Here is a quick overview of these categories:

1) **Security** – Devices that help protect homes, such as doorbell cameras, smart locks, motion detectors, and alarm systems, fall under this category. Security systems are getting smarter as the usage grows. Some systems can detect when the owner is away from home and automatically lock the home, detect intruders, integrate with smoke or carbon monoxide detectors, or detect water leakages. Nest Protect, the Ring doorbell camera, the Schlage smart lock, Canary Home Security and the Arlo camera are a few examples.

2) **Heating and cooling** – Keeping the home at an optimal temperature while it is too hot or too cold outside is one of the key elements of making it livable. For a

long time, manual thermostats had to be set by people to control the heating system or the air conditioner. Smart thermostats make this automated by learning about the system's usage, saving a lot of energy in the process. The Nest thermostat and Ecobee are an examples of such devices.

3) **Lighting** – Smart lighting systems allow users to control lighting inside or outside the home remotely. Some systems allow lights to be controlled using the voice through smart speakers. Lights could automatically turn on when someone is in the room or gradually turn on during the morning, or even change color based on music or mood. These systems generally need smart bulbs that connect to a central hub. An example of this type of system is the Philips Hue lighting system.

4) **Appliances** – Refrigerators were one of the first appliances that became popular as a smart appliance. Some refrigerators keep a tab on the inventory of items inside them and notify users (Sripan *et al.* 2012). Many appliances are now smart devices, such as microwave ovens, dishwashers, and coffee makers. Often Wi-Fi-connected devices integrate well with systems such as Amazon's Alexa and can operate under voice commands.

5) **Entertainment** – Smart TVs, smart music systems, and other devices controlled by voice fall under this category. Most major manufacturers like Sony, Samsung and Vizio have smart entertainment systems.

Also, a smart home can be viewed as a system that houses other smart ecosystems. A smart car is a system by itself that connects directly to the Internet. A person wearing implantable and other devices forms a BSN (Body Sensor Network) with its own hub (different from the gateway for the smart home devices) or might connect to a phone, which connects to the Internet. Both the smart car and BSN are in the home though they may not be categorized as smart home systems.

2.3. Smart home security

The mere fact that a smart home system is connected to the Internet means that it is exposed to a hostile environment. Any system that needs to be secure on the Internet should make an effort to address the seven key concepts in the area of computer security (Daswani *et al.* 2007):

1) Authentication – Authentication is an act of verifying someone's identity using "something you know", "something you have", or "something you are", or a combination of these factors.

2) Authorization – Authorization is the act of making sure that a user, generally an authenticated user, has the authority to perform a specific action.

3) Confidentiality – Confidentiality ensures that the data at rest or in transit is kept secret from unauthorized users.

4) Data/message integrity – Data integrity ensures that the data is not tampered with during transmission.

5) Accountability – Accountability ensures that the system can identify who the attacker is in case someone has tried to tamper with the data or attack the system.

6) Availability – Availability ensures that the system is available to perform its functions.

7) Non-repudiation – Non-repudiation ensures that the sender or receiver cannot deny the message.

2.3.1. *Threats*

For smart home systems, threats and vulnerabilities can come from any of the seven concepts mentioned above. However, some areas are more critical than others. One key difference between a smart home system and an enterprise system is that the average user of a smart home system may not have in-depth technical knowledge of the system and may not be aware of the threats. A 2014 report published by mashable.com stated that 73,000 webcams were exposed to the Internet because people had not changed the default passwords (Moh and Raju 2019). There are many such instances where the naivety and ignorance of users has led to security issues.

Komninos *et al.* (2014) listed confidentiality, resilience, reliability and availability as the fundamental security properties that threaten smart home systems. Lin and Bergmann (2016) listed confidentiality, authentication and access as the three critical threats faced by smart home systems. They note the threats to access or authorization as the most severe of these since unauthorized access, especially as an administrator, is potentially catastrophic for the household. Nawir *et al.* (2016) listed data integrity, privacy, non-repudiation and authorization as the critical threat areas.

From the existing literature, we could summarize the following as the key security goals that are compromised by various threats to a smart home system. Threats could be in the form of eavesdropping, traffic analysis, message modification, replay attack, impersonation, repudiation, physical tampering/ removal, illegal software update, interception, traffic load, and so on.

– Data integrity – An adversary could access data in transit and tamper with it, resulting in erroneous measurements and actions. It could be a malicious attacker eavesdropping on traffic from home to an external network or even from the internal network if the attacker has gained access. One way of achieving integrity is MAC (Machine Authentication Code) (Mantas *et al.* 2011).

– Data confidentiality – The daily life patterns of residents at home could become exposed due to unauthorized viewing or usage of data from smart home devices. There have been instances of thieves getting to know when residents are at home or not by gaining access to electricity meter readings (Komninos *et al.* 2014). If attackers can gain access to more data, there is no mention of the harm they could inflict. Confidentiality can be achieved by encrypting data at rest and in flight.

– Authentication – A smart home system has different types of interactions – user-to-device, device-to-device and device-to-external network (Mantas *et al.* 2011). Customer impersonation and device impersonation are the chief threats to authentication (Komninos *et al.* 2014). Weak authentication leads to easy access to the system for adversaries, and this is a considerable threat. The model of authentication at the gateway and free access at the device levels does not work. The best option is to have a Zero Trust security model (Gilman and Barth 2017), assuming that the adversary is inside the internal network, and insist on authentication at every device. However, due to resource constraints, this may not be possible for all devices.

– Authorization/access threats – Unauthorized devices connecting to the home network, unauthorized users gaining administrator-level access to the smart devices and thereby to other systems in the network, are perilous scenarios. The system should to configured to have different types of users with different access levels so that most users will not have access to resources that they are not authorized for (Mantas *et al.* 2011). The important thing is to restrict elevated access to a smaller set of users.

2.3.2. *Vulnerabilities*

Many researchers have categorized vulnerabilities in smart home systems. The following are a few of them.

Lin and Bergmann (2016) listed the following vulnerabilities for a smart home system – network accessibility, physical accessibility, constrained system resources, system heterogeneity, fixed firmware, slow uptake of standards, and lack of dedicated security professionals to manage the complexities of a smart home network. Many issues like constrained system resources, system heterogeneity, fixed firmware, and slow uptake of standards have been there and are becoming more of an issue due to the increased adoption. Though miniature sensing devices are becoming more powerful with every passing year, they still do not have the computing capabilities to leverage more robust security paradigms. Also, the existence of multiple vendors in the market creates a heterogeneous system with different operating systems and interfaces.

Ali and Awad (2018) applied the OCTAVE (Operationally Critical Threat, Asset, and Vulnerability Evaluation) Allegro methodology to assess the security risks of smart homes. They listed ten different areas of vulnerability with threats for each of the areas. User credentials, device information and metadata, log information, video feed, system setup information, location tracking, and so on are the areas that lead to user impersonation threats, denial-of-service (DoS) attacks, information modification, and spying.

Davis *et al.* (2020) conducted a comprehensive review of the known vulnerability studies of smart home devices. They classified the vulnerabilities into four categories – physical, network, software and encryption. Physical attacks occur when adversaries gain physical access to devices and tamper with them. The network is vulnerable to attacks like man-in-the-middle and DoS. Software attacks exploit the bugs in the software, especially in systems that have not been patched. Encryption attacks occur when an attacker breaks the encryption mechanism by gaining access to the keys or using machines powerful enough to crack a weakly encrypted system or data.

There are common themes in all these vulnerability areas. Attackers are always on the lookout to hijack a device in the network to steal data or an identity or cause a DoS attack. Also, in most homes, smart devices are not integrated when the home is built. They are gradually added one by one, as and when new systems come onto the market or when the residents in the house become aware of or are able to afford these devices. As mentioned above, devices could be from different manufacturers who may have different standards when it comes to security. Even if a home is secure at a point in time, when a new device is added, the system must be re-evaluated to ensure that the initial assumptions about security have been maintained. The hope is that, as newer systems begin to roll out features like security and privacy labels (Emami-Naeini *et al.* 2020), consumers will be able to make informed decisions.

The following table summarizes the threats and challenges across the seven key security concepts discussed in section 3.1.

Security Goal	Security Threats	Security Challenges
Authentication	– Impersonation – Eavesdropping – Traffic analysis – Replay attack	– Default passwords – Lack of UI – Lightweight authentication protocols
Authorization	– Impersonation – Unauthorized access due to lack of tiered access levels	– Physical access – Lack of local authentication – Lightweight protocols for authorization
Confidentiality	– Impersonation – Eavesdropping – Traffic analysis	– Lack of encryption for data in transit due to low-capability devices – Hardware attacks
Data integrity	– Message modification – Replay attack – Interception	– Spoofing due to lack of attestation – Lack of comprehensive checks due to low-capability devices
Accountability	– Impersonation – Anonymous access	– Devices with hardware or software vulnerabilities exposed to the Internet. – Delayed patching of security issues due to heterogeneity of devices.
Availability	– DDoS attack – Physical Tampering	– Prone to DDoS – Physically accessible
Non-Repudiation	– Forgery	– Lack of secure identity and signatures – No secure local storage

Table 2.1. *Summary of security threats and challenges for a smart home*

2.3.3. *IoT communication protocols*

IoT devices are connected to the Internet but may not always leverage the protocols used by web applications and other devices on the Internet. The main challenge has been that IoT devices are low energy, limited-memory devices and are not as powerful as the general desktop and laptop computers. IETF (Internet Engineering Task Force) has established lightweight communication protocols at different layers over the past few years to overcome these limitations. Some of the most commonly used protocols are 6LoWPAN at the physical layer, RPL at the routing layer, and CoAP at the application layer.

Here is a short explanation of these three protocols:

– **6LoWPAN (IPv6 over Low-Power Wireless Personal Area Networks)** – The IEEE wireless standard 802.15.4 defines how the physical and MAC layers should operate under low-rate wireless personal area networks (LR-WPANs). 6LoWPAN was designed by IEFT and defined in RFC 4944 (Montenegro *et al.* 2007) to define how the IPv6 version of the Internet Protocol could be transmitted using the IEEE 802.15.4 protocol.

– **RPL (Routing Protocol for Low-Power and Lossy Networks)** – RPL is a routing protocol designed by IETF and defined in RFC 6550 (Winter *et al.* 2012) for wireless networks with low power and in a lossy network. It is a protocol based on distance vectors and is mainly used in 6LoWPAN networks.

– **CoAP (Constrained Application Protocol)** – CoAP is an application layer protocol designed by IETF and defined in RFC 7252 (Shelby *et al.* 2014) for networks of constrained devices. It provides multi-cast support and adopts UDP (User Datagram Protocol) since it is better suited for low-bandwidth connections than TCP (Transfer Control Protocol) used in web-based communications. The communication is also based on the REST (Representational State Transfer) model, making data exchange semantics simple. CoAP uses DTLS (Datagram Transport Layer Security) for secure communications. DTLS is a variant of TLS (Transport Layer Security), used for secure communication over HTTP in web applications. DTLS is based on UDP, while TLS is based on TCP since the implementation of TLS is complicated for constrained devices.

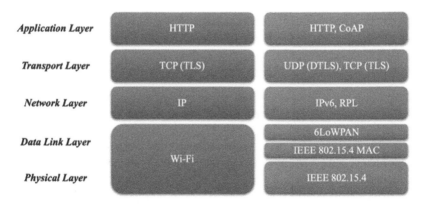

Figure 2.2. *Comparison of IoT protocol stack with Wi-Fi at different layers of the simplified OSI model. For a color version of this figure, see www.iste.co.uk/khatoun/cybersecurity.zip*

The figure below compares the IoT protocol stack with Wi-Fi at different layers of the simplified OSI model (Olsson 2014).

	Protocol	Transport	Security
Application	COAP	UDP	DTLS
	MQTT	TCP	SSL
	XMPP	TCP	SSL
	AMQP	TCP	SSL
	DDS	TCP UDP	SSL TLS
	HTTP	TCP	SSL
	Protocol	**Functionality**	
Network Layer	mDNS	Service Discovery	
	DNS-SD	Service Discovery	
	RPL	Routing	
	6LoWPAN	Encapsulation	
	6TiSCH	Encapsulation	
	Protocol	**Spreading technique**	**MAC Access**
Physical Layer	IEEE 802.15.4	DSSS	TDMA, CSMA/CA
	BLE	FHSS	TDMA
	LTE-A	Multiple CC	OFDMA
	Z-Wave	–	CSMA/CA
	Sigfox	BPSK	Unslotted ALOHA
	NB-IoT	QPSK	FDMA/OFDMA

Table 2.2. *Summary of protocols across different IoT layers (Kalla* et al. *2020)*

2.3.4. *Enhancements to IoT communication protocols*

Over the last decade, many enhancements and variants of the protocols mentioned above have been proposed by researchers in this field. Some of them are listed below:

– IPSec (Internet Protocol Security) – A secure version of IP that provides secure encrypted communication between two nodes over an IP network.

– Raza *et al.* proposed an enhancement over IPSec by compressing the AH (Authentication Headers) and ESP (Encapsulating Security Payloads) (Raza *et al.* 2011).

– Yue *et al.* proposed EAKES6Lo, an enhanced authentication and key establishment scheme for 6LoWPAN (Yue *et al.* 2015).

– Rajesh *et al.* proposed an improvement in energy consumption and communication delay of 6LoWPAN devices using Lamport's algorithm in the MAC layer (Rajesh *et al.* 2019).

– Perrey *et al.* proposed a topology authentication scheme named TRAIL (Trust Anchor Interconnection Loop), which improved RPL (Perrey *et al.* 2013). It could discover and isolate forged nodes and thus prevent topological inconsistency attacks.

– Kenji *et al.* proposed a secure parent node selection scheme in route construction to exclude attacking nodes from the RPL network (Kenji *et al.* 2015).

– Kamgueu *et al.* surveyed RPL enhancements focused on three areas - topology optimization, security, and mobility (Kamgueu *et al.* 2018). Topology optimization concentrated on metrics like buffer occupancy, MAC reliability, residual energy, expected lifetime, and average delay. Security focused on attacks like DoS, isolation, replay attacks and spoofing. RPL extensions like mRPL, mRPL+, ME-RPL, mod-RPL and co-RPL, which took mobility into account, were the third area of RPL enhancements in the survey.

– CoAP enhancements – CoCoA, CoCoA+ (Betzler *et al.* 2015) and pCoCoA (Bolettieri *et al.* 2018) were proposed to improve upon the issues in the default congestion control mechanism of CoAP. CoCo-RED (Suwannapong *et al.* 2019) was proposed to improve response time and packet loss. Genetic CoCoA++ (Yadav *et al.* 2020) was proposed to improve packet failure rate.

2.3.5. *IoT security architectures*

There has been much research into IoT security, and multiple architectures have been proposed over the past couple of decades. Many of them provide good security postures and have been implemented in multiple systems. Many middleware systems exist since that is the easiest way to use existing infrastructure to communicate with and support IoT devices (Fremantle and Scott 2017). Cloud-based architecture, also known as Cloud of Things (CoT), offers solutions where complex processing happens in the cloud and triggers are sent to the IoT devices. Fog computing and Edge computing attempt to move this processing closer to the devices to get near-real-time reactions. Gateway architecture provides for a central hub to connect and coordinate with all the devices. Even in the absence of an Internet connection, a gateway could provide proxy support to shield IoT devices from an attack.

Secure Architecture	AuthN	AuthZ	Cf'ty	D In'ty	Acb'ty	Av'ty	N-R'ion
SOCRADES (2008)	Y		Y	Y			
SMEPP (2009)	Y		Y	Y			
FIWARE (2011)	Y	Y	Y	Y	Y		
Privacy-preserving smart meter system (2011)			Y				
INCOME (2012)	Y	Y	Y	Y			Y
VIRTUS (2012)	Y	Y	Y	Y			
Webinos (2012)	Y	Y	Y	Y			
SBIOTA (2012)	Y		Y				
Device Cloud (2014)	Y	Y	Y	Y	Y		
DREMS (2014)	Y	Y	Y	Y			
NAPS (2014)	Y	Y			Y		
IoT Cloud on CoAP (2014)	Y		Y	Y			
Cloud of Things for Smart Home (2014)			Y	Y			
Message Integrity using DH and RC4 (2014)			Y	Y			
Lattice-based homomorphic aggregation (2014)			Y	Y			
&Cube (2015)	Y	Y	Y	Y			
Cloud-Sensor Secure architecture (2015)	Y	Y					
SEA (2015)			Y	Y			
IoT-MP (2016)	Y	Y					
NOS (2016)	Y	Y	Y	Y			
IAGW (2016)	Y	Y	Y	Y			
Secure firmware validation (2016)	Y	Y					
AllJoyn (2016)	Y	Y	Y	Y	Y		Y
TBSA for Smart Home (2017)			Y	Y			
SH-BlockCC (2019)	Y		Y	Y		Y	Y

Table 2.3. *Matrix of security architectures and security goals (Authentication (AuthN), Authorization (AuthZ), Confidentiality (Cf'ty), Data Integrity (D In'ty), Accountability (Acb'ty), Availability (Av'ty), Non-Repudiation (N-R'ion))*

The following is a list of a few of the secure IoT architectures:

– **SOCRADES** (De Souza *et al.* 2008) is a web services based middleware designed for IoT in manufacturing plants. It utilizes Web Service Security standards for encryption and message integrity.

– **SMEPP** (Secure Middleware for P2P) (Benito *et al.* 2009) is an IoT middleware designed to provide secure peer-to-peer communication.

– **FIWARE** (Glikson 2011; Fazio *et al.* 2015) is an IoT middleware with a framework that supports a variety of plugins. Security is implemented through plugins for identity management, authorization policy, and policy enforcement points.

– **Privacy-preserving smart meter system** (Ács and Castelluccia 2011) provided a differential privacy model where the data is shared by maintaining the patterns while withholding the actual information.

– **INCOME** (Arcangeli *et al.* 2012) is an IoT middleware framework for multi-scale context management. It uses context data from multiple levels to make decisions related to privacy, trust and security.

– **VIRTUS middleware** (Conzon *et al.* 2012) is an XMPP (eXtensible Messaging and Presence Protocol) based architecture for secure IoT communications. It uses an SASL (Simple Authentication and Security Layer) protocol for authentication and TLS for security. It attempts to guarantee a (near) real-time, secure and reliable communication channel among heterogeneous devices.

– **Webinos** (Desruelle *et al.* 2012) is a framework where each user has a Personal Zone Hub (PZH), which is in their control to protect. Users authenticate into the PZH using the OpenID protocol. The PZH acts as a certificate authority (CA), issuing certificates to the devices used for mutual authentication using TLS.

– **SBIOTA** (Server-Based Internet-Of-Things Architecture) (Bergmann and Robinson 2012) proposed a separate network port for authentication and communication between the gateway and devices. Before connecting a device to the network, it is authenticated to ensure that only legitimate devices are connected to the network.

– **Device Cloud** (Renner *et al.* 2014) is an architecture where Cloud Computing concepts are applied to IoT device middleware. It supports OAuth2.0 to provide tokens to devices that are used for encryption and access control.

– **DREMS** (Distributed REaltime Managed Systems) (Levendovszky *et al.* 2013) is a middleware runtime for IoT that has the concept of multi-level security (MLS) for communications between an actor and a device.

– **NAPS** (Naming, Addressing and Profile Server) (Liu *et al.* 2014) is a middleware IoT architecture to support heterogeneous IoT devices to communicate with each other. It has a central component to handle AAA (Authentication, Authorization and Accounting), and the security design uses on the Network Security Capability model.

– **IoT Cloud on CoAP** (Kovatsch *et al.* 2014) is an IoT cloud architecture based on CoAP protocol that uses DTLS for security.

– **Cloud of Things for smart home** (Alohali *et al.* 2014) is a secure Cloud of Things architecture for smart homes where symmetric key encryption is applied to encrypt end-to-end communications.

– **Message Integrity using DH and RC4** (Mantoro *et al.* 2014) is a security model consisting of AES256, Ephemeral Diffie-Hellman key exchange, and RC4-based hash function to secure the authentication and assure the integrity of message communicated between devices. This is used to authenticate smartphones and send messages safely in a Smart Home environment.

– **Lightweight lattice-based homomorphic privacy-preserving aggregation** (Abdallah and Shen 2014) for Home Area Networks uses a lightweight lattice-based homomorphic cryptosystem to encrypt messages.

– **&Cube** (Yun *et al.* 2015) is a middleware that provides REST APIs and MQTT connections to integrate with IoT devices. Encryption, authentication and access control are provided by a component named Security Manager.

– **Cloud-Sensor Secure architecture** (Razvi *et al.* 2015) has the automation of processes and data analysis done in the Cloud. The slave server manages the security of the sensors and devices on the edge.

– **SEA** (Secure and Efficient Authentication and Authorization) (Moosavi *et al.* 2015) is a secure architecture for IoT-based healthcare using smart gateways. It is based on DTLS and uses a more secure key management scheme between the sensor nodes and the smart gateway.

– **IoT-MP** (IoT Management Platform) (Elkhodr *et al.* 2016) is an IoT middleware that offers a security module that implements attribute-based access control.

– **NOS** (Networked Smart Objects) (Sicari *et al.* 2016) is a quality-aware architecture for IoT where the system provides a reputational score based on data from components like "Quality Analyser" and "Security Analyser". The score is computed by a machine learning algorithm that learns from the systems' behavior in the network.

– **IAGW** (Integrated Access Gateway) architecture (Ding *et al.* 2016) proposes standard interfaces for Smart Home environments, through which various application nodes are connected. The system upward connects with the operator machine-to-machine platform (M2M P/F) and includes a security module to implement the authentication, authorization, and encryption.

– **Secure firmware validation** (Choi *et al.* 2016) performs ID-based authentication between devices in a smart home environment and uses a key derivation algorithm for firmware image distribution.

– **AllJoyn IoT framework at home** (Tomanek and Kencl 2016) is a framework based on the open-source framework "AllJoyn" and contains the AllJoyn core, permission module, and policy certificate trust anchor.

– **Smart Home automation using WSN** (Pirbhulal *et al.* 2017) uses Triangle Based Security Algorithm (TBSA) to ensure energy-efficient data encryption, thus providing a secure IoT-based Smart Home automation system.

– **SH-BlockCC** (Singh *et al.* 2019) is a secure IoT smart home architecture based on cloud computing and blockchain technology. The model utilizes the MCA (Multivariate Correlation Analysis) technique to analyze the network traffic and identify the correlation between traffic features.

The following table summarizes the security architectures listed above and the security goals that each promises to protect.

2.4. Smart home authentication mechanisms

Since its inception, there have been many methods of authentication and authorization for smart devices. The identity of a person or a system could be established using different factors usually categorized into three buckets:

– something that a person **knows**, like a password, private information or secret code (proof by knowledge);

– something that a person **is**, like a fingerprint, retina pattern or signature (proof by property);

– something that a person **has**, like a smart card, digital key or token (proof by possession).

The authentication mechanism could be of two broad types – intra-domain (within-network authentication) and inter-domain (outside-network authentication). Intra-domain authentication could be done by any one of the above mechanisms – proof by knowledge, proof by possession, or proof by property (Mantas *et al.* 2011). Inter-domain authentication should ideally involve additional factors, say, a combination of proof by knowledge and proof by possession, but that is not the case many times.

The ID-password-based authentication mechanism, where authentication is based on a password provided by the user, has to date been the most widely used proof of identity and has not served very well. To reduce friction during onboarding, most manufacturers supply devices with factory-default passwords that remain unchanged by the user. A 2015 study of 50 smart home devices found that none of the devices enforced strong passwords or used other mechanisms to make the devices more secure (Barcena and Wueest 2015). Thus, IoT devices have become the weak link in many systems, and analyses of major breaches have pointed to bad actors leveraging this vulnerability in the past decade. Many home networks that were previously secure have become insecure just by adding a device like a security camera to their network.

Since password guessing is the leading cause of security breaches due to people using default passwords or weak passwords, employing stricter password requirements is often the first step towards improved smart home systems security. However, that may not be enough since adversaries could obtain passwords through phishing or other mechanisms. Hence, to make the system more secure, it is essential to choose not only a strong password but also use additional factors of authentication. For access patterns where a person is physically present, some biometric factors could be used. However, for remote access of the smart devices through APIs (Application Platform Interfaces), that may not work.

2.4.1. *Stages of defining an authentication protocol for IoT*

Ferrag *et al.* defined different stages that an IoT system provider should go through to realize an authentication protocol. The first step is to define a network model, which could be IoS (Internet of Sensors) in the case of a smart home system. The second step is to define an authentication model that could be any of the authentication mechanisms. Examples are password-based authentication, smart-card-based authentication, biometric authentication, mutual authentication, and RFID authentication. The third step is to define an attack model that is most relevant to the network model. Examples include replay attack, privileged-insider attack, and impersonation attack. The fourth step is to select a list of countermeasures. Examples are cryptographic methods, biometric methods, and the fuzzy extractor technique. The fifth step is to identify the phase in which a specific authentication protocol would be used. The authentication protocol used in the initialization phase may be different from that in the message transmission phase. The sixth step is to perform a security analysis using formal security verification tools like ProVerif, BAN-logic (Burrows-Abadi-Needham-Logic) or AVISPA (Automated Validation of Internet Security Protocols and Application). The last step is to do a performance evaluation based on factors like communication overhead, storage cost or computation complexity (Ferrag *et al.* 2017).

Stage	Description
Step 1	Definition of Network Model
Step 2	Definition of Authentication Model
Step 3	Definition of Attack Model
Step 4	Selection of Countermeasures
Step 5	Identification of Phases where specific authentication protocols would be used
Step 6	Security Analysis using formal tools
Step 7	Performance Analysis

Table 2.4. *Stages of defining an authentication protocol for IoT (Ferrag* et al. *2017)*

2.4.2. *Taxonomy of authentication schemes for IoT*

In Step 2 of the stages of defining an authentication protocol, choosing an authentication model was briefly discussed. Based on the security requirements at different levels, a specific scheme that suits the requirement or a combination of different schemes is chosen. The following table summarizes different types of authentications grouped by authentication factors and types.

Mutual authentication or two-way authentication is one of the authentication procedures mentioned above. In this, both entities involved in communication authenticate each other, thus making sure that anonymous users will not be able to read or modify the state of a device. Mutual authentication can be implemented in many ways – through a shared secret, through public keys, or using a timestamp.

Authentication Scheme	Type	Description
Authentication factor	Identity	Information presented by the client to identify itself. E.g. password-based authentication.
	Context	Context could be physical or behavioral. Biometric authentication is an example of physical context. Authentication based on keystroke analysis or gait analysis are examples of using behavioral context.
Use of tokens	Token-based	Authentication based on a token generated by the server using schemes like OAuth2 protocol or open ID.
	Non-token based	Re-authentication for every call.
Authentication procedure	One-way authentication	The client authenticates the server but not vice-versa.
	Two-way (mutual) authentication	Client and server authenticate each other.
	Three-way authentication	A central authority authenticates client and server.
Authentication architecture	Distributed	Authentication is distributed to nodes closer to the clients.
	Centralized	Authentication is done using a centralized server or a trusted third-party.
	Hierarchical	Authentication using a multi-level hierarchy.
	Flat	Authentication using policies defined in a flat structure.
Hardware-based	Implicit	Authentication using physical characteristics of hardware to improve security posture. E.g. Physical Unclonable Function (PUF), True Random Number Generator (TRNG).
	Explicit	Using devices like TPM (Trusted Platform Module) which are hardware designed to store keys and perform hardware authentication.

Table 2.5. *IoT authentication schemes (El-Hajj* et al. *2019)*

Reference	Purpose	Type of Authentication	Pros/Cons
Huth *et al.* (2015)	Authenticate end devices deployed in smart homes based on the combination of PUF and Physical Key Generation (PKG).	Implicit hardware-based, centralized architecture with mutual authentication, asymmetric encryption.	**Pros** – Resistance to device compromise since PUF provides a secure key based on the physical parameters of the end device. **Cons** – Vulnerable to variations in environmental conditions.
Sun *et al.* (2015)	The architecture allows a remote user to communicate with end devices in the smart home network.	Implicit hardware-based, centralized architecture with mutual authentication, symmetric encryption.	**Pros** – Resistance to impersonation and replay attacks. **Cons** – Privacy preservation is not considered.
Zhao *et al.* (2016)	Mutual authentication based on PUF and introduction of object life cycle (OLC) to track the roadmap of a device from manufacture to end-user.	Implicit hardware-based, centralized hierarchical architecture with mutual authentication, symmetric and asymmetric encryption.	**Pros** – Resistance to impersonation and replay attacks. **Cons** – Machine learning attacks or environmental variations not considered.
Muhal *et al.* (2018)	Used CRP data stored inside the gateway to provide mutual authentication between the end device and the gateway.	Implicit hardware-based, centralized architecture with mutual authentication, symmetric encryption.	**Pros** – Efficient in computation, resistant to replay attacks. **Cons** – Machine learning attacks or environmental variations not considered.
Jan *et al.* (2019)	Mutual authentication based on lightweight features of CoAP.	Implicit hardware-based, centralized architecture with mutual authentication, symmetric encryption.	**Pros** – Resistance to replay attacks, DoS attacks, low communication cost. **Cons** – Privacy preservation is not considered; the pre-shared key should be provisioned as a pre-requisite.

Table 2.6. *Examples of smart home authentication proposals*

Mutual authentication using shared key – In this method, when party A wants to communicate with party B, they use a key that is shared securely ahead of time. At a high level, it works as follows: Party A sends a message to party B. After receiving this message, party B sends a random challenge (R1) to party A. After receiving this, party A encrypts R1 using the shared key and sends it to party B. Party A also sends a random challenge R2 to party B. After receiving the encrypted message, party B checks if they could decrypt and obtain R1 from the message. Party B also encrypts R2 and sends the encrypted message to party A who checks it at their end. This completes the authentication, and they are ready to exchange messages.

Mutual authentication using public key (certificate-based mutual authentication is an authentication) – This uses a PKI (Public Key Infrastructure) cryptography framework. In public-key cryptography, when party A needs to communicate with party B, each has a pair of keys – a public key shared with everyone and a private key. When A needs to send a message to B, A either encrypts the message with B's public key or with a randomly generated key using the public key. B then decrypts the message using its private key. Moreover, A can create a digital signature with its private key and sign its message with this key.

Mutual authentication using timestamp – In this method, when party A wants to communicate with party B, party A sends their user name with the current timestamp encrypted with a shared symmetric key K1 to party B. Party B decrypts the timestamp, adds 1 to it, and encrypts the new timestamp with another shared key K2 and sends it to party A along with their user name.

The following table has a few examples of smart home architectures that use mutual authentication.

The next section discusses mutual authentication using PKI and key management fundamentals in detail.

2.5. A primer on mutual authentication and key management terminologies

During the Internet's explosive growth phase, one of the main concerns was the secure transport of data, especially sensitive financial data like credit card numbers. One of the first widely used solutions to the problems of data tampering or eavesdropping was SSL (Secure Sockets Layer), developed by Netscape, which was later the basis for the TLS (Transport Layer Security) standard (Dierks and Rescorla 2006) defined by the IETF (Internet Engineering Task Force). TLS 1.2 was defined later by the IETF in RFC 5246 (Dierks and Rescorla 2008), and the current version is TLS 1.3 defined in RFC 8446 (Rescorla 2018).

TLS is a general-purpose protocol that sits between the application layer (HTTP) and transport layer (TCP), and this automatically ensures that the features of TCP like reliability, flow control, and congestion control are available to the application (Shinzaki *et al.* 2016). At a high level, an application that TLS secures has three properties that may be used independently or in combination:

1) Client can authenticate the server using public-key cryptography.

2) The connection between the client and server is secure and reliable because symmetric cryptography is used to encrypt the communication and each message includes a message integrity check.

3) Server can authenticate the client using public-key cryptography.

In general, TLS usage in the web involves authenticating the server and communicating securely. In mutual authentication, also known as two-way authentication, both steps 1 and 3 listed above occur. The client and server authenticate each other before actual communication occurs by providing digital certificates to prove their identities.

2.5.1. *X.509 certificate*

X.509 is a specification standard for public-key certificates. It contains a public key and an identity and is either signed by a CA (Certificate Authority) or is self-signed. The mutual authentication process generally involves the following certificates:

– Root CA certificate – A self-signed X.509 certificate used to identify a CA that signed a client's certificate. In IoT setup, the administrators deploy a root CA certificate or chain to the edge servers.

– Server SSL certificate – Deployed in the server and server sends it over to the client during TLS handshake.

– Client SSL certificate – Deployed in the client and client sends it over to the server during mutual authentication.

Many industrial IoT trust implementations use the X.509 digital certificate format (Russel and Van Duren 2018). In the new IoT devices, the device manufacturer certifies and signs the keys they assign to the devices.

The fields in an X.509 Certificate are as follows:

– Version.

– Certificate serial number: unique serial number that is created for each certificate that a CA creates.

– Certificate issuer's signature: the algorithm used to generate the signature.

– Issuer: the DN of the issuing CA.

– Validity period.

– Subject: the DN of the entity to which the certificate is issued.

– Subject public-key info: the public-key algorithm and value (RSA, DSA or Diffie-Hellman).

– Issuer unique identifier (optional).

– Subject unique identifier (optional).

– Extensions (optional).

– CA's digital signature.

X.509 certificates provide strong identity and access control, but they require the devices to have sufficient computational power, which may not be present in IoT devices. This prevents many miniature devices from being part of public-key cryptography. Fortunately, this is becoming solved in two ways: newer devices are being manufactured with more computational power, and at the same time, newer standards are being defined for devices with computational constraints. The IEEE 1609.2 certificate format has approximately half the typical X.509 certificate and still uses elliptic curve cryptographic algorithms.

The sequence of certificate exchanges and establishment of an encrypted channel for communication using mutual certificate-based authentication is depicted in Figure 2.3.

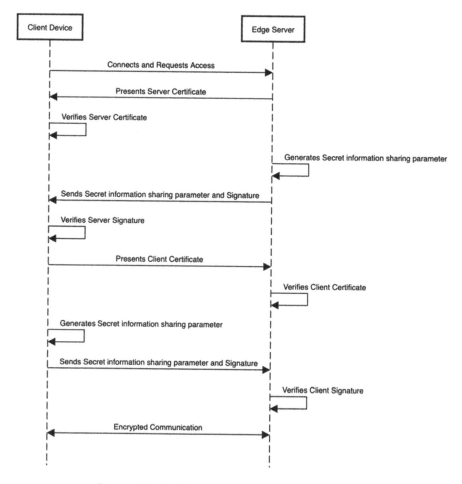

Figure 2.3. *Certificate-based mutual authentication*

2.5.2. *CoAP and DTLS*

As mentioned earlier, CoAP (Constrained Application Protocol) is an application layer protocol defined in RFC 7252 (Shelby *et al.* 2014) for networks of constrained devices. It can integrate with HTTP (HyperText Transfer Protocol) for communication via the web and relies on the request/response paradigm using REST (Representational State Transfer). For security, CoAP uses the DTLS (Datagram Transport Layer Security) protocol (Rescorla and Modadugu 2012). DTLS is a variant of TLS (Transport Layer Security), used for secure communication over HTTP in web applications. DTLS is based on UDP, while TLS is based on TCP since the implementation of TLS is complicated for constrained devices. The endpoint is of the form coaps://<url> for secure communication in lieu of coap://<url>. Though it is based on UDP, which can have packet losses, DTLS overcomes this by including a sequence number in the message and retransmissions and timeouts.

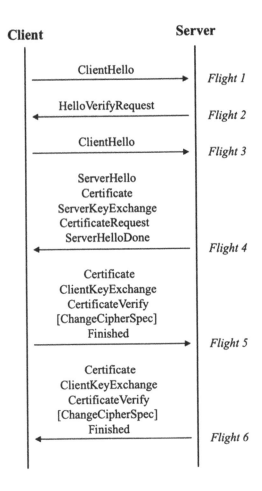

Figure 2.4. *DTLS handshake, client-server authentication*

Three security modes are available in DTLS: pre-shared key, raw public key, and certificate (Tiloca and Raza 2018).

1) Pre-shared key – In this mode, a set of devices is whitelisted to use a specific set of keys shared ahead of time.

2) Raw public key – In this mode, each device has a pair of asymmetric private-public keys, the identity of each device is computed from the public key, and each device has a list of devices that it can communicate with.

3) Certificate – In this mode, similar to the raw public key mode, each device has a pair of asymmetric private-public keys. The difference is that each device also contains an X.509 certificate, which has a digital signature from a well-known trust root (Tiloca and Raza 2018).

A typical DTLS handshake and message transmission depicted in RFC 6347 (DTLS 1.2) is shown in Figure 2.4.

– Flight 1 – Client sends a ClientHello message to the server.

– Flight 2 – Server responds with a HelloVerifyRequest and stateless cookie value. HelloVerifyRequest is designed to prevent DoS attacks.

– Flight 3 – Client sends ClientHello message to the server with the cookie from HelloVerifyRequest attached.

– Flight 4 – Flight 6 – The server responds with ServerHello, and its certificate and client and server authenticate each other, establish mutual trust, and are ready to communicate securely.

2.5.3. *TLS 1.3*

TLS 1.3 (Rescorla 2018) was introduced with IoT use-cases in mind, i.e. to secure connections to and between low-capability devices. One of the main goals was the reduction of n-RTT (number of round trip time) required for the handshake. TLS 1.3 requires only one round trip for a full handshake in comparison to 2-RTT for TLS 1.2. This cuts the encryption latency in half. This is done by sending the key agreement algorithm the server might use and the KeyShare in the ClientHello. If the server is ok with that, it sends back its KeyShare for the same algorithm, thus completing the handshake. Also, the *ServerConfiguration* packet is introduced, which enables remembering previous connections, and this reduces it to 0-RTT for future connections. Most certificates use the RSA algorithm, but lightweight schemes use ECC (elliptic curve cryptography), which uses smaller keys with the same security level as RSA.

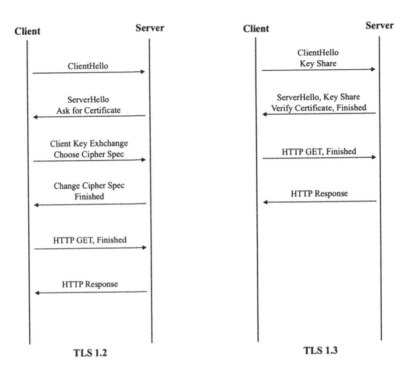

Figure 2.5. *TLS 1.2 and 1.3 comparison*

2.5.4. *Key management fundamentals*

Key management is the process of managing the lifecycle of keys used in cryptographic modules. The lifecycle could include generating, storing, transporting, protecting and revoking keys. A good security practice is to use one type of key for one purpose (Daswani *et al.* 2007). Keys used for authentication are generally called "identity keys". Other types of keys are "session/transport keys" used for communication between two entities using TLS/IPSec, and "integrity keys" used to compute MACs (message authentication codes) for performing integrity checks on IoT messages.

Key generation

Key generation refers to using the mechanism in which keys are generated. Depending on the type of the algorithm and the usage, the key generation scheme might be different. The key generation method for symmetric algorithms is different from that of asymmetric algorithms, where public/private pair of keys need to be generated. One must be careful not to generate weak keys that could be exploited. General rules of thumb are to carefully choose the random number generation algorithm, use passwords and salts to generate a key, not reinvent the wheel and utilize tried-and-tested utilities and libraries to generate keys.

Key generation can be performed directly on the machine or in a centralized key management system. One aspect to remember is to be careful with the location of the key generation. It is safer to generate keys in a machine that is not connected to a network and temporarily store them in a place that is not shared and wipe the memory once the key generation is completed (Daswani *et al.* 2007).

Key storage

Key storage refers to the process of securely storing keys. Keys themselves can be encrypted using KEKs (key encryption keys). Though different systems use varied key storage methods like storing parts of the keys at different places in the code, storing on the disk, storing on a PDA, or a smart card, the safest mechanism is to store in an HSM (hardware security module). HSMs are cryptographic modules that provide extensive physical and logical security protections and are specifically designed to be very difficult to hack (Russel and Van Duren 2018). If hacked or tampered with, they automatically wipe the data stored within.

Key agreement and transport

Key agreement refers to the process of two parties agreeing to use a shared symmetric key or agree upon a scheme of using a pair of public/private keys to communicate. When A needs to send a message to B, A either encrypts the message with B's public key or a randomly generated key using the public key. B then decrypts the message using its private key.

Key transport refers to the process of sending a cryptographic key from one party to another. The key is generally encrypted with a key encryption key (KEK), which may be symmetric or asymmetric.

Key revocation

Sometimes keys could be compromised and in that scenario they will have to be revoked or deleted. Securely deleting cryptographic keys from memory is called zeroization, in which the memory location is overwritten with zeros or random data instead of just deleting the key. The key deletion could also involve physical destruction of the hard drives so that it does not fall into the wrong hands.

Other concepts related to key management that one must be aware of are "key escrow", where keys are stored securely with a third party to be prepared for a disaster recovery scenario, "key lifetime", which refers to how long a key should be in use, "key accounting" which refers to tracking the usage of a key during its lifetime.

2.6. Mutual authentication in smart home systems

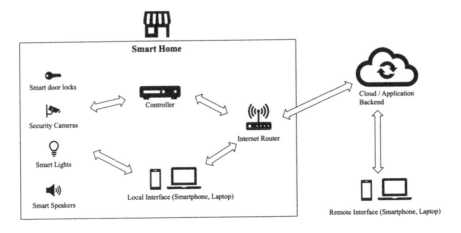

Figure 2.6. *High level overview of a smart home system*

Figure 2.6 shows a smart home network consisting of various communication channels between devices in the home. Though the figure shows a single gateway connecting all the devices, there could be multiple in reality. There could be one gateway for all the bulbs in the home, and another for the security sensors since they are from different manufacturers. Devices like smart speakers could connect to a smartphone through Bluetooth.

For the sake of simplicity, we could consider a gateway connecting to all the devices and a smartphone being able to connect to these devices through the gateway. Moreover, as per our earlier review of security architectures, gateway architecture was the most preferred option. The gateway can provide the translation between varied IoT standards, help maintain a common security scheme and connect the devices to the Internet. The gateway acts as a bridge between the smart home devices and the user. The user can connect to any of the smart home devices from anywhere in the world if they can connect to the gateway through the Internet.

Mutual authentication during the initiation phase can be described as follows. When a new device is added to a system that has a gateway, authentication happens during the first pairing. At this stage, a certificate is created, issued and verified with a manufacturer's private key (Kang *et al.* 2017). Once the pairing process is completed, the "authentication module" returns the module Id and relevant values to indicate whether the new connection is permitted or not. The user registers themselves with the trusted registration authority. The devices are already registered with a trusted authority. Thus, the gateway acts as the special node responsible for controlling the network data, device and network interoperability, and secure management. After successful and secure registration, the trusted authority stores this information in the memory of the smartphone and the gateway used during the authentication process.

Three categories of mutual authentication occur: a) between the user and the gateway, b) between the gateway and the smart devices, c) between the user and the smart devices. In addition, they establish a secret session key between them to protect exchanged messages. A symmetric session key is established for future secure communications using a symmetric cipher such as AES-CBC.

2.6.1. *Device and user onboarding*

The first step in device onboarding is device provisioning, which is the process of a device registering itself to the IoT platform when it first comes online. The process is as follows:

– At the manufacturer – Using the root CA registered to the platform, a certificate that is unique to the device is created. This is then stored in the device firmware.

– At the user – When the device comes online and connects to the platform, the platform validates the certificate against its root CA. After this, the device can connect multiple times to the platform.

The next step is device onboarding, which is the process of linking a user identity to a device. The process is as follows:

– the user gets an activation code from the device (it could be on the device or on the packaging from the manufacturer, provided through the phone, etc.);

– the user submits the code to the platform, and it associates the user with the device and sends this information to the gateway or the device.

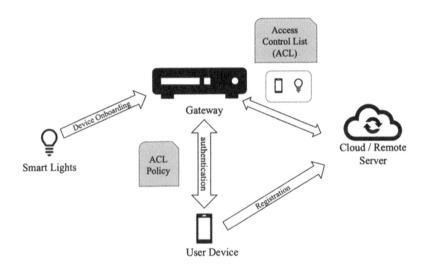

Figure 2.7. *Device onboarding and authentication*

2.6.2. *Flow of user authentication and authorization*

When a device is trying to get access to a sensor through the gateway, it gets authenticated first. Key exchanges occur, and credentials are validated by the gateway or, in some instances, the remote server. When the authentication is complete, the platform generates a session id to keep track of all the actions during that specific session.

After authentication is completed, the gateway checks the ACLs for authorization when the user performs any action. ACLs are checked to make sure that the user is authorized to perform that specific action.

2.6.3. *Examples of mutual authentication schemes*

There have been many designs and implementations of the usage of mutual authentication in a smart home ecosystem. Over a decade ago, SPS (Secure Profile Server) was proposed, which had the inter-node communication as TLS enabled, and provided payload encryption and certificate-based authentication based on X.509 certificates. SPS was a middleware for smart home systems to ensure the security of personal profiles by allowing access only for relevant stakeholders in a specific situation. Mutual authentication was made mandatory to prevent anyone from spoofing their identity to the Security Manager, and it used a ticketing system. A ticket comprises the six entries – a) Application's identifier, b) Application's public key, c) Issuer's public key, d) ACL (Access Control List), e) Timestamp with expiry, and f) Digital Signature.

There are a number of works on mutual authentication for home networks in smart grids, collectively called SG-HANs (Smart Grid Home Area Networks). Fouda *et al.* proposed a mutual authentication and a lightweight message authentication mechanism for smart grids (Fouda *et al.* 2011). This system had less communication overhead and message decryption delay than other systems of the day (Ferrag *et al.* 2017). Nicanfar *et al.* proposed SGMA (Smart Grid Mutual Authentication protocol) and SGKM (Smart Grid Key Management) (Nicanfar *et al.* 2013) in which the smart meter in a home network was mutually authenticated with an authentication server in the smart grid. The protocol used an initial password and provided efficiency by decreasing the number of steps in the remote password protocol from five to three, and the number of exchanged packets from four to three. The mutual authentication scheme prevented brute-force attacks, replay attacks, man-in-the-middle attacks, and DoS attacks. The proposal also contained an efficient key management protocol for key management of unicast and multicast communications in the smart grid based on enhanced identity-based cryptography using the PKI (Ferrag *et al.* 2017). Other examples are the ECC-based authenticated key establishment (EAKE) protocol proposed by Li (Li 2013), another ECC-based device authentication protocol for smart energy home area networks by Vaidya (Vaidya *et al.* 2011), and device authentication mechanisms for the SG-HANs based on symmetric-key cryptography proposed by Ayday and Rajagopal (Ayday and Rajagopal 2013).

There are also many examples of mutual authentication for machine-to-machine (M2M) communications. The LGTH (Lightweight Group authentication protocol) (Lai *et al.* 2013) implemented mutual authentication for M2M communications. To reduce the authentication overhead of the public-key cryptosystems, LGTH proposed a lightweight group authentication protocol based on aggregate message authentication codes (MACs) (Lai *et al.* 2013a, 2013b). The SE-AKA (secure and efficient authentication and key agreement) protocol (Lai *et al.* 2013a, 2013b) proposed implementing mutual authentication between devices in a home network domain, among others. The protocol was an enhancement over the existing AKA protocols with lower authentication message delivery overhead (Ferrag *et al.* 2017). It used elliptic curve Diffie-Hellman (ECDH) to realize key forward/key backward secrecy. It used the ProVerif tool, an automatic cryptographic protocol verifier, for security analysis and formal verification of the mutual authentication between the mobile equipment and its serving network (Ferrag *et al.* 2017). The SEGR (secure and efficient group roaming) protocol (Lai *et al.* 2014) addressed the secure and efficient access authentication for a group of MTC (machine type communication) devices during roaming. This protocol proposed the implementation of mutual authentication and key agreement between a group of devices that perform M2M (machine-to-machine) communication within 3GPP and WiMAX networks. The M2M application model using TDSCDMA (time division-synchronous code division multiple access) (Sun *et al.* 2015) achieved mutual authentication in machine-to-machine home network communication by connecting a mobile user with the home network using the TDSCDMA network. After connection, the communicating parties were identified by password-based authentication and key establishment protocol. It was efficient in terms of the number of calculations needed and communication volume (Ferrag *et al.* 2017). GLARM (group-based lightweight authentication scheme for resource-constrained M2M communications) (Lai *et al.* 2016) focused on group authentication and key agreement but for M2M devices in 3GPP networks. Here the mutual authentication and secure key agreement happened in the initialization and group authentication and key agreement phases.

There are also many mutual authentication schemes focused on WSNs, which are a broader class of sensors that include smart home sensors. PAWN (payload-based mutual authentication scheme for wireless sensor networks) (Jan *et al.* 2017) is one such example. This scheme proposed an extremely lightweight payload-based mutual authentication protocol for a cluster-based hierarchical WSN. It operated in two steps. In the first step, an optimal percentage of cluster heads was selected, authenticated, and allowed to communicate with neighboring nodes. In the second step, each cluster head acted as a server and authenticated nearby nodes to form clusters. PAWN could detect Sybil attacks based on the cluster formation between neighboring nodes and their nearest cluster head (Ferrag *et al.* 2017). Kumari *et al.* proposed a mutual authentication and key agreement scheme between a user and a sensor node within a WSN (Kumari *et al.* 2016). It used BAN-Logic to verify that the proposed protocol could establish a session key between user and sensor node

(Ferrag *et al.* 2017). Similar proposals that provided mutual authentication and session key agreement securely for WSNs used tools like BAN-logic (Chung *et al.* 2016), ProVerif (Mahmood *et al.* 2016), and AVISPA (Amin and Biswas 2016) security analyzer for verification. The improved three-factor remote authentication scheme for WSN (Wu *et al.* 2018) used mutual authentication to protect data between the sensor node, users, and gateway node. This scheme was an improvement over an earlier three-factor authentication scheme (Das *et al.* 2016), which lacked user anonymity and strong forward security.

Many mutual authentication schemes have been proposed for systems with smart card-based authentication, along with additional features like perfect forward secrecy (Chang and Le 2015), anonymity, untraceability (Jiang *et al.* 2016), and authentication using biohashing (Srinivas *et al.* 2017).

Other proposals to note are ID-based encryption by Shinzaki *et al.* and "mutual authentication for IoT-enabled devices in distributed Cloud Computing environment" by Amin *et al.* In 2016, a team from Fujitsu Laboratories published a paper that outlined a lightweight mutual authentication mechanism. It evaluated two variants of the TLS protocol, named TLS-PSK and TLS-DHE-RSA. TLS-PSK used pre-shared keys (PSK), while TLS-DHE-RSA used public-key cryptographic methods. The downside of using public-key cryptography was that it required all the devices to have a certificate, which had a considerable effort estimate. In order to overcome this difficulty, Fujitsu proposed a public-key cryptography technology called ID-based cryptography. The proposal allowed the use of information (ID) associated with a user, device or server, such as a device ID, e-mail address or a fully qualified domain name (FQDN), as a public key. The proposal by Amin *et al.* contained an architecture applicable for a distributed cloud environment using a smart card. It was based on elliptic curve cryptography (ECC) and provided mutual authentication between registered users and IoT devices (Amin *et al.* 2018).

Considering the low capacity of the devices, many authentication schemes use symmetric key cryptography. Several lightweight authentication protocols have been proposed to solve this issue. The anonymous authentication scheme by Banerjee *et al.* is an authentication protocol that used one-way hashing and XOR functions to make the protocol lightweight (Banerjee *et al.* 2020). This was an improvement over the ECC-based anonymous authentication protocol by Shuai *et al.* (2019). Dey and Hossain proposed a lightweight and secure session-key establishment scheme for smart home networks and incorporated the Diffie-Hellman (DH) key exchange.

Reference	Name	Details of Authentication
Schaefer et al. (2006)	SPS (Secure Profile Server)	Payload encryption and certificate-based authentication based on X.509 certificates.
Fouda et al. (2011)	Mutual Authentication for Smart Grid	Mutual authentication and a lightweight message authentication mechanism for smart grid.
Lai et al. (2013)	LGTH (Lightweight Group authentication protocol)	Mutual authentication for M2M communications based on aggregate MACs.
Lai et al. (2013)	SE-AKA (Secure and Efficient Authentication and Key Agreement protocol)	Mutual authentication b/w mobile and device network, used elliptic curve Diffie-Hellman (ECDH) to realize key forward/key backward secrecy.
Lai et al. (2014)	SEGR (Secure and Efficient Group Roaming protocol)	Mutual authentication and key agreement between a group of devices that do M2M communication within 3GPP and WiMAX networks.
Nicanfar et al. (2013)	SGMA (Smart Grid Mutual Authentication protocol) and SGKM (Smart Grid Key Management)	Smart meter in a home network was mutually authenticated with an authentication server in the smart grid.
Sun et al. (2015)	M2M application model using TDSCDMA (Time Division-Synchronous Code Division Multiple Access)	Mutual authentication in M2M home network communication by connecting a mobile user with the home network using the TDSCDMA network.
Lai et al. (2016)	GLARM (Group-based Lightweight Authentication scheme for Resource-constrained Machine-to-machine communications)	Group authentication and key agreement for M2M devices in 3GPP networks.
Farash et al. (2016)	Improved UAKAS (User Authentication and Key Agreement Scheme)	A user could authenticate with an IoT sensor node within the Smart Home network without connecting to the gateway.
Jan et al. (2017)	PAWN (Payload-based mutual Authentication scheme for Wireless sensor Networks)	Mutual authentication protocol for a cluster-based hierarchical WSN.
Jiang et al. (2016)	Smart card-based authentication protocol	Smart card-based authentication with additional features like perfect forward secrecy, anonymity and untraceability.

Reference	Name	Details of Authentication
Kumari *et al.* (2016)	Mutual authentication scheme using chaotic maps	Mutual authentication and key agreement scheme between a user and a sensor node within a WSN.
Qiu and Ma (2016)	Enhanced mutual authentication for 6LoWPAN networks	A 6LoWPAN device securely authenticates the remote server with a session key established between them.
Shinzaki *et al.* (2016)	ID-based encryption	Use of information (ID) associated with a user, device, or server, such as a device ID, e-mail address, or a fully qualified domain name (FQDN), as a public key.
Srinivas *et al.* (2017)	Smart card-based authentication protocol	Authentication scheme using biohashing.
Wu *et al.* (2018)	Improved three-factor remote authentication scheme	Mutual authentication to protect data between the sensor node, users and gateway node.
Amin *et al.* (2018)	Mutual authentication in distributed Cloud Computing environment	Mutual authentication between registered users and IoT devices in a distributed Cloud environment using a smart card.
Shuai *et al.* (2019)	Anonymous authentication scheme for Smart Home	An ECC-based anonymous authentication protocol for smart home environments.
Dey and Hossain (2019)	Session-Key Establishment and Authentication in a Smart Home Network	Lightweight and secure session-key establishment scheme for smart home networks and incorporates the Diffie-Hellman (DH) key exchange as an alternative method.
Varghese and Vinnarasi (2020)	Session key authentication system for smart homes	A secure key establishment scheme which also allows each entity to perform a mutual authentication before being able to participate in the home network.
Xiang and Zheng (2020)	Situation-Aware Scheme for Authentication in SG-HAN	Utilized the situational awareness of smart home systems for efficient device authentication in Smart Grid Home Area Networks (SG-HANs).
Oh *et al.* (2021)	Secure and lightweight authentication protocol for smart homes	An improvement over the Situation-aware scheme (Xiang and Zheng 2020) ensuring secure mutual authentication and lower computational costs.

Table 2.7. *Examples of mutual authentication schemes*

2.7. Challenges and open research issues

As discussed earlier, the crucial issues in IoT devices, especially for smart homes, are that many of them are connected directly to the Internet, which opens the devices to a hostile environment. Even if the network is made secure, the addition of every new device or upgrade (or lack of upgrade) of a device can put the system at risk. It is a nascent field, and there are many players in the market, leading to fragmentation and devices that have different standards and use differing protocols. Another issue of being an emerging technology is that companies compete to be the pioneers in a sector and give much importance to time-to-market. Devices are being made with futuristic features and secured with solutions to existing security and privacy challenges, which means that the industry is continuously in a catch-up mode.

To summarize, here are the key areas where more research focus is needed:

1) *Smartness in routers and modems that connect smart home devices to the Internet* – Many security solutions for smart home devices are in gateways/hubs that cater to devices of specific companies. For example, Philips Hue bulbs connect to a Philips Hub, which connects to the Internet through a wired connection to the router, while the Ring doorbell connects to the Internet through a wireless connection to the router. An intrusion detection system could be a feature in the Philips Hub or similar gateways but not in the home router or modem. Hence the possibility of a universal router that could perform the function of a hub by plugging in a software module could make things more secure for the user. At the same time, the consumer may not have to deal with the complexity of multiple hubs. Research and new products in this area or similar to "Interconnecting Wi-Fi devices with IEEE 802.15.4 devices without using a gateway" (Yin *et al.* 2015) will benefit customers immensely.

2) *Auto configuration support* – As mentioned before, a lack of technical knowledge and support is one of the biggest challenges. Consumers are burdened by error-prone manual steps to add and manage smart devices (Lin and Bergmann, 2016) and mostly leave default settings as-is to get things done fast, which opens the door to security issues. Hence research into secure auto-configuration will make smart home device installations much more straightforward and improve the security posture (Lin and Bergmann 2016).

3) *Standardization of device upgrades* – IoT devices generally do not get the security patches and operating system upgrades that desktop or mobile devices get (Lin and Bergmann 2016). There are many reasons for this. There are too many devices, the heterogeneity of versions is vast, many devices need software and firmware upgrades, and so on. Research into the standardization of devices, interfaces, and easier updates would be beneficial.

4) *Built-in security and privacy goals during design* – There should be guidelines for manufacturers of devices to incorporate security into smart devices in the design phase or earlier. The goal should be to design systems that mitigate automated attack risks, where integration points are secure, protect confidentiality and privacy, have availability and redundancy built-in, are resilient, and are compliant (Russel and Van Duren 2018). Research into this area would help in standardization, reduce heterogeneity, and remove problems at the root.

5) *Bring regulation to the industry* – Due to the lack of standardization and regulation, the consumer is not fully aware of the amount of data being collected or shared by smart devices. Ideas like adopting a "nutrition label" on boxes that sell smart devices (Emami-Naeini *et al.* 2020) are great. Those will bring the much-needed transparency and force the manufacturers to factor in privacy and security. Research on the types of labels and their usefulness is one of the most critical areas that need focus.

6) *Improved awareness and knowledge among common people* – It is time to treat smart home devices as public utility tools similar to smart meters. Utility companies run paid ads to promote devices like smart meters. In the same way, different manufacturers or governments need to run influencer campaigns or publish educational material in social media about the security and privacy aspects of smart home devices. Research in the area of correlating "improvement of tech-savviness of consumers" to "reduction in cyberattacks on Smart Home devices" would be beneficial for policymakers and companies in the industry.

2.8. Conclusion

In this chapter, we focused on security issues within IoT devices in a smart home environment. We also reviewed the security threats and vulnerabilities, the communication protocols generally used in smart home systems highlighting protocols like 6LoWPAN, RPL, and CoAP as well as their variants. We then reviewed key security architectures for IoT systems listing out middlewares, cloud-based, and gateway solutions. These reviews set the context to perform a deep dive into one of the mechanisms for securing smart home devices – mutual authentication. Before going into mutual authentication for smart homes, we reviewed the basics of mutual authentication with TLS and the practices involved in security key management. We then reviewed mutual TLS and mutual DTLS for IoT.

We concluded that mutual TLS offers several security advantages both for user-to-machine communication as well as machine-to-machine communications. In particular, mutual TLS authentication protects against credential theft through phishing; it also protects against brute force attacks on passwords, man-in-the-middle attacks, DoS attacks, and many others. In addition, client certificates provide a clear chain of trust.

We then reviewed over 20 mutual authentication systems from over the past decade such as SPS (secure profile server), LGTH (lightweight group authentication protocol), SE-AKA (secure and efficient authentication and key agreement protocol), SEGR (secure and efficient group roaming protocol), SGMA (smart grid mutual authentication protocol), GLARM (group-based lightweight authentication scheme for resource-constrained M2M communications), PAWN (payload-based mutual authentication scheme for wireless sensor networks) and so on. Many of these were mutual authentication for machine-to-machine communications. Rightfully so, since machine identities have far outpaced human identities in the IoT era.

After that, we reviewed protocols and architectures for mutual authentication in different areas like SG-HAN (smart grids), WSN focused mechanisms, card-based authentication, methods used in distributed cloud computing, and also many lightweight protocols. There is no one-size-fits-all solution, and different solutions would be apt in different situations. The seven stages of identifying an authentication protocol defined by Ferrag *et al.* (Ferrag *et al.* 2017) can be used as a baseline to ask the right questions and narrow them down to specific schemes. The stages involve understanding the entire ecosystem well and defining the network, authentication, and attack models. It also involves verification by using formal tools like BAN-logic or AVISPA.

Finally, we concluded by reviewing the challenges and open research items for smart home security, including "smartness" in routers and modems that connect smart home devices to the Internet, support for auto configuration, standardization of device upgrades, building in security and privacy goals during design, bringing regulation to the industry, and improving awareness and knowledge among the general population.

2.9. References

Abdallah, A.R. and Shen, X.S. (2014). Lightweight lattice-based homomorphic privacy-preserving aggregation scheme for home area networks. *2014 Sixth International Conference on Wireless Communications and Signal Processing (WCSP)*, IEEE.

Ács, G. and Castelluccia, C. (2011). I have a DREAM! (DiffeRentially privatE smArt Metering). *Information Hiding*, Filler, T., Pevný, T., Craver, S., Ker, A. (eds). Springer, Cham, Switzerland.

Aldrich, F.K. (2003). *Smart Homes: Past, Present and Future. Inside the Smart Home*. Springer, Berlin, Heidelberg.

Ali, B. and Awad, A.I. (2018). Cyber and physical security vulnerability assessment for IoT-based smart homes. *Sensors*, 18(3), 817.

Alohali, B., Merabti, M., Kifayat, K. (2014). A secure scheme for a smart house based on Cloud of Things (CoT). *2014 6th Computer Science and Electronic Engineering Conference (CEEC)*, IEEE.

Amin, R. and Biswas, G.P. (2016). A secure light weight scheme for user authentication and key agreement in multi-gateway based wireless sensor networks. *Ad Hoc Networks*, 36, 58–80.

Amin, R., Kumar, N., Biswas, G.P., Iqbal, R., Chang, V. (2018). A light weight authentication protocol for IoT-enabled devices in distributed cloud computing environment. *Future Generation Computer Systems*, 78, 1005–1019.

Arcangeli, J.P., Bouzeghoub, A., Camps, V., Canut, M.F., Chabridon, S., Conan, D., Desprats, T., Laborde, R., Lavinal, E., Leriche, S., Maurel, H. (2012). INCOME–multi-scale context management for the Internet of Things. *International Joint Conference on Ambient Intelligence*, Springer, November.

Ayday, E. and Rajagopal, S. (2013). Secure device authentication mechanisms for the smart grid-enabled home area networks. Technical report, Infoscience EFPL scientific publications [Online]. Available at: https://infoscience.epfl.ch/record/188373.

Banerjee, U., Juvekar, C., Fuller, S.H., Chandrakasan, A.P. (2017). eeDTLS: Energy-efficient datagram transport layer security for the Internet of Things. *GLOBECOM 2017–2017 IEEE Global Communications Conference*, IEEE.

Banerjee, S., Odelu, V., Das, A.K., Chattopadhyay, S., Park, Y. (2020). An efficient, anonymous and robust authentication scheme for smart home environments. *Sensors*, 20(4), 1215.

Barcena, M.B. and Wueest, C. (2015). Insecurity in the Internet of Things. Report, Symantec, Mountain View, CA, USA.

Benito, R.J.C., Márquez, D.G., Tron, P.P., Castro, R.R., Martín, N.S., Martín, J.L.S. (2009). Smepp: A secure middleware for embedded P2P. *Proceedings of ICT-Mobile Summit*, 9.

Bergmann, N.W. and Robinson, P.J. (2012). Server-based Internet of Things architecture. *2012 IEEE Consumer Communications and Networking Conference (CCNC)*, 360–361, IEEE.

Betzler, A., Gomez, C., Demirkol, I., Paradells, J. (2015). CoCoA+: An advanced congestion control mechanism for CoAP. *Ad Hoc Networks*, 33, 126–139.

Betzler, A., Gomez, C., Demirkol, I., Paradells, J. (2016). CoAP congestion control for the Internet of Things. *IEEE Communications Magazine*, 54(7), 154–160.

Bolettieri, S., Tanganelli, G., Vallati, C., Mingozzi, E. (2018). pCoCoA: A precise congestion control algorithm for CoAP. *Ad Hoc Networks*, 80, 116–129.

Bugeja, J., Jacobsson, A., Davidsson, P. (2018). Smart connected homes. In *Internet of Things A to Z: Technologies and Applications*, Hassan Q.F. (ed.). John Wiley & Sons, New York.

Chang, C.C. and Le, H.D. (2015). A provably secure, efficient, and flexible authentication scheme for ad hoc wireless sensor networks. *IEEE Transactions on Wireless Communications*, 15(1), 357–366.

Choi, B.C., Lee, S.H., Na, J.C., Lee, J.H. (2016). Secure firmware validation and update for consumer devices in home networking. *IEEE Transactions on Consumer Electronics*, 62(1), 39–44.

Chung, Y., Choi, S., Lee, Y., Park, N., Won, D. (2016). An enhanced lightweight anonymous authentication scheme for a scalable localization roaming service in wireless sensor networks. *Sensors*, 16(10), 1653.

Cisco (2020). Solutions – Securely onboarding IoT devices onto your network: Challenges and opportunities white paper [Online]. Available at: https://www.cisco.com/c/en/us/solutions/collateral/internet-of-things/white-paper-c11-743623.html?dtid=osscdc000283. [Accessed 21 November 2020].

Conzon, D., Bolognesi, T., Brizzi, P., Lotito, A., Tomasi, R., Spirito, M.A. (2012). The virtus middleware: An xmpp based architecture for secure IoT communications. *2012 21st International Conference on Computer Communications and Networks (ICCCN)*, IEEE.

Das, A.K., Kumari, S., Odelu, V., Li, X., Wu, F., Huang, X. (2016). Provably secure user authentication and key agreement scheme for wireless sensor networks. *Security and Communication Networks*, 9(16), 3670–3687.

Daswani, N., Kern, C., Kesavan, A. (2007). *Foundations of Security: What Every Programmer Needs to Know*. Apress, New York.

Davis, B.D., Mason, J.C., Anwar, M. (2020). Vulnerability studies and security postures of IoT Devices: A smart home case study. *IEEE Internet of Things Journal*, 7(10), 10102–10110.

De Souza, L.M.S., Spiess, P., Guinard, D., Köhler, M., Karnouskos, S., Savio, D. (2008). SOCRADES: A web service based shop floor integration infrastructure. *The Internet of Things*, Floerkemeier, C., Langheinrich, M., Fleisch, E., Mattern, F., Sarma, S.E. (eds). Springer, Berlin, Heidelberg.

Desruelle, H., Lyle, J., Isenberg, S., Gielen, F. (2012). On the challenges of building a web-based ubiquitous application platform. *Proceedings of the 2012 ACM Conference on Ubiquitous Computing*, 733–736.

Dey, S. and Hossain, A. (2019). Session-key establishment and authentication in a smart home network using public key cryptography. *IEEE Sensors Letters*, 3(4), 1–4.

Dierks, T. and Rescorla, E. (2006). The Transport Layer Security (TLS) Protocol Version 1.1. RFC 4346 [Online]. Available at: http://www.ietf.org/rfc/rfc4346.txt.

Dierks, T. and Rescorla, E. (2008). The Transport Layer Security (TLS) Protocol Version 1.2. RFC 5246 [Online]. Available at: http://www.ietf.org/rfc/rfc5246.txt.

Ding, F., Song, A., Tong, E., Li, J. (2016). A smart gateway architecture for improving efficiency of home network applications. *Journal of Sensors*, Special issue [Online]. Available at: https://doi.org/10.1155/2016/2197237.

El-Hajj, M., Fadlallah, A., Chamoun, M., Serhrouchni, A. (2019). A survey of Internet of Things (IoT) authentication schemes. *Sensors*, 19(5), 1141.

Elkhodr, M., Shahrestani, S., Cheung, H. (2016). A middleware for the Internet of Things. arXiv preprint, arXiv:1604.04823.

Emami-Naeini, P., Agarwal, Y., Cranor, L.F., Hibshi, H. (2020). Ask the experts: What should be on an IoT privacy and security label? *2020 IEEE Symposium on Security and Privacy (SP)*, IEEE.

Farash, M.S., Turkanović, M., Kumari, S., Hölbl, M. (2016). An efficient user authentication and key agreement scheme for heterogeneous wireless sensor network tailored for the Internet of Things environment. *Ad Hoc Networks*, 36, 152–176.

Fazio, M., Celesti, A., Marquez, F.G., Glikson, A., Villari, M. (2015). Exploiting the FIWARE cloud platform to develop a remote patient monitoring system. *2015 IEEE Symposium on Computers and Communication (ISCC)*, IEEE.

Ferrag, M.A., Maglaras, L.A., Janicke, H., Jiang, J., Shu, L. (2017). Authentication protocols for Internet of Things: A comprehensive survey. *Security and Communication Networks* [Online]. Available at: https://doi.org/10.1155/2017/6562953.

Fouda, M.M., Fadlullah, Z.M., Kato, N., Lu, R., Shen, X. (2011). Towards a light-weight message authentication mechanism tailored for smart grid communications. *2011 IEEE Conference on Computer Communications Workshops (INFOCOM WKSHPS)*, IEEE.

Fremantle, P. and Scott, P. (2017). A survey of secure middleware for the Internet of Things. *PeerJ Computer Science*, 3, p.e114.

Ghaffarianhoseini, A., Tookey, J., Omrany, H., Fleury, A., Naismith, N., Ghaffarianhoseini, M. (2016). The essence of smart homes: Application of intelligent technologies towards smarter urban future. *Artificial Intelligence: Concepts, Methodologies, Tools, and Applications*, Information Resources Management Association (ed.). IGI Global, Hershey, PA, USA.

Gilman, E. and Barth, D. (2017). *Zero Trust Networks*. O'Reilly Media, Sebastopol, CA, USA.

Glikson, A. (2011). Fi-ware: Core platform for future internet applications. *Proceedings of the 4th Annual International Conference on Systems and Storage*, New York, USA.

Greenstein, S. (2019). The aftermath of the Dyn DDOS Attack. *IEEE Micro*, 39(4), 66–68.

Guido, D. (2008). An overview of modern web authentication methods [Online]. Available at: http://cryptocity.net/files/papers/modern_web_auth_overview.pdf.

Gyarmathy, K. (2020). Comprehensive guide to IoT statistics you need to know in 2019 [Online]. Available at: https://www.vxchnge.com/blog/iot-statistics.

Hall, F., Maglaras, L., Aivaliotis, T., Xagoraris, L., Kantzavelou, I. (2020). Smart homes: Security challenges and privacy concerns. arXiv preprint, arXiv:2010.15394.

Hui, J. and Thubert, P. (2011). Compression format for IPv6 datagrams over IEEE 802.15. 4-based networks. RFC 6282 [Online]. Available at: https://tools.ietf.org/html/rfc6282.txt.

Hussain, A.M., Oligeri, G., Voigt, T. (2020). The dark (and bright) side of IoT: Attacks and countermeasures for identifying smart home devices and services. arXiv preprint, arXiv:2009.07672.

Huth, C., Zibuschka, J., Duplys, P., Güneysu, T. (2015). Securing systems on the Internet of Things via physical properties of devices and communications. *2015 Annual IEEE Systems Conference (SysCon) Proceedings*, IEEE.

Iuchi, K., Matsunaga, T., Toyoda, K., Sasase, I. (2015). Secure parent node selection scheme in route construction to exclude attacking nodes from RPL network. *2015 21st Asia-Pacific Conference on Communications (APCC)*, 299–303, IEEE.

Jan, M., Nanda, P., Usman, M., He, X. (2017). PAWN: A payload-based mutual authentication scheme for wireless sensor networks. *Concurrency and Computation: Practice and Experience*, 29(17), e3986.

Jan, M., Khan, F., Alam, M., Usman, M. (2019). A payload-based mutual authentication scheme for Internet of Things. *Future Generation Computer Systems*, 92, 1028–1039.

Jiang, Q., Ma, J., Wei, F., Tian, Y., Shen, J., Yang, Y. (2016). An untraceable temporal-credential-based two-factor authentication scheme using ECC for wireless sensor networks. *Journal of Network and Computer Applications*, 76, 37–48.

Kalla, A., Prombage, P., Liyanage, M. (2020). Introduction to IoT. *IoT Security: Advances in Authentication*, 1–25.

Kamgueu, P.O., Nataf, E., Ndie, T.D. (2018). Survey on RPL enhancements: A focus on topology, security and mobility. *Computer Communications*, 120, 10–21.

Kang, W.M., Moon, S.Y., Park, J.H. (2017). An enhanced security framework for home appliances in smart home. *Human-Centric Computing and Information Sciences*, 7(1), 6.

Komninos, N., Philippou, E., Pitsillides, A. (2014). Survey in smart grid and smart home security: Issues, challenges and countermeasures. *IEEE Communications Surveys & Tutorials*, 16(4), 1933–1954.

Kovatsch, M., Lanter, M., Shelby, Z. (2014). Californium: Scalable cloud services for the Internet of Things with CoAP. *2014 International Conference on the Internet of Things (IOT)*, 1–6, IEEE.

Kumari, S., Li, X., Wu, F., Das, A.K., Arshad, H., Khan, M.K. (2016). A user friendly mutual authentication and key agreement scheme for wireless sensor networks using chaotic maps. *Future Generation Computer Systems*, 63, 56–75.

Lai, C., Li, H., Lu, R., Jiang, R., Shen, X. (2013a). LGTH: A lightweight group authentication protocol for machine-type communication in LTE networks. *2013 IEEE Global Communications Conference (GLOBECOM)*, IEEE.

Lai, C., Li, H., Lu, R., Shen, X.S. (2013b). SE-AKA: A secure and efficient group authentication and key agreement protocol for LTE networks. *Computer Networks*, 57(17), 3492–3510.

Lai, C., Li, H., Lu, R., Jiang, R., Shen, X. (2014). SEGR: A secure and efficient group roaming scheme for machine to machine communications between 3GPP and WiMAX networks. *2014 IEEE International Conference on Communications (ICC)*, IEEE.

Lai, C., Lu, R., Zheng, D., Li, H., Shen, X.S. (2016). GLARM: Group-based lightweight authentication scheme for resource-constrained machine to machine communications. *Computer Networks*, 99, 66–81.

Lazakidou, A., Siassiakos, K., Ioannou, K. (eds) (2010). *Wireless Technologies for Ambient Assisted Living and Healthcare: Systems and Applications: Systems and Applications*. IGI Global, Hershey, PA, USA.

Lee, J.P., Lee, S.H., Lee, J.G., Lee, J.K. (2018). Design of device mutual authentication protocol in smart home environment. *International Conference on Computational Science/Intelligence & Applied Informatics*, 135–148, Springer.

Levendovszky, T., Dubey, A., Otte, W.R., Balasubramanian, D., Coglio, A., Nyako, S., Emfinger, W., Kumar, P., Gokhale, A., Karsai, G. (2013). Distributed real-time managed systems: A model-driven distributed secure information architecture platform for managed embedded systems. *IEEE Software*, 31(2), 62–69.

Li, Y. (2013). Design of a key establishment protocol for smart home energy management system. *2013 Fifth International Conference on Computational Intelligence, Communication Systems and Networks*, IEEE.

Lin, H. and Bergmann, N.W. (2016). IoT privacy and security challenges for smart home environments. *Information*, 7(3), 44.

Liu, C.H., Yang, B., Liu, T. (2014). Efficient naming, addressing and profile services in Internet-of-Things sensory environments. *Ad Hoc Networks*, 18, 85–101.

Logue, J.D., Supramaniam, S., Hardison, O.B., Luxemberg, J.A., Nest Labs Inc. (2013). Multi-tiered authentication methods for facilitating communications amongst smart home devices and cloud-based servers. US Patent 8,539,567.

Lueth, K.L. (2020). IoT 2019 in review: The 10 most relevant IoT developments of the year [Online]. Available at: https://iot-analytics.com/iot-2019-in-review.

Mahmood, K., Chaudhry, S.A., Naqvi, H., Shon, T., Ahmad, H.F. (2016). A lightweight message authentication scheme for smart grid communications in power sector. *Computers & Electrical Engineering*, 52, 114–124.

Maleh, Y., Shojafar, M., Darwish, A., Haqiq, A. (eds) (2019). *Cybersecurity and Privacy in Cyber Physical Systems*. CRC Press, Boca Raton, FL, USA.

Mantas, G., Lymberopoulos, D., Komninos, N. (2011). Security in smart home environment. *Wireless Technologies for Ambient Assisted Living and Healthcare: Systems and Applications*, Lazakidou, A., Siassiakos, K., Ioannou, K. (eds). IGI Global, Hershey, PA, USA.

Mantoro, T., Ayu, M.A., Binti Mahmod, S.M. (2014). Securing the authentication and message integrity for smart home using smart phone. *2014 International Conference on Multimedia Computing and Systems (ICMCS)*, IEEE.

Moh, M. and Raju, R. (2018). Machine learning techniques for security of Internet of Things (IoT) and fog computing systems. *2018 International Conference on High Performance Computing & Simulation (HPCS)*, IEEE.

Moh, M. and Raju, R. (2019). Using machine learning for protecting the security and privacy of Internet of Things (IoT) systems. *Fog and Edge Computing: Principles and Paradigms*, 30, 223–257.

Möller, D.P. and Haas, R.E. (2019). Advanced driver assistance systems and autonomous driving. *Guide to Automotive Connectivity and Cybersecurity*, Springer, Cham, Switzerland.

Montenegro, G., Kushalnagar, N., Hui, J., Culler, D. (2007). Transmission of IPv6 packets over IEEE 802.15. 4 networks. RFC 4944 [Online]. Available at: https://tools.ietf.org/html/rfc4944.txt.

Moosavi, S.R., Gia, T.N., Rahmani, A.M., Nigussie, E., Virtanen, S., Isoaho, J., Tenhunen, H. (2015). SEA: A secure and efficient authentication and authorization architecture for IoT-based healthcare using smart gateways. *Procedia Computer Science*, 52, 452–459.

Muhal, M.A., Luo, X., Mahmood, Z., Ullah, A. (2018). Physical unclonable function based authentication scheme for smart devices in Internet of Things. *2018 IEEE International Conference on Smart Internet of Things (SmartIoT)*, IEEE.

Müller, D. (2017). Reference security guide for app-controlled smart home systems. Master's thesis, University of Bremen, Bremen, Germany.

Nag, A., Alahi, M.E.E., Afsarimanesh, N., Prabhu, S., Mukhopadhyay, S.C. (2019). IoT for smart homes. *Sensors in the Age of the Internet of Things: Technologies and Applications*, 171.

Nawir, M., Amir, A., Yaakob, N., Lynn, O.B. (2016). Internet of Things (IoT): Taxonomy of security attacks. *2016 3rd International Conference on Electronic Design (ICED)*, IEEE.

Nicanfar, H., Jokar, P., Beznosov, K., Leung, V.C. (2013). Efficient authentication and key management mechanisms for smart grid communications. *IEEE Systems Journal*, 8(2), 629–640.

Oh, J., Yu, S., Lee, J., Son, S., Kim, M., Park, Y. (2021). A secure and lightweight authentication protocol for IoT-based smart homes. *Sensors*, 21(4), 1488.

Olsson, J. (2014). 6LoWPAN demystified. *Texas Instruments*, 13 [Online]. Available at: https://www.ti.com/lit/wp/swry013/swry013.pdf.

Panwar, N., Sharma, S., Mehrotra, S., Krzywiecki, Ł., Venkatasubramanian, N. (2019). Smart home survey on security and privacy. arXiv preprint, arXiv:1904.05476.

Park, N. and Kang, N. (2016). Mutual authentication scheme in secure Internet of Things technology for comfortable lifestyle. *Sensors*, 16(1), 20.

Perrey, H., Landsmann, M., Ugus, O., Schmidt, T.C., Wählisch, M. (2013). TRAIL: Topology authentication in RPL. arXiv preprint, arXiv:1312.0984.

Peterson, L.L. and Davie, B.S. (2007). *Computer Networks: A Systems Approach.* Elsevier, Burlington, MA, USA.

Pirbhulal, S., Zhang, H., Alahi, M.E.E., Ghayvat, H., Mukhopadhyay, S.C., Zhang, Y.T., Wu, W. (2017). A novel secure IoT-based smart home automation system using a wireless sensor network. *Sensors*, 17(1), 69.

Qiu, Y. and Ma, M. (2015). An authentication and key establishment scheme to enhance security for M2M in 6LoWPANs. *2015 IEEE International Conference on Communication Workshop (ICCW)*, IEEE.

Qiu, Y. and Ma, M. (2016). A mutual authentication and key establishment scheme for M2M communication in 6LoWPAN networks. *IEEE Transactions on Industrial Informatics*, 12(6), 2074–2085.

Ra, G.J. and Lee, I.Y. (2018). A study on KSI-based authentication management and communication for secure smart home environments. *KSII Transactions on Internet and Information Systems*, 12, 892–905. 10.3837/tiis.2018.02.021.

Rajesh, R., Annadurai, C., Nirmaladevi, K. (2019). Performance enhancement of IPv6 low power wireless personal area networks (6LoWPAN) by Lamport's algorithm. *Cluster Computing*, 22(4), 7745–7750.

Raju, R., Moh, M., Moh, T.S. (2018). Compression of wearable body sensor network data using improved two-threshold-two-divisor data chunking algorithms. *2018 International Conference on High Performance Computing & Simulation (HPCS)*, IEEE.

Raza, S., Duquennoy, S., Chung, T., Yazar, D., Voigt, T., Roedig, U. (2011). Securing communication in 6LoWPAN with compressed IPsec. *2011 International Conference on Distributed Computing in Sensor Systems and Workshops (DCOSS)*, IEEE.

Razvi, S.A.M., Al-Dhelaan, A., Al-Rodhaan, M., Sulaiman, R.A.B. (2015). IoT cloud-sensor secure architecture for smart home. *Proceedings of the International Conference on Security and Management (SAM)*, The Steering Committee of the World Congress in Computer Science, Computer Engineering and Applied Computing (WorldComp).

Renner, T., Kliem, A., Kao, O. (2014). The device cloud-applying cloud computing concepts to the Internet of Things. *2014 IEEE 11th International Conference on Ubiquitous Intelligence and Computing and 2014 IEEE 11th International Conference on Autonomic and Trusted Computing and 2014 IEEE 14th International Conference on Scalable Computing and Communications and Its Associated Workshops*, IEEE.

Rescorla, E. (2018). The Transport Layer Security (TLS) Protocol, Version 1.3. RFC 8446 [Online]. Available at: https://tools.ietf.org/html/rfc8446. txt.

Rescorla, E. and Modadugu, N. (2012). Datagram transport layer security version 1.2. RFC 6347 [Online]. Available at: https://www.ietf.org/rfc/rfc6347.txt.

Russell, B. and Van Duren, D. (2018). *Practical Internet of Things Security: Design a Security Framework for an Internet Connected Ecosystem*. Packt Publishing Ltd, Birmingham, UK.

Sandler, D. and Wallach, D.S. (2008). Input type="password"> must die. *Proceedings of W2SP*.

Santoso, F.K. and Vun, N.C. (2015). Securing IoT for smart home system. *2015 International Symposium on Consumer Electronics (ISCE)*, IEEE.

Schaefer, R., Ziegler, M., Mueller, W. (2006). Securing personal data in smart home environments. *Workshop on Privacy-Enhanced Personalization (PEP2006)*, Quebec, Montreal.

Shelby, Z., Hartke, K., Bormann, C. (2014). The Constrained Application Protocol (CoAP). RFC 7252 [Online]. Available at: https://tools.ietf.org/html/rfc7252.txt.

Shinzaki, T., Morikawa, I., Yamaoka, Y., Sakemi, Y. (2016). IoT security for utilization of big data: Mutual authentication technology and anonymization technology for positional data. *Fujitsu Scientific & Technical Journal*, 52(4), 52–60.

Shuai, M., Yu, N., Wang, H., Xiong, L. (2019). Anonymous authentication scheme for smart home environment with provable security. *Computers & Security*, 86, 132–146.

Sicari, S., Rizzardi, A., Miorandi, D., Cappiello, C., Coen-Porisini, A. (2016). A secure and quality-aware prototypical architecture for the Internet of Things. *Information Systems*, 58, 43–55.

Singh, S., Ra, I.H., Meng, W., Kaur, M., Cho, G.H. (2019). SH-BlockCC: A secure and efficient Internet of Things smart home architecture based on cloud computing and blockchain technology. *International Journal of Distributed Sensor Networks*, 15(4), 1550147719844159.

Srinivas, J., Mukhopadhyay, S., Mishra, D. (2017). Secure and efficient user authentication scheme for multi-gateway wireless sensor networks. *Ad Hoc Networks*, 54, 147–169.

Sripan, M., Lin, X., Petchlorlean, P., Ketcham, M. (2012). Research and thinking of smart home technology. *International Conference on Systems and Electronic Engineering (ICSEE'2012)*, December 18–19.

Stickle, B. and Felson, M. (2020). Crime rates in a pandemic: The largest criminological experiment in history. *American Journal of Criminal Justice*, 45(4), 525–536.

Sun, X., Men, S., Zhao, C., Zhou, Z. (2015). A security authentication scheme in machine-to-machine home network service. *Security and Communication Networks*, 8(16), 2678–2686.

Suwannapong, C. and Khunboa, C. (2019). Congestion control in CoAP observe group communication. *Sensors*, 19(15), 3433.

Tariq, M.A., Khan, M., Raza Khan, M.T., Kim, D. (2020). Enhancements and challenges in CoAP – A survey. *Sensors*, 20(21), 6391.

Tiloca, M. and Raza, S. (2018). Security mechanisms and technologies for constrained IoT devices. *Internet of Things A to Z: Technologies and Applications*, 221, 219–254, doi: 10.1002/9781119456735.ch8.

Tomanek, O. and Kencl, L. (2016). Security and privacy of using AllJoyn IoT framework at home and beyond. *2016 2nd International Conference on Intelligent Green Building and Smart Grid (IGBSG)*, IEEE.

Vaidya, B., Makrakis, D., Mouftah, H.T. (2011). Device authentication mechanism for smart energy home area networks. *2011 IEEE International Conference on Consumer Electronics (ICCE)*, IEEE.

Varghese, K.J. and Vinnarasi, A. (2020). A session key authentication system for smart homes. *IOP Conference Series: Materials Science and Engineering*, 912(6), 062014.

Wazid, M., Das, A.K., Odelu, V., Kumar, N., Susilo, W. (2017). Secure remote user authenticated key establishment protocol for smart home environment. *IEEE Transactions on Dependable and Secure Computing*, 17(2), 391–406.

Winter, T., Thubert, P., Brandt, A., Hui, J.W., Kelsey, R., Levis, P., Pister, K., Struik, R., Vasseur, J.P., Alexander, R.K. (2012). RPL: IPv6 routing protocol for low-power and lossy networks. RFC 6550 [Online]. Available at: https://tools.ietf.org/html/rfc6550.txt.

Wu, F., Xu, L., Kumari, S., Li, X. (2018). An improved and provably secure three-factor user authentication scheme for wireless sensor networks. *Peer-to-Peer Networking and Applications*, 11(1), 1–20.

Xiang, A. and Zheng, J. (2020). A situation-aware scheme for efficient device authentication in smart grid-enabled home area networks. *Electronics*, 9(6), 989.

Yadav, R.K., Singh, N., Piyush, P. (2020). Genetic CoCoA++: Genetic algorithm based congestion control in CoAP. *2020 4th International Conference on Intelligent Computing and Control Systems (ICICCS)*, IEEE.

Yin, S., Li, Q., Gnawali, O. (2015). Interconnecting wifi devices with IEEE 802.15. 4 devices without using a gateway. *2015 International Conference on Distributed Computing in Sensor Systems*, IEEE.

Yun, J., Ahn, I.Y., Sung, N.M., Kim, J. (2015). A device software platform for consumer electronics based on the Internet of Things. *IEEE Transactions on Consumer Electronics*, 61(4), 564–571.

Zhao, M., Yao, X., Liu, H., Ning, H. (2016). Physical unclonable function based authentication protocol for unit IoT and ubiquitous IoT. *2016 International Conference on Identification, Information and Knowledge in the Internet of Things (IIKI)*, IEEE.

3

SRAM Physically Unclonable Functions for Smart Home IoT Telehealth Environments

Fayez GEBALI[1] and Mohammad MAMUN[2]

[1]*Department of Electrical and Computer Engineering,*
University of Victoria, Canada
[2]*National Research Council of Canada, Government of Canada, Canada*

One main application of smart home IoT networks is telehealth, which is timely given the current pandemic situation and increasing healthcare costs. To ensure security of IoT smart homes, it has been suggested that silicon-based physically unclonable functions (PUF) be incorporated in the IoT devices themselves. PUFs are used as the main technique for establishing device authentication and secure key exchange as well as any higher level security protocols. This chapter provides an analysis of the characteristics and performance of SRAM physically unclonable functions. The analysis takes into account several factors such as the static or slowly-varying random process variations as well as the dynamic CMOS noise sources. The main parameters affecting the performance are identified and techniques used to measure them at the fabricator and in the field are explained. Three algorithms are proposed for choosing the set of challenges and the corresponding responses. The three algorithms are: Algorithm #1: single challenge; Algorithm #2: repeated challenge; and Algorithm #3: repeated challenge with bit selection. The last algorithm manages to eliminate the bit errors in the response and hence will not require the use of error correction coding often used in secure sketch or fuzzy extractor methods that have previously been proposed. The use of physically unclonable functions, coupled

Cybersecurity in Smart Homes,
coordinated by Rida KHATOUN. © ISTE Ltd 2022.

with the proposed algorithms, provide a layer of protection against the common IoT attacks and the novel deep learning attacks that EW claimed to be a serious security threat to IoT devices in telehealth applications.

3.1. Introduction

An emerging application of smart homes is telehealth, where healthcare delivery is extended to serve stay-at-home patients and remote or isolated communities. Telehealth is motivated by the escalating healthcare costs and the fact that many patients can not afford long-term hospital stays and prefer staying in their homes or within their remote communities. Telehealth relies very heavily on equipping the home with smart IoT devices that can sense the patient's vitals and can also deliver medication in a secure environment that is immune to cyber attacks. This approach allows us to reach out to many disadvantaged communities, thereby democratizing healthcare, as well as leading to reduced costs and speedy patient recovery times (Ellenbecker *et al*. 2008; National Institute on Aging 2020).

IoT devices used in smart homes are considered the weakest link in the security protocols implemented. As a result, contemplating the implementation of critical telehealth services in a smart home is very risky due to the device limitations of the Internet of Things (IoT). Some of the limitations include:

1) Limited resources, such as computer processing capabilities, which often prevent the implementation of secure key exchange algorithms that use complex elliptic functions.

2) Storing secret keys in non-volatile memory (NVRAM) is considered a security gap since simple memory attacks can reveal those secret keys. Furthermore, these secret keys are are hard to update since the NVRAM must be reprogrammed.

3) Users often do not customize or update each IoT device password or operating system firmware and rely solely on factory-set defaults. This is what system attackers first look for to launch their attacks.

4) IoT devices are located in unsecured premises and can be subject to theft, counterfeiting and reverse engineering.

These limitations impact the effectiveness of security protocols for both authentication and secure key exchange. A very promising technique for endowing a simple IoT device with a unique identity and the ability to secure secret keys without using NVRAM is to use silicon-based physically unclonable functions (PUF).

There are many types of PUFs based on different physical phenomena such as optical, acoustical and electrical. However only silicon PUFs implemented as electric circuits are practical for inexpensive implementations on simple IoT devices. Silicon PUFs are practical means of adding unique, unclonable identities to IoT devices. This is equivalent to biometrics in humans, such as iris, retina, voice, facial or fingerprint. PUFs not only help to authenticate IoT devices, but also aid in storing secret keys in the way a PUF is constructed. Traditionally, secret keys are stored in IoT devices using NVRAM. The disadvantage of NVRAM is the ability of an attacker to extract the secret keys, using many techniques such as memory persistence, reverse engineering, etc. A very attractive property of PUFs is their tamper-resistance which provides immunity from reverse engineering attacks that aim to extract the unique device response. The unique response of the PUF prevents the manufacturer, the user and the attacker from duplicating the PUF function, even when the PUF hardware design and structure are known.

Authentication using PUFs is based on establishing a challenge-response pair (CRP) where a set of challenges and their associated unique response is established by the device manufacturer. This dataset is then shared with a trusted certification authority (CA) for later use by administrators of the telehealth system to construct a secure and trusted system.

There are several criteria for CRP establishment:

1) Several CRP must be established so that each CRP is used only once to prevent attackers from forging a valid response by observing past CRP activities.

2) The number of bits for each response must be "large enough" to be able to establish enough Hamming distance (HD) separation between valid devices and counterfeit ones.

3) Techniques must be established to remove the inevitable dynamic noise from the PUF response to be able to match the noisy response to the one provided by the manufacturer and stored at a CA.

4) Algorithms must be provided to extract a high-entropy stable and repeatable secret key from a noisy low-entropy response.

The ability to construct inexpensive PUFs for IoT edge devices allows us to impart a unique device identity (ID), which is used for device authentication and developing stable and secure session keys. A very significant advantage is that the session key is obtained at the beginning of each session without the use of NVRAM. The key will be shared between the device and the authenticator through the use of publicly available helper data that will not compromise either the key or the device response.

Ensuring security of telehealth systems is hard, since many devices are distributed in insecure locations. Many types of attacks become feasible, such as eavesdropping, theft, tampering, man-in-the-middle, denial of service, etc. Central to ensuring security is authentication and key exchange. Cryptographic protocols are based on primitive operations such as block ciphers, stream ciphers and cryptographic hash functions. These primitive operations rely on storing a secret key stored in non-volatile memory, which proves to be their Achilles heel, especially for unsecured IoT devices (Delvaux 2017b).

The use of PUFs for mutual authentication in IoT devices has been the recognized solution to endowing IoT devices with a unique identity, akin to a fingerprint or retina image for human users. A PUF serves to authenticate a device and also provides a measure of tamper resistance (Gassend *et al.* 2002; Ravikanth *et al.* 2002; Guajardo *et al.* 2007; Suh and Devadas 2007; Maes *et al.* 2009, 2012; Maes 2013; Herder *et al.* 2014; Delvaux 2017b). Operation of the PUF relies on a challenge-response pair (CRP), where the server issues a challenge and the IoT device, or client, provides a response that is unique to the device. The problem with PUF response is it is noisy but has low entropy. Therefore, techniques have been developed to recover reliable and stable response from the noisy response using fuzzy extractors or secure sketch (Linnartz and Tuyls 2003; Boyen 2004; Dodis *et al.* 2004, 2008). The advantage of the fuzzy extractor is that it also serves to generate a secret key with high entropy from the low-entropy noisy response.

Contributions: The contributions of this chapter can be summarized as follows:

1) Novel statistical modeling and analysis of SRAM PUFs is presented. The model includes the effects of static random process variations and dynamic CMOS noise.

2) The main physical, device and system parameters affecting the PUF response are identified and techniques to estimate them are presented for both the IoT device manufacturer and for the IoT device user in the field.

3) A novel NOR-based SRAM PUF cell design is proposed that enables rapid device resetting at a speed matching the operating speed of the system and does not require the waste of too much delay or energy resetting the entire SRAM.

4) Three algorithms are proposed for generating the challenge response pairs. The techniques illustrate the impact of system parameters in uniquely identifying valid devices from counterfeit ones.

5) A discussion is provided on how to harden SRAM PUF against typical IoT attacks and deep learning attacks in particular.

Organization: The rest of this chapter is structured as follows. In section 3.2 we discuss the literature related to the use of PUFs for authentication and secure key exchange. In section 3.3 we review the architecture of a telehealth system where the smart home is the target for the healthcare delivery. In section 3.4 we discuss physically unclonable functions and using secure sketch and fuzzy extractors to remove the dynamic noise from the PUF response. In section 3.5 we discuss the use of convolutional coding as a means of generating the helper data without revealing the IoT device response when a challenge is issued. In section 3.6 the structure of SRAM PUFs is presented and a novel NOR-based SRAM is discussed. A statistical model of the SRAM PUF is also developed. In section 3.7 we propose three algorithms for issuing the PUF challenge-response pair (CRP) data and their effect on system design. In section 3.8 we discuss the attacks targeting smart homes, especially deep learning attacks.

3.2. Related literature

A high-level authentication and key exchange protocol for a smart home IoT system was recently proposed by Fakroon *et al.* (2020, 2021). The protocol used a two-factor authentication scheme that preserved user anonymity and untraceability. In the 2020 publication, the IoT edge devices were assumed to have secret keys stored in NVRAM. On the other hand, the 2021 publication assumed the secret keys could be derived from a built-in PUF that gave the IoT edge devices unique IDs. Security analysis of the scheme was conducted through formal analysis using the Burrows-Abadi-Needham logic (BAN), informal analysis and model check using the automated validation of Internet security protocols and applications (AVISPA) tool. A review of PUF-based security techniques can be found in Dodis *et al.* (2004, 2008). The authors discussed how to use a low-entropy PUF response to generate secure keys with high entropy. Secret key extraction techniques used fuzzy extractors to obtain session keys from the noisy PUF responses.

PUFs are classified as strong PUFs and weak PUFs as explained by Delvaux *et al.* (2014) and Delvaux (2017b). The discussion discussed the impact of strong and weak PUFs on device authentication and secure key exchange. A discussion was also provided about the helper data algorithm and how it can be used to obtain high-entropy stable keys from noisy, low-entropy PUF responses. At a different level, the abstraction of PUF operation as a one-way functions can be found in Ravikanth (2001) and Ravikanth *et al.* (2002). They compared algorithmic one-way functions (e.g. RSA encryption) with physical one-way functions (e.g. PUFs). A discussion of silicon PUFs can be found in Gassend *et al.* (2002). The discussion focused mainly on delay-based PUFs such as arbiter PUF and ring oscillator PUF. The authors also discussed helper data, which is used to generate session keys from PUF responses.

An initial attempt at analyzing delay-based PUFs can be found in Suh and Devadas (Suh and Devadas 2007). The analysis considered the need to use each CRP only once. Techniques were proposed to generate a sufficiently large number of responses through increasing the number of options to configure the circuit delays. The authors also discussed low-cost authentication techniques that do not require the use of the more expensive cryptographic primitives.

It is interesting to explore how PUFs can be incorporated using the popular FPGA technology. This is especially true for SRAM PUFs, which could make use of the built-in block RAM provided in many FPGA modules. However, resetting the SRAM might not be a simple matter, since this was not part of the design requirements of an FPGA block RAM (Xilinx 2021). Guajardo *et al.* (2007) studied SRAM PUF structures implemented in FPGA technology. To overcome noise associated with the response of the PUF a fuzzy extractor was used. This also helped extract secure and stable session keys with high entropy.

In a series of publications, Maes *et al.* (2012, 2009) and Maes (2013) discussed seven silicon-based as well as non-silicon-based PUFs. The authors also discussed the secure sketch techniques used to generate session keys that were proposed by Dodis *et al.* (2004, 2008).

Reviewing the published literature, we can make several conclusions about the current state of the art in using PUFs for IoT authentication and secure exchange:

1) The literature discusses, sometimes implicitly, one algorithm for issuing the CRP pairs: a single challenge is issued and the device response is observed. This is a simple algorithm that does not utilize the IoT device statistical characteristics to its advantage. Perhaps the only advantage of this algorithm is that it maximizes the number of CRP pairs, which is critical, especially for weak PUFs.

2) The parameters that define the response of the IoT PUF device are not identified in most published works. General statements are typically stated such as: "a large number of response bits are needed to differentiate valid from counterfeit devices". At best a sketch is provided about the desired Hamming distance (HD) separation between valid devices and counterfeit devices.

3) Values of the PUF circuit parameters, the statistical parameters and the choice of overall system parameters are not studied to see how the response of the PUF can be controlled and optimized. A lack of accurate logical PUF models explains why this is the accepted view of using PUFs.

3.3. System design considerations

Telehealth Network Model: Figure 3.3 shows the architecture of the telehealth system. The main agents in the system include:

– **Network Server (S):** The network server is usually located in a hospital. We can consider the server to be a root-of-trust (RoT) since it contains tamper-resistant hardware like a trusted platform module (TPM).

– **Mobile User (M):** This can be thought of as the smart devices or telephones used by the healthcare professionals such as doctors and nurses.

– **IoT Edge Device (D):** The IoT edge devices include Internet-enabled sensors/actuators that could be located in a remote health care unit or could be located in a body area network (BAN) attached to a stay-at-home patient.

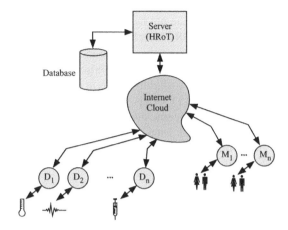

Figure 3.1. *Telehealth network model. For a color version of this figure, see www.iste.co.uk/khatoun/cybersecurity.zip*

3.4. Silicon physically unclonable functions (PUF)

Silicon static random access memory (SRAM) used to construct a PUF is a practical technique to give a unique "fingerprint" or identity to a silicon device and the ability to generate a secret key without the need to store it in NVRAM. The main advantages of silicon SRAM PUF are several:

1) Silicon SRAM based on CMOS technology does not require any extra processing steps which makes them practical to implement at no additional costs or delays (Holcomb *et al.* 2009).

2) The area cost is less than that required by an identity stored in NVRAM since circuits often require extra hardware such as charge pump to program the NVRAM.

3) The identity can not be cloned or reverse-engineered without destroying the fingerprint itself and removing the possibility of any device recyling.

4) The number of CRP goes beyond the number of words of the memory. In fact, the number of challenge-response pairs (CRP) is given by equation [3.6] or equation [3.7] later in this chapter.

In addition, a PUF provides tamper resistance since any changes to the device physical parameters will lead to a corrupted identity (Maes *et al.* 2009). The concept of silicon PUF was first proposed by Gassend *et al.* (2002). Silicon PUF operation relies on the inevitable random variations that are introduced during the fabrication of semiconductor devices. This gives the means to uniquely identify the individual devices. Furthermore, such a PUF can not be replicated through reverse engineering even by the device manufacturer. SRAM cells provide an compact way to create a silicon PUF through the unique startup values of the individual words in the memory (Guajardo *et al.* 2007; Boehm and Hofer 2009; Schrijen 2020). The SRAM content each time the SRAM PUF starts up is slightly different due to the inevitable dynamic noise (Su *et al.* 2008; Yu *et al.* 2011). Dodis was the first to propose using forward error correcting codes (FEC) to overcome the noisy inconsistent SRAM PUF output (Dodis *et al.* 2004, 2008). This was later improved upon by other authors (Boyen 2004; Bosch *et al.* 2008; Maes *et al.* 2009, 2012; van der Leest *et al.* 2012; Maes 2013; Delvaux *et al.* 2014; Hiller 2016; Delvaux 2017a, 2017b; Gao *et al.* 2018, 2019; Schrijen 2020).

3.4.1. *Mutual authentication and key exchange using PUF*

Figure 3.2 shows the basic structure of the secure sketch at the server and client. The server selects a challenge c and uses the database supplied by the manufacturer to extract the expected response r. The server also performs forward error correction coding (FEC) on the response to produce helper data w. The secure sketch also produces a hashed value h for the response. This value will serve to establish mutual authentication between the server (gateway provided by Internet service provider, in our case) and the client (IoT edge device, in our case).

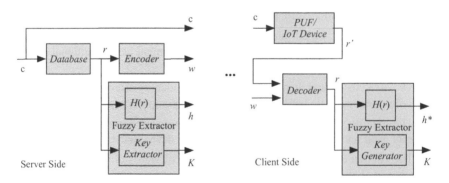

Figure 3.2. *Basic structure of the secure sketch at the server (on the left) and client (on the right). For a color version of this figure, see www.iste.co.uk/khatoun/cybersecurity.zip*

The client receives the challenge c and helper data w and in response produces the actual noisy response r', and with the help of w it decodes r' to produce the error-free response r. The client then hashes this value and sends h^* to the server to be authenticated.

3.4.2. *Fuzzy extractor*

At the server side, the fuzzy extractor uses the expected response w to generate the secret key K and helper data w as shown on the left in Figure 3.3. The helper data r can be made public without divulging the secret key. On the right side of Figure 3.3, the IoT device with the PUF is the client which, upon receiving the challenge c and helper data P, generates the noisy response r'. As long as the Hamming distance between r and r' is less than a certain threshold, the fuzzy extractor uses the corrected response r and helper data w to generate the secret key K.

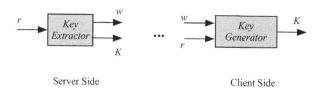

Server Side   Client Side

Figure 3.3. *Basic structure of the fuzzy extractor at the server and client. For a color version of this figure, see www.iste.co.uk/khatoun/cybersecurity.zip*

It should be noted that the secret key changes each time a new challenge c is issued. In this chapter we will use this feature to generate a nonce which could be K or a hashed value of K to increase its entropy. This will serve to construct a secret key shared among the entities of our system: mobile device (M), server (S), and IoT edge device (D).

The key regeneration using the fuzzy extractor process can be expressed by the equation

$$(K_d, N_d) = \text{key\_regen}(c, w) \tag{3.1}$$

where K_d is the secret key and N_d is the secret random number.

Some implementations were done in FPGA platforms (Herrewege *et al.* 2012; Maes *et al.* 2012) and some were implemented on microcontrollers (Aysu *et al.* 2015). Gao *et al.* (2019) proposed an SRAM-based PUF key generator on a microcontroller using RF energy harvesting.

3.5. Convolutional encoding and Viterbi decoding the SRAM words

As explained in section 3.4.1, the PUF response is inherently noisy due to the CMOS dynamic noise. Means have to be provided for removing this noise from the response. This is the job of the secure sketch which is derived from forward error correcting coding (FEC) theory. The helper data w in Figure 3.2 is used to remove the dynamic noise. However, the system designer must ensure that w does not reveal any information about the device response since w will be sent across unsecured channels. Furthermore, the error correcting capability of the secure sketch must be limited to a certain number of bit errors. If it exceeds that limit, there is a danger of inadvertently converting the response from a counterfeit device to that of a valid device.

Convolutional codes are a powerful FEC technique that is the only FEC that can handle both random errors and bust errors. The error correcting capability can be increased or decreased by increasing or decreasing the code rate, respectively.

A rate k/n convolutional encoder accepts k message bits and adds redundant bits to produce n output bits for each message with $n > k$. A convolutional encoder is specified by the three-tuple (n, k, m) where:

1) n: number of bits of the message after encoding;

2) k: number of information bits of the message before encoding;

3) m: order of the code or number of storage registers.

The code rate is defined by the first two parameters k/n. We can write the convolutional encoder as

$$\mathbf{y}_i[n] = \sum_{j=0}^{k-1} \mathbf{h}_i[j]\, \mathbf{x}[n-j] \tag{3.2}$$

where $\mathbf{x}[n]$ is the k-bit input symbol, $\mathbf{y}_i[n]$ is the ith k-bit output symbol with $0 \le i < n$, and $\mathbf{h}_i[j]$ is the k-bit generator polynomial weight with $0 \le j < m$ the number of delay elements. $\mathbf{x}[n]$ represents the input symbol stream and $\mathbf{y}[n]$ represents the output symbol stream.

Figure 3.4 shows a 1/2 convolutional encoder. The disadvantage of the structure in Figure 3.4 is the delay incurred to add m inputs using XOR gates. The constraint length for the k/n encoder with the structure in Figure 3.4 is km, which indicates the number of delay elements needed to generate the outputs from k inputs.

Figure 3.5 shows an alternative form for a 1/2 convolutional encoder. This form has the advantage of pipelining the partial output results at the expense of doubling the number of delay elements. The constraint length for the k/n encoder with the structure in Figure 3.5 is knm, which indicates the number of delay elements needed to generate the outputs from k inputs.

The generator polynomial for the structure in Figure 3.4 or 3.5 is defined as

$$p_1(x) = h_1[0]x^3 + h_1[1]x^2 + h_1[2]x^1 + h_1[3] \tag{3.3}$$

$$p_2(x) = h_2[0]x^3 + h_2[1]x^2 + h_2[2]x^1 + h_2[3] \tag{3.4}$$

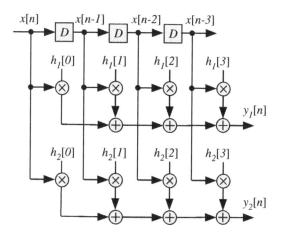

Figure 3.4. *Structure of a (2, 1, 3) convolutional encoder. For a color version of this figure, see www.iste.co.uk/khatoun/cybersecurity.zip*

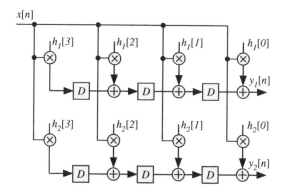

Figure 3.5. *Structure of an alternative form for a (2, 1, 3) convolutional encoder. For a color version of this figure, see www.iste.co.uk/khatoun/cybersecurity.zip*

Typically the generator polynomial is represented in matrix form as an $n \times (m+1)$ matrix $\mathbf{G}$. For the (2, 1, 3) encoder we can write

$$\mathbf{G} = \begin{bmatrix} h_1[0] & h_1[1] & h_1[2] & h_1[3] \\ h_2[0] & h_2[1] & h_2[2] & h_2[3] \end{bmatrix} \tag{3.5}$$

For a degree 3 polynomial in GF(2) we can use several primitive polynomials such as

$$p(x) = \begin{cases} x^3 + x^2 + x + 1 \\ x^3 + x + 1 \end{cases}$$

The golden SRAM words are defined according to the rules in [3.18]. These criteria will determine which bits of a given SRAM word are to be used for encoding/decoding and which ones will be overpassed according to the algorithms discussed in section 3.7.

The manufacturer applies convolutional coding to the golden SRAM data word before transmission. The ICs in the field use Viterbi decoding on the actual PUF output to generate the corrected SRAM word. The decoder uses hard decision algorithm, where each bit is interpreted as either '0' or '1'.

3.6. CMOS SRAM PUF construction

The basic structure of an SRAM CMOS cell is shown in Figure 3.6, which is basically two cross-coupled CMOS inverters. An excellent discussion of the operation of the CMOS SRAM memory is found in (Prince 1991, section 5.5). As we shall see in section 3.6.2, part of the requirement for an SRAM PUF is to perform repeated resetting of the SRAM. An SRAM PUF might have to be reset over 1,000 or more times to obtain a dependable response free of dynamic noise. This is a basic feature of the proposed algorithm discussed in sections 3.7.2 and 3.7.3 later in this chapter. The basic SRAM can be reset in one of two ways

1) Disconnect then reconnect the power supply V_{DD}. This will force the initial state of the two outputs of the cell to be 0 simultaneously. However, this is a slow process since the power supply rails usually have very large parasitic capacitances.

2) Ground the bit lines $B = \overline{B} = 0$ and set the word line $W = 1$. This will ensure the initial state of the two outputs of the cell to be 0 simultaneously. This option requires modifying the word lines W and $\overline{W}$ for the entire SRAM module. This approach is not feasible if the SRAM block is used to store data in addition to the PUF function.

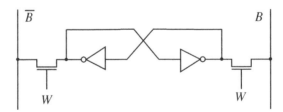

Figure 3.6. *Basic cell structure for a 6-transistor SRAM CMOS cell*

A third alternative is to modify the cell structure so that resetting the cell can be done at a speed matching the write speed of an SRAM. Figure 3.7 shows the basic cell structure of a NOR gate-based SRAM PUF and Figure 3.8 shows the details of the cell structure. In Figures 3.7 and 3.8, the contents of the cell are obtained through the bit lines B and $\overline{B}$ for the bit value and its complement, respectively. Signal W is usually referred to as the word line and, when asserted, connects the outputs of the cell to the bit lines. Finally, signal R is the reset signal and when it is asserted to '1', both NOR gates' outputs will be 0. As soon as $R = 0$, the storage cell stores '1' or '0' depending on several factors such as:

1) Threshold voltage values for the n-MOS and p-MOS transistors of the NOR gates and the pass-gate controlled by signal W.

2) Delay between the signal R and the lower inputs to the NOR gates.

3) Parasitic capacitances seen by the outputs of the two NOR gates.

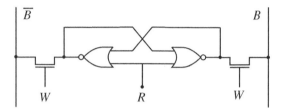

Figure 3.7. *Basic cell structure for NOR gate-based SRAM PUF*

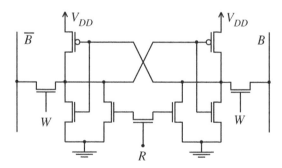

Figure 3.8. *Detail of the basic cell structure for NOR gate-based SRAM PUF*

The cell structure in Figure 3.8 was first simulated using the analog device simulator QUCS (Jahn and Borrás 2007). The simulator confirmed the basic operation of the SRAM cell under normal operation when $R = 0$ and $W = 1$. When the cell was reset ($R = 1$), both outputs B and $\overline{B}$ both reached the same reset value due to symmetry conditions. When the reset was not asserted $R = 0$, the SRAM cell assumed a random value 1 or 0.

It should be mentioned that the cell design can use two NOR gates or two inverters. The inverter-based design, also known as the 6-transistor design, must add enough pass-gates to allow for breaking up the feedback path and setting the inputs of the two inverters to equal values, whether 0 or 1. There is therefore no saving in terms of the MOS transistor count to using the 6-transistor cell design.

Assuming the number of words in the SRAM PUF to be N and that a challenge selects addresses of k words, the number of challenge-response pairs (CRP) is given by the permutation

$$CRP = N^k \gg N \qquad [3.6]$$

when repetitions are allowed. Alternatively we have

$$CRP = \frac{N!}{(N-k)!} \gg N \qquad [3.7]$$

when repetitions are not allowed. Adopting this strategy, one can construct strong PUF out of NOR-based SRAM PUF, especially if the order of the response bits is pre-arranged and can be securely varied at the start of each session.

3.6.1. *SRAM PUF statistical model*

The operation of SRAM PUF relies to two random physical phenomena: random processing variations and dynamic noise, which are analog processes. Both these phenomena control the digital binary value of the stored bits after SRAM initialization. Random process variation is static for a given device and facilitates creation of the device "biometric" or unique fignerprint. Random dynamic noise, on the other hand, is dynamic and introduces noise to the device identity (ID).

One way to analyze an SRAM-based PUF is to accurately model the devices and wire delays of the basic cell. However, this will not account for all the factors, such as doping variations, oxide thickness variations, random parasitic loading capacitances, etc. Instead we resort here to developing a logical model that encompasses all these physical phenomena. This approach is akin to the logical modeling of faults instead of modeling all possible physical faults in an integrated circuit.

The random variable we choose to model should be amenable to measurements under mass production settings by the device manufacturer. In the context of using an SRAM PUF, an appropriate random variable is the content of the SRAM memory cells. This is a binary random variable that is characterized by the two probabilities a and b denoting the probability that the SRAM cell is '1' or '0', respectively. Ideally random process variations and CMOS noise are absent and the structure of each

SRAM cell is completely symmetric making the ideal probabilities a_i and b_i satisfy the equality

$$a_i = b_i = 0.5$$

Due to the central limit theorem, the random process variation (RPV) effect on the pair (a_i, b_i) follows the biased Gaussian distribution whose pdf is given by

$$f_{A_p} = \frac{1}{\sigma_p \sqrt{2\pi}} e^{-(a_p - a_i)^2 / 2\sigma_p^2} \qquad [3.8]$$

where a_p is the adjusted value of a_i due to RPV and σ_p^2 is the variance of the RPV process. We should note that a_i and σ_p are identical for all SRAM bits within a device or among different devices.

The value of a_p is given by

$$a_p = G(a_i, \sigma_p) \qquad [3.9]$$

where $G(a_i, \sigma_p)$ is a Gaussian random process with mean a_i and variance σ_p^2. Figure 3.9 shows the different types of distributions due to the random processes involved in determining the bit value probabilities.

Figure 3.9(a) shows the pdf of the random variable a_p due to RPV which is a biased Gaussian process with mean a_i and variance σ_p^2.

There are several sources of dynamic or short-term noise in CMOS devices including:

1) Thermal noise as additive white Gaussian noise (AWGN), showing flat spectral distribution.

2) Shot noise due to charge carrier flow across p-n junctions.

3) Flicker noise due to charge trapping in the device, showing $1/f$ spectral distribution.

These noise sources introduce variations in the value of transition probability a each time the CMOS inverter undergoes a transition.

Figure 3.9(b) shows the pdf of the random dynamic noise n which is given by

$$f_{A_n}(a_n) = \frac{1}{\sigma_n \sqrt{2\pi}} e^{-a_n^2 / 2\sigma_n^2} \qquad [3.10]$$

where σ_n^2 is the variance of the dynamic noise process. On the other hand, the pdf for the additive white Gaussian noise (AWGN) is common to all bits within a device and also for all devices.

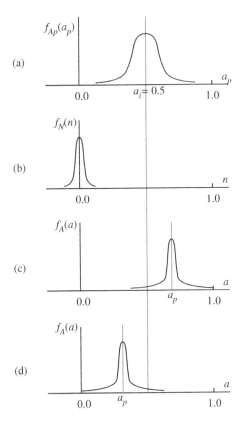

Figure 3.9. *The pdf distributions of transition probability a due to the different physical phenomena. (a) pdf of a_p due to random process variations (RPV). (b) pdf of n due to random dynamic noise. (c) pdf of a due to the combined effects of RPV and random dynamic noise when $a_p > a_i$. (d) pdf of a due to the combined effects of RPV and random dynamic noise when $a_p < a_i$*

The combined effects of RPV and dynamic CMOS noise generate a pdf given by

$$f_A(a) = \frac{1}{\sigma_n\sqrt{2\pi}} e^{-(a-a_p)^2/2\sigma_n^2} \qquad [3.11]$$

where a_p is the contribution of RPV and σ_n is the contribution of random dynamic noise.

Figure 3.9(c) shows the pdf of the transition probability a when both RPF and dynamic noise are present and the mean value $\mu_p > \mu_i$. Figure 3.9(d) shows the pdf of the transition probability a when both RPF and dynamic noise are present and the mean value $\mu_p < \mu_i$. For either case, the probability a is given by:

$$a = G(a_p, \sigma_n) \tag{3.12}$$

3.6.2. *Extracting the SRAM cell statistical parameters*

The value of the a bit at location b in word w is denoted by $v(w, b)$ with w denoting the SRAM word and b denoting the location b in the word. The range of the indices w and b is given by

$$0 \leq w < W \qquad \text{and} \qquad 0 \leq b < B$$

where W is the total number of words in the SRAM and B is the word size.

The values of W and B are set during the fabrication phase of the device. The values of the probability a_p and variance σ_p^2 can be extracted by the manufacturer during the pre-deployment phase by following these steps:

1) The manufacturer performs N initializations and observes the stored values of $v_k(w, b)$ in the tagged bit at each step k.

2) The probability a_p is obtained as

$$a_p(w, b) = \frac{1}{N} \sum_{k=0}^{N-1} v_k(w, b) \tag{3.13}$$

3) The variance σ_n^2 due to dynamic noise is obtained as

$$\sigma_n^2(w, b) = \frac{1}{N} \sum_{k=0}^{N-1} [v_k(w, b) - a_p(w, b)]^2 \tag{3.14}$$

Alternatively, the overall σ_n^2 can be estimated as

$$\sigma_n^2 = \frac{1}{W B N} \sum_{w=0}^{W-1} \sum_{b=0}^{B-1} \sum_{k=0}^{N-1} [v_k(w, b) - a_p(w, b)]^2 \tag{3.15}$$

In order to measure the RPV parameters a_i and σ_i the manufacturer now studies the contents of all the bits in the SRAM memory.

1) The values $a_p(w, b)$ for all bits in the SRAM memory are obtained previously.

2) The value a_i is obtained as:

$$a_i = \frac{1}{WB} \sum_{w=0}^{W-1} \sum_{b=0}^{B-1} a_p(w, b) \tag{3.16}$$

3) The value σ_i is obtained as:

$$\sigma_i^2 = \frac{1}{WB} \sum_{w=0}^{W-1} \sum_{b=0}^{B-1} [a_p(w,b) - a_i]^2 \qquad [3.17]$$

3.6.3. *Obtaining the golden SRAM PUF memory content*

The manufacturer of the SRAM PUF can run N initialization steps on each device to obtain the values of a_i, σ_i, a_p, and σ_n, as explained in section 3.6.2. The digitization, or analog-to-digital conversion, step gives the golden or reference stored value $v(w,b)$ of each bit in the SRAM PUF where $0 \leq w < W$ is the SRAM row index or word address and $0 \leq b < B$ is the bit index within a word. The assignment of golden or reference memory content is given by the rules:

$$v(w,b) = \begin{cases} 0, & 0 \leq a_p(w,b) \leq a_i \\ 1, & a_i < a_p(w,b) \leq 1 \end{cases} \qquad [3.18]$$

The conditions in equation [3.18] indicate the cell is skewed toward 0 or 1, respectively, and the effect of dynamic noise is negligible. Such cells provide the desired randomness that make the PUF hard to clone or reverse engineer (Holcomb *et al.* 2009).

The manufacturer now prepares a dataset for each device's SRAM PUF. The dataset contains the following information:

1) W the number of words in the SRAM PUF.

2) B the number of bits in each word.

3) Golden value $v(w,b)$ associated with each bit in the SRAM PUF based on criteria in equation [3.18].

The user now has the ability to choose the challenge/response pairs to use.

3.6.4. *Bit error rate (BER)*

The bit error rate of an SRAM cell is due to two mutually exclusive events: the bit is measured as '0' when it should be '1' or it is measured as '1' when it should be '0'. We can write the BER as

$$p_e = A + B \qquad [3.19]$$

where A is the probability that the SRAM bit is measured '0' when it should be '1' because $a_p > a_i$ and B is the probability that the SRAM bit is measured '1' when it should be '0' because $a_p < a_i$. The two probabilities are

$$A = \int_{a=0}^{a_i} \frac{1}{\sigma_n \sqrt{2\pi}} e^{-(a-a_p)^2/2\sigma_n^2}\, da \qquad [3.20]$$

for the case when $a_p > a_i$, and

$$B = 1 - \int_{a=0}^{a_i} \frac{1}{\sigma_n \sqrt{2\pi}} e^{-(a-a_p)^2/2\sigma_n^2} \, da \tag{3.21}$$

for the case when $a_p < a_i$.

3.6.5. Signal-to-noise ratio (SNR) for SRAM PUF

The term "signal" in the context of this work refers to the probability a_p. More specifically, we take the *absolute difference* $|a_p - a_i|$ as the definition of our signal for the following reasons:

1) When $a_p = a_i$ the SRAM cell value has equal probability of being 1 or 0 and this value totally depends on the effects of dynamic noise.

2) When $a_i < a_p \leq 1$ the SRAM cell value is biased to be 1 with little effects from dynamic noise especially when $a_p \to 1$.

3) When $0 \leq \mu_p < a_i$ the SRAM cell value is biased to be 0 with little effects from dynamic noise especially when $a_p \to 0$.

We can now define the system-level signal-to-noise ratio (SNR) of a tagged SRAM cell as the ratio of the energy due random process variations relative to dynamic noise energy:

$$SNR = 10 \log \left(\frac{(a_p - a_i)^2 + \sigma_p^2}{\sigma_n^2} \right) \tag{3.22}$$

where the contribution of the random process variations (through a_p and σ_p) and dynamic noise (through σ_n) are beyond the control of the device manufacturer.

Bits in an SRAM word, and for that matter, all bits in the SRAM, do not have the same SNR. The mininum SNR is when $\mu_p = a_i$:

$$SNR_{min} = 10 \log \left(\frac{\sigma_p^2}{\sigma_n^2} \right)$$

$$= 20 \log \left(\frac{\sigma_p}{\sigma_n} \right) \tag{3.23}$$

On the other hand, maximum SNR occurs when either $a_p = 0$ or when $a_p = 1$. Since $a_i = 0.5$, we can write:

$$SNR_{max} = 10 \log \left(\frac{a_i^2 + \sigma_p^2}{\sigma_n^2} \right) \tag{3.24}$$

When $SNR \approx SNR_{min}$, the response to the challenge is noisy. Similarly when $SNR \approx SNR_{max}$, the response to the challenge is more stable and less dependent on noise.

3.7. Algorithms for issuing CRP

In this section we propose and analyze several algorithms for issuing the CRP data and their effect on system design.

3.7.1. *Algorithm #1: single-challenge*

The single-challenge algorithm used to authenticate a device follows the steps depicted in Figure 3.10. Four steps are required for authenticating the device and generating the session key.

1: Server selects a single CRP (c, r)

2: Server generates w, K and h

3: Client uses (c, w) to generate r_1', K, and h^*

4: Server authenticates device

Server	Channel	Client
# 1. Select CRP (c, r)		
# 2. Generate w, K, h	$\xrightarrow{(c,w)}$	# 3. Use (c, w) to generate r_1', K, and h^*
# 4. Verify $h^* = h$	$\xleftarrow{h^*}$	

Figure 3.10. *Algorithm #1 for the authentication of an IoT edge device and secure key exchange*

Table 3.1 shows the maximum intra Hamming distance and inter Hamming distance for different word sizes B for the case when $W = 1K$ words, $N = 1024$ initialization operations and $SNR_{max} = 20$ dB.

We observe from Table 3.1 that the number of errors in the PUF response increases as B increases, as indicated by the intra Hamming distance. The errors are due to the effects of dynamic noise. We also observe from Table 3.1 that word lengths $B \geq 256$ are required to ensure clear separation between different device IDs.

B (bits)	32	64	128	256	512
Maximum Intra Hamming Distance (bits)	0	0	52	92	171
Inter-Intra Hamming Distance Separation (bits)	-12	-6	-3	10	49

Table 3.1. *The Algorithm #1 maximum intra Hamming distance and inter Hamming distance for the case when $W = 1K$ words, $N = 1024$ initialization operations and $SNR_{max} = 20$ dB*

Algorithm #1 is vulnerable to effects of dynamic noise which leads to a large intra Hamming distance and a small, or even negative, inter Hamming distance. The former leads to developing error correction codes capable of correcting a large number of bits. The latter might lead to false positive that declares or accepts a device as being authentic while it is, in fact, fake.

To be able to mitigate the above effects, the system designer must be able to ensure that the distribution of the intra Hamming distance is sufficiently separated from the inter Hamming distance. This approach is expensive since it requires:

1) Using large SRAM word size.

2) Being able to correct a large number of error bits through using many redundancy bits.

Figure 3.11 shows the histograms for intra and inter Hamming distance distributions for the case when $W = 1K$ words, $B = 128$ bits, $N = 1024$ initialization operations and $SNR_{max} = 20$ dB. We notice that when $B = 128$ bits the inter and intra Hamming distance histograms are touching. It would be hard to distinguish between a valid device and a fake one.

Figure 3.12 shows the histograms for intra and inter Hamming distance distributions for the case when $W = 1K$ words, $B = 512$ bits, $N = 1024$ initialization operations and $SNR_{max} = 20$ dB. When $B = 256$ the the inter and intra Hamming distance histograms are well separated. It would be easy to distinguish between a valid device and a fake one.

Figure 3.13 shows the histograms for intra and inter Hamming distance distributions for the case when $W = 1K$ words and $B = 512$ bits. When $B = 512$ the separation between inter and intra Hamming distances is increased compared to the case when $B = 256$.

It might prove expensive to implement an SRAM PUF with a word size of 512 bits. This problem can be simply solved by changing the challenge c to use multiple words that need not be consecutive. For example, if the SRAM PUF is a memory with word size $B = 64$, then generating a 512-bit response is feasible by simply having the challenge c correspond to addressing 8 words. This actually allows us to enrich the space of possible challenges by being able to generate all possible permutations so that we have $8! = 40,032$ possible challenges that use the same 8 words of the SRAM.

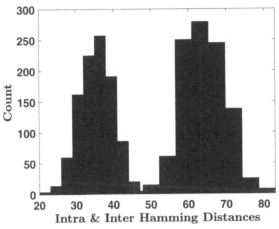

Figure 3.11. *The Algorithm #1 histogram on the left shows the intra Hamming distance distribution. The histogram on the right shows the inter Hamming distance distribution. The case when $W = 1K$ words, $B = 128$ bits, $N = 1024$ initialization operations and $SNR_{max} = 20$ dB*

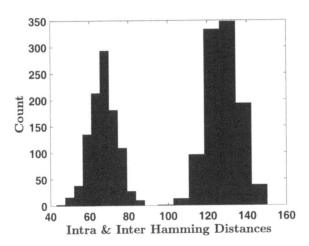

Figure 3.12. *The Algorithm #1 histogram on the left shows the intra Hamming distance distribution. The histogram on the right shows the inter Hamming distance distribution. The case when $W = 1K$ words, $B = 256$ bits, $N = 1024$ initialization operations and $SNR_{max} = 20$ dB*

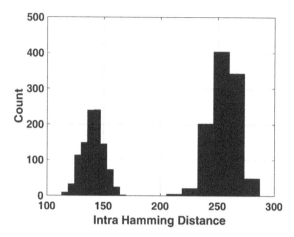

Figure 3.13. *The Algorithm #1 histogram on the left shows the intra Hamming distance distribution. The histogram on the right shows the inter Hamming distance distribution. The case when $W = 1K$ words, $B = 0.5K$ bits, $N = 1024$ initialization operations and $SNR_{max} = 20$ dB*

3.7.2. *Algorithm #2: repeated challenge*

The basic idea behind Algorithm #2 is to eliminate dynamic noise by repeating the steps used by the manufacturer to obtain the golden reference SRAM as discussed in section 3.6.2.

Algorithm #2 performs N initializations of the SRAM PUF and prepares an $N \times B$ response matrix $\mathbf{R}'$ whose rows are the individual responses $r'[n]$ for the same challenge c. A row vector $\mathbf{x}$ is obtained as the sum of columns of $\mathbf{R}'$.

$$\mathbf{x} = \frac{1}{N} \times \text{SumColumns}(\mathbf{R}') \qquad\qquad [3.25]$$

where $SumColumns(\mathbf{R}')$ sums the individual B columns of matrix $\mathbf{R}'$ to produce a row B-vector $\mathbf{x}$. The sum operation effectively cancels out the random dynamic noise which effectively performs repetition coding or majority voting.

The response of the device being authenticated is estimated in bitwise fashion. The bit at location b of w_2' is obtained as:

$$v_2'[b] = \begin{cases} 0 \text{ when } 0 \le \mathbf{x}[b] < a_i \\ 1 \text{ when } a_i \le \mathbf{x}[b] < 1 \end{cases} \qquad\qquad [3.26]$$

Using the helper data w, the error-corrected response r_2 is obtained. The steps used by Algorithm #2 are shown in Figure 3.14. Four steps are required for authenticating the device and generating the session key.

\# 1: Server selects a CRP (c, r_2, N)

\# 2: Server generates w, K and h

\# 3: Client uses (c, w, N) to generate r'_2, K, and h^*

\# 4: Server authenticates device

Server	Channel	Client
\# 1. Select CRP (c, r_2, N)		
\# 2. Generate w, K, h	$\xrightarrow{(c,w,N)}$	\# 3. Use c, w to generate $\mathbf{R'}$, r'_2, K, and h^*
\# 4. Verify $h^* = h$	$\xleftarrow{h^*}$	

Figure 3.14. *Algorithm #2 for the authentication of an IoT edge device and secure key exchange.*

Table 3.2 shows the maximum intra Hamming distance and inter Hamming distance for different word sizes B for the case when $W = 1K$ words, $N = 1024$ initialization operations and $SNR_{max} = 20$ dB.

B (bits)	32	64	128	256	512
Maximum Intra Hamming Distance (bits)	0	2	4	7	12
Inter-Intra Hamming Distance Separation (bits)	7	21	42	211	207

Table 3.2. *The Algorithm #2 maximum intra Hamming distance and inter Hamming distance for the case when $W = 1K$ words, $N = 1024$ initialization operations and $SNR_{max} = 20$ dB*

We see from the table that the intra Hamming distance is at least an order of magnitude less that the case for Algorithm #1. The inter Hamming distance, of course, remained the same as in Algorithm #1.

From Table 3.2 we make a very interesting discovery which is the ability to reduce the word size B and yet be able to authenticate devices. Table 3.2 shows that we are able to authenticate IoT devices even when $B \approx 32$ bits. This would not be possible with Algorithm #1.

3.7.3. *Algorithm #3: repeated challenge with bit selection*

Algorithm #3 is derived from Algorithm #2. The main idea of this algorithm is to consider or select the response bits that have high SNR in a further attempt to reduce the effects of dynamic noise. The criterion to select a response bit to be part of the filtered response is given by

$$w'_3[b] = w'_2[b] \quad \text{when} \quad \begin{cases} 0 \le \mathbf{x}[b] < a_i - \Delta \\ \text{or} \\ a_i + \Delta < \mathbf{x}[b] \le 1 \end{cases} \quad [3.27]$$

The steps used by Algorithm #3 are shown in Figure 3.15 where A is the vector of bit addresses selected according to equation [3.27]. Four steps are required for authenticating the device and generating the session key.

1: Server selects a CRP (c, r_3, N, A, Δ)

2: Server generates w, K and h

3: Client uses (c, w, N, A, Δ) to generate r'_3, K, and h^*

4: Server authenticates device

Server	Channel	Client
# 1. Select CRP (c, r_3, N, A, Δ)		
# 2. Generate w, K, h	$\xrightarrow{(c,w,N,A,\Delta)}$	# 3. Use c, w, N, A, Δ to generate $\mathbf{W'}, r'_3, K$, and h^*
# 4. Verify $h^* = h$	$\xleftarrow{h^*}$	

Figure 3.15. *Algorithm #3 for the authentication of an IoT edge device and secure key exchange.*

Table 3.3 shows the maximum intra Hamming distance and inter Hamming distance for the case when $W = 1K$ words, $N = 1024$ initialization operations and $SNR_{max} = 20$ dB and $\Delta = 0.3$.

Table 3.3 shows that we are able to authenticate IoT devices even when $B \approx 32$ bits. This would not be possible with Algorithm #1.

B (bits)	32	64	128	256	512
Maximum Intra Hamming Distance (bits)	0	0	4	6	9
Inter-Intra Hamming Distance Separation (bits)	7	21	40	95	213

Table 3.3. *The Algorithm #3 maximum intra Hamming distance and inter Hamming distance for different word sizes B for the case when $W = 1K$ words, $N = 1024$ initialization operations, $SNR_{max} = 20$ dB and $\Delta = 0.3$.*

3.8. Security of PUF-based IoT devices

The smart home is the target of several attacks such as (Fakroon *et al.* 2020):

1) replay;

2) eavesdropping;

3) device loss;

4) impersonation;

5) man-in-the-middle;

6) forward-backward secrecy;

7) user credentials;

8) session key guessing;

9) user identification and tracking;

10) side-channel;

11) over-production and counterfeiting;

12) deep learning and machine learning;

13) reverse engineering;

14) nonvolatile memory attacks.

We should note several general principles to ensure the security of the telehealth system, which includes smart home and IoT devices.

– The attacks mentioned above depend on getting the secret key associated with each IoT device through targeting the NVRAM content. Here this is prevented through storing the secret keys within the circuit structure of the PUF.

– Studying the CRP responses is thwarted by hiding the IoT device response r and never sending it between the communicating entities. This provides a level of protection against using deep learning to mimic the PUF function.

– Secret session keys K and hash values h are based on chaining and context such that a previous hash value or current device environment are used to generate a session K and h in addition to the response r (Fakroon *et al.* 2021).

– The use of PUFs in IoT devices constitutes an inexpensive means of providing tamper-proofing to a certain degree. It is not expected that each IoT device would be a root of trust (RoT) but at least it provides immunity to reverse engineering and tampering.

– Security measures must be layered starting from the physical layer (PUFs), then the communication layer and ending with the application layer. Multifactor authentication is also feasible here since each PUF can provide some of these factors.

3.9. Conclusions

This chapter developed novel statistical models for SRAM PUF performance. The main parameters affecting the SRAM PUF performance were identified and techniques to measure them were proposed. These parameters can be estimated by the manufacturer at the pre-deployment phase and can also be measured in the field. This chapter also proposed three algorithms for generating CRP and establishing device authentication and secure key exchange. Algorithm #1 is based on a single challenge. Algorithm #2 is based on repeated challenge. Algorithm #3 is based on repeated challenge with bit selection. We noted that Algorithm #1 can be used when the SRAM word size is $B > 256$ bits. Further, Algorithm #1 introduces a rather large number of bits in error in the response. Two new algorithms are proposed in this chapter: Algorithm #2 and Algorithm #3. These two algorithms solved the two main problems associated with noisy PUF responses: the need to use a large number of bits B and the large number of errors in the response.

3.10. Acknowledgements

This research was supported by a grant from the National Research Council of Canada (NRC) through the Collaborative R&D Initiative.

3.11. References

Aysu, A., Gulcan, E., Moriyama, D., Schaumont, P., Yung, M. (2015). End-to-end design of a PUF-based privacy preserving authentication protocol. *International Workshop on Cryptographic Hardware and Embedded Systems*, 556–576.

Boehm, C. and Hofer, M. (2009). Using SRAMs as physical unclonable functions. *17th Austrian Workshop on Microelectronics – Austrochip*, 117–122.

Bosch, C., Guajardo, J., Sadeghi, A.-R., Shokrollahi, J., Tuyls, P. (2008). Efficient helper data key extractor on FPGAs. In *Cryptographic Hardware and Embedded Systems (CHES)*, Oswald, E. and Rohatgi, P. (eds). Springer, Heidelberg.

Boyen, X. (2004). Reusable cryptographic fuzzy extractors. *11th ACM Conference on Computer and Communications Security – CCS*, October.

Delvaux, J. (2017a). Machine-learning attacks on PolyPUF, OB-PUF, RPUF, and PUF–FSM. *IACR Cryptology*, November.

Delvaux, J. (2017b). Security analysis of PUF-based key generation and entity authentication. PhD Thesis, University of KU Leuven and Shanghai Jiao Tong University.

Delvaux, J., Gu, D., Schellekens, D., Verbauwhede, I. (2014). Helper data algorithms for PUF-based key generation: Overview and analysis. *IEEE Transactions on Computers*, 34(6), 889–902.

Dodis, Y., Reyzin, L., Smith, A. (2004). Fuzzy extractors: How to generate strong keys from biometrics and other noisy data. In *EUROCRYPT*, Cachin, C. and Camenisch, J. (eds). Springer, Heidelberg.

Dodis, Y., Ostrovsky, R., Reyzin, L., Smith, A. (2008). Fuzzy extractors: How to generate strong keys from biometrics and other noisy data. *SIAM Journal on Computing*, 38(1), 97–139.

Ellenbecker, C.H., Samia, L., Cushman, M.J., Alster, K. (2008). Patient safety and quality in home health care. In *Patient Safety and Quality: An Evidence-Based Handbook for Nurses*, Hughes, R.G. (ed.). Agency for Healthcare Research and Quality, Rockville [Online]. Available at: https://www.ncbi.nlm.nih.gov/books/NBK2651/.

Fakroon, M., Alshahrani, M., Gebali, F., Traorè, I. (2020). Secure remote anonymous user authentication scheme for smart home environment. *Springer's Internet Things*, 9 [Online]. Available at: https://doi.org/10.1016/j.iot.2020.100343.

Fakroon, M., Gebali, F., Mamun, M. (2021). Multifactor authentication scheme using physically unclonable functions. *Springer's Internet Things*, 13 [Online]. Available at: https://doi.org/10.1016/j.iot.2020.100343.

Gao, Y., Ma, H., Al-Sarawi, S.F., Abbott, D., Ranasinghe, D.C. (2018). PUF-FSM: A controlled strong PUF. *IEEE Transactions on Computer-Aided Design of Integrated Circuits and Systems*, 37(5), 1104–1108.

Gao, Y., Su, Y., Yang, W., Chen, S., Nepal, S., Ranasinghe, D.C. (2019). Building secure SRAM PUF key generators on resource constrained devices. *The Third Workshop on Security, Privacy and Trust in the Internet of Things*, 912–917.

Gassend, B., Clarke, D., Dijk, M.V., Devadas, S. (2002). Silicon physical random functions. *Proceedings of the 9th ACM Conference on Computer and Communications Security*, 148–160.

Guajardo, J., Kumar, S., Schrijen, G., Tuyls, P. (2007). FPGA intrinsic PUFs and their use for IP protection. In *Cryptographic Hardware and Embedded Systems – CHES*, Paillier, P. and Verbauwhede, I. (eds). Springer, Heidelberg.

Herder, C., Yu, M.-D., Koushanfar, F., Devadas, S. (2014). Physical unclonable functions and applications: A tutorial. *Proceedings of the IEEE*, 102(8), 1126–1141.

Herrewege, A.V., Katzenbeisser, S., Maes, R., Peeters, R., Sadeghi, A.-R., Verbauwhede, I., Wachsmann, C. (2012). Reverse fuzzy extractors: Enabling lightweight mutual authentication for PUF-enabled RFIDs. *International Conference on Financial Cryptography and Data Security*, 374–389.

Hiller, M. (2016). Key derivation with physical unclonable functions. PhD Thesis, Universität München, Munich.

Holcomb, D.E., Burleson, W.P., Fu, K. (2009). Power-up SRAM state as an identifying fingerprint and source of true random numbers. *IEEE Transactions on Computers*, 58(9), 1198–1210.

Jahn, S. and Borrás, J.C. (2007). Qucs: A tutorial getting started with Qucs [Online]. Available at: http://qucs.sourceforge.net/docs/tutorial/getstarted.pdf.

van der Leest, V., Preneel, B., van der Sluis, E. (2012). Soft decision error correction for compact memory-based PUFs using a single enrollment. In *Cryptographic Hardware and Embedded Systems (CHES)*, Prouff, E. and Schaumont, P. (eds). Springer, Heidelberg.

Linnartz, J.P. and Tuyls, P. (2003). New shielding functions to enhance privacy and prevent misuse of biometric templates. In *Audio- and Video-Based Biometric Person Authentication*, Kittler, J. and Nixon, M.S. (eds). Springer, Heidelberg.

Maes, R. (2013). *Physically Unclonable Functions: Constructions, Properties and Applications*. Springer, Heidelberg.

Maes, R., Tuyls, P., Verbauwhede, I. (2009). Low-overhead implementation of a soft decision helper data algorithm for SRAM PUFs. In *Cryptographic Hardware and Embedded Systems (CHES)*, Clavier, C. and Gaj, K. (eds). Springer, Heidelberg.

Maes, R., van Herrewege, A., Verbauwhede, I. (2012). PUFKY: A fully functional PUF-based cryptographic key generator. In *Cryptographic Hardware and Embedded Systems (CHES)*, Prouff, E. and Schaumont, P. (eds). Springer, Heidelberg.

National Institute on Aging (2020). Aging in place: Growing older at home [Online]. Available at: https://www.nia.nih.gov/health/aging-place-growing-older-home.

Prince, B. (1991). *Semiconductor Memories*, 2nd edition. John Wiley, New York.

Ravikanth, P. (2001). Physical one-way functions. PhD Thesis, Massachussetts Institute of Technology, MA.

Ravikanth, P., Recht, B., Taylor, J., Gershenfeld, N. (2002). Physical one-way functions. *Science*, 297(5589), 2026–2030.

Schrijen, G.-J. (2020). SRAM PUF: A closer look at the most reliable and most secure PUF [Online]. Available at: https://www.design-reuse.com/articles/47782/sram-puf-a-closer-look-at-the-most-reliable-and-most-secure-puf.html.

Su, Y., Holleman, J., Otis, B. (2008). A digital 1.6 pJ/bit chip identification circuit using process variations. *IEEE Journal of Solid-State Circuits*, 43(1), 69–77.

Suh, G.E. and Devadas, S. (2007). Physical unclonable functions for device authentication and secret key generation. *Design Automation Conference*, 9–14.

Xilinx, Inc. (2021). UltraScale architecture memory resources user guide, Xilinx [Online]. Available at: https://www.xilinx.com/support/documentation/user_guides/ug573-ultrascale-memory-resources.pdf.

Yu, M., M'Raihi, D., Sowell, R., Devadas, S. (2011). Lightweight and secure PUF key storage using limits of machine learning. In *Cryptographic Hardware and Embedded Systems (CHES)*, Preneel, B. and Takagi, T. (eds). Springer, Heidelberg.

4

IoT Network Security
in Smart Homes

Manju LATA[1] and Vikas KUMAR[2]

[1] *Chaudhary Bansi Lal University, Bhiwani, India*
[2] *Central University of Haryana, Mahendergarh, India*

IoT smart home automation is gradually becoming an attractive aspect of everyday life around the world. However, these applications generate numerous concerns and challenges. Data is used to observe, manage and transmit information to other devices through the Internet. This enables certain actions to be performed remotely in order to acheive certain conditions. The majority of IoT smart home automation devices use applications (apps) or voice-based instructions. There are therefore a number of management and technical concerns that need to be mapped properly in order to use these applications effectively. Monitoring, energy management and transformation processes require a prominent and well-built control and management strategy. In addition, the data controls and management come from a wide range of resources, which further complicate the procedure for data protection, in order to create secure real time networks. As we move towards significant deployment of smart home IoT infrastructure and applications, smart home IoT network security systems have been recognized as a major concern. Therefore, the implications of network interconnection and security need to be a top priority. This chapter discusses the most significant IoT network challenges and their implications for smart home security. The challenges for the networks are presented, with reference to existing practices and available standards and initiatives, along with the relevant global standards.

4.1. Introduction

The Internet of Things (IoT) is now a buzzword that is spreading amongst the general public. It is a rapidly developing area that is constantly evolving, and many applications are expected to appear in the near future (Yousuf *et al.* 2019). The most commonly-used description of the IoT is "a cluster of things that are well-established or embedded through electric energy, actuators, sensors, software, and connected devices, using the Internet to bring together and replace data throughout the home and all other devices" (Yang *et al.* 2017). The relationships between a large number of things and the Internet makes it possible to steer the world away from detachment (Broll *et al.* 2009). The most valuable aspect of IoT processes is their ability to connect people with other people, objects with other objects, things with other things, and people with things. IoT devices are created using processing power and sensors that make it possible for them to be controlled in a number of surroundings (Li *et al.* 2017). IoT devices develop a network of smart things that allow the general public to connect and communicate with objects within the infrastructure of the Internet (Padyab and Stahlbrost 2018). The increasing accessibility and variety of IoT devices provide opportunities for people to use Internet services that are self-designed, self-configured, self-controlled and self-managed through smart tools and techniques, anytime or anywhere (Atzori *et al.* 2010). The IoT can be viewed as a collection of unified objects and devices that enable the community and things to connect to anyone and anything, anywhere and at any time, with any service or network (Balte *et al.* 2015). According to Statista, in 2017 the number of devices connected to the Internet reached over 20 billion units (Gyarmathy 2020).

Within a short period of time, the IoT has become more intelligent and has therefore been proven as a promising area for new cutting-edge technology and applications. The world is turning into an IoT universe, where several technologies work together with the IoT to connect things or devices. This is having a transformative effect on the way the world currently operates across several areas, including connected smart homes with energy management and home automation, smart health, industrial process management and public protection (Yousuf *et al.* 2019). However, with the growing number of IoT devices, interoperability between IoT systems is now crucial. In 2023, up to $1.1 trillion is expected to be spent on the IoT worldwide (Gyarmathy 2020). Several industries have formerly recognized IoT devices as an obvious valuable asset for the business. This not only drives innovation, but also supports enhanced security and privacy (James *et al.* 2015).

Models or standards are essential for existing businesses, protecting customers against the threats of proprietary resolutions. Standards reduce the level of threat for stockholders and help in the wide-spread application and sustainable development of IoT systems (Guillemin *et al.* 2013; Brass 2018). According to International Data Corporation (IDC), the overall global cost of IoT deployment reached $745 billion in 2019, with an increase of 15.4% from the previous year. Smart home IoT devices are being used to automate climate control, lighting, electrical devices, entertainment and home security systems. The IoT market is steadily growing, as IoT is now known as an enabler in terms of enhancing efficiency in different fields through logistics and transformation, automation, transportation, and so on (Miorandi *et al.* 2012).

IoT is enabling the smart home to support the automation in a number of ways. IoT devices connect things and objects from different surroundings to a particularly large network using an Internet Protocol (IP); this then becomes the basis for the development of smart homes, smart environments, smart industrial units, and so on. IoT enables home devices to be extra smart, remote, convenient and integrated (Alaa *et al.* 2017). Smart home IoT devices allow data to be collected in real time, offering valuable services to the people using them; for instance, reduced energy consumption and therefore energy savings, protection, communication, transportation, home automation and numerous innovations within the forthcoming environment (Padyab and Stahlbrost 2018). IoT-based smart home environments with key components and interrelated connectivity are presented in Figure 4.1 (Vinodhan *et al.* 2016; Jian *et al.* 2017). In IoT and smart home automation, the devices are connected through a local area network (LAN) and the Internet. The LAN allows communication between the devices and outer surface of the applications. A server and its database is also connected through the LAN, with the server controlling and managing the devices and activity logs, generating reports, replying to queries and performing the relevant command lines. For comprehensive or common tasks, the smart home server transfers the data to the cloud and remotely activates tasks with the use of APIs.

Additionally, the database stores and processes data collected from cloud services and sensors. The Internet connection enables the end user to communicate with the smart home to obtain existing information and execute tasks remotely. The Rivest–Shamir–Adleman (RSA) cryptography algorithm is commonly used in the communication, encrypting or decrypting messages using a public or private key (Mao *et al.* 2018; Domb 2019). To deal with this, power from the local smart home processors is used for the RSA calculation and more complex computing tasks are processed through the cloud. The results will subsequently be transferred to the IoT sensor to be assembled and compiled, in order to produce the RSA encryption or decryption code, hence supporting the IoT security (Li *et al.* 2011; Jian *et al.* 2017).

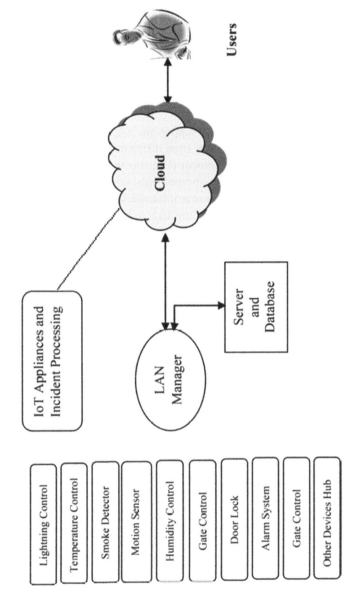

Figure 4.1. *Smart home system using IoT*

Devices such as thermostats, lights, windows or doors, along with numerous others are the typical components of smart homes (see: https://iot5.net/iot-applications/smart-home-iot-applications/) (Alaa *et al.* 2017). Smart home automation through IoT devices enables people to manage their lives; the main objective of IoT designers and producers is to revolutionize controlling and monitoring systems to support smart home applications. These include devices such as power plugs, weather sensors, smart lights, door sensors, vibration sensors, motion sensors, smart gateways, smoke detectors and inlet switches (Yang *et al.* 2018). However, as this is a relatively new objective, and associated technologies are still under development, substantial challenges need to be overcome (Joo and Choi 2017). The general idea behind smart homes centers around the electronic networking technology used to integrate appliances, devices and protection to create a fully integrated home, controlled and monitored centrally through a particular mechanism (Froiz-Míguez *et al.* 2018).

IoT based home automation also highlights the challenges associated with the varied access, sensing, processing of data and information, services, applications and other sections related to network security (Yousuf *et al.* 2019). The data or information collected with reference to persons and devices represent the probable security breaches. This makes it a complex task to encourage the adoption of IoT enabling home devices (Gubbi *et al.* 2013; Dutton 2014). IoT enabled home devices can make life more straightforward, however these devices have become vulnerable to a number of security threats. Consequently, it is particularly important to offer better security and access control, and include a high level of data integrity to secure the devices of a smart home (Li *et al.* 2017; Yousuf *et al.* 2019). Currently, a vast amount of secure, sensitive or confidential data is susceptible to leakage through the convenient IoT techniques.

4.2. IoT and smart home security

Using IoT-based devices and sensors, a smart home is able to remotely control, monitor and make services available, as requested by customers (Perrig *et al.* 2002; Yim and Choi 2012). The initial smart home tools and technology became accessible to customers at the beginning of the 21st century (Morris *et al.* 2013). Each type of tool and technology related to smart homes enables customers to monitor and control the associated home devices via smart home apps or other networked devices (D'Ulizia *et al.* 2010). The IoT provides devices with plans and procedures to increase their security potential. All appliances or devices that have varying functions (smart sensors, smart cars and smart appliances) become fairly susceptible to attacks by hackers, while the existing procedures fail to offer complete control of security. Thus the growth of secure IoT systems with lightweight security apps will resolve the most important requirements in the future.

Technology has changed the community conversation on buying and selling products, education, medication, farming, as well as the security. Consequently, IoT based smart home systems contain inbuilt security to combat the threats. Hence the numerous wireless network solutions, such as wireless Ethernet, ultra wide band (UWB), Bluetooth and others related to the field of home networking come into play (Yashwant *et al.* 2020). In view of the fact that Bluetooth is now widespread in mobile devices, it provides a cost-effective and secure solution to support the wireless network for IoT-based home systems. With increased growth in smart homes and improvements to a considerable number of manufactured smart home goods on the market, home security has become extremely fashionable (Manyika *et al.* 2013). Additionally, the prototype implementation system would be an excellent solution to support access monitoring and the control system for smart home security in IoT. A number of scenarios are involved in the development of communications procedures for the purpose of smart home security, leveraging standard procedures and encoding the interfaces, along with providing automation platforms that reduce the number of threats within dissimilar computing platforms and appliances (Drahansky *et al.* 2016). Consequently, smart homes contain appliances such as refrigerators, thermostats, home security, self-operating vacuum cleaners, clean-up and safeguarding devices, as well cameras, light sensors and motion sensors, which also collect data and information (Drahansky *et al.* 2016). A large amount of confidential information and susceptible data exists, such as: addresses, locations, representations and network related information. The information can be available to the device manufacturer, mobile application holder, and intermediary dealers or the community, depending on their rights. There are small numbers of offerings that deal with confidentiality in the environment of smart home security (Kraemer *et al.* 2018).

However, numerous modification techniques are in place to analyze the confidentiality and security associated with IoT-related information processing and threats (Almusaylim and Zaman 2019). Considering the publicly authorized aspects of security in IoT related areas, government associations are becoming heavily involved in IoT based security and interoperability from a standards perspective. When customers obtain IoT-based smart home devices openly from service providers, they may possibly work with the extremely insignificant knowledge while approving the terms and conditions (Ts and Cs), and privacy policy (PP). A significant number of standards have been specified by the Open Connectivity Foundation (OCF). For most of the standards, interoperability is key to increasing security in smart homes and allowing customers and commercial organizations to communicate (Philippe *et al.* 2011). With the growing needs, the IoT marketplace is witnessing an increase in the technology and tools that would support the reliable security approach (ENISA 2017). The most important technological concerns include:

– **Regulations:** Government directives protect the computer systems, as well as other information technology components, with the intention of improving security. A lot of associations and companies pitch for regulations to secure the information systems from cyber-attacks and governments issue regulations. For example, NERC-CIP for power efficiency in North America, and also instruction on security of Network Information Systems (NIS Directive) in Europe. Associations need to follow the regulations to plan the new devices and processes.

– **Standards:** Facts and reports on how certain approaches should be relayed in a reliable way are very important. Methods are usually standardized in a published resource, in an attempt to improve the cyber security and cyber surroundings of a consumer or association. The main concern is reducing the risk, together with preventing and mitigating the attacks. Conforming to standards is regularly required to make sure that a satisfactory level of excellence is achieved. For instance, the IEC-62443 standard is well regarded in the control of industrial and smart home systems.

– **Guidelines:** Detailed instructions on the usage and implementation of techniques are required to protect smart home systems and their surroundings. Guidelines are related to standards and need measured references and approval from the stakeholders. For instance, the NISTIR 7628 guidelines are in place to support smart grid-based home security (Pillitteri 2014).

– **Policies:** Guiding principles and procedures meet the security requirements of smart homes, organizations, as well as the society at large. Compliance with the policies has become compulsory. Policies offer top-down requests in support of smart home, business and commerce, in order to secure the information and assets. They work with the set of laws, regulation and authorized requests.

– **Procedures:** In order to apply standards and policies, detailed procedures need to be defined. Procedures contain sequences of detailed steps and instructions that should be followed in order to achieve a target. These become mandatory to illustrate and guide the end users. For instance, the maximum amount of time for a user account password to become obsolete and indicating the new requests to be produced.

It is important to note that standards are not yet mandatory at the time of implementing and designing the systems and platforms of IoT based smart home security. However, the general procedure should become easier and foster the development of a capacity to establish innovative tools and techniques (Brass *et al.* 2018). Similar application-related techniques on security may include facial recognition, fingerprint scanning and password protection. These applications observe the behavior of customers and consequently improve security. The amalgamation of technologies such as machine learning, omnipresent wireless communications, embedded systems, and real-time analytics has led to the development of new applications with IoT potential to support a large number of domains (Hoque *et al.* 2019).

Latent IoT applications include the remote based monitoring and control of smart home devices, energy consumption and managing smart light and smart lock type devices (Ahmed *et al.* 2016; Davidson *et al.* 2018; Hoque *et al.* 2019). For example, the customer details needed to access the smart lock must be mentioned and stored within the server, together with a time and date schedule. This schedule is able to further utilize to foresee the date and time when the customer will come into the house and handle the security. When the door is locked, the lights should turn off automatically, and when the door is unlocked, the lights should turn on automatically. Anyone can set holidays or vacations on the devices and the system will be on the highest security until the customer returns. Users are also able to set provisional keys in support of the household or in favor of visitors (Davidson *et al.* 2018). A smart home security system design has been presented in Figure 4.2. This kind of smart home security system can be very cost effective (Hoque *et al.* 2019). The procedures that need to be used to control and monitor each component of a smart home include the following.

– Control and monitor components:

- *Android application*: This application makes the interface between the customer and smart home devices available, such as locks. This application is used to control and monitor each component of a smart home system.

- *Web server database*: This is used to keep records of customer based activities. In addition, anyone is allowed to access a device and store the approved person or customer's identification, for example, their login ID or password.

- *Control unit*: This becomes the central monitoring unit, used to control and communicate with all of the related components in use within the smart home system. To build a low cost smart home security system, inexpensive components can be used, such as the microcontrollers from Elegoo and the Raspberry PI and RF signals as a communication channel between devices.

– Window or door component:

- *Camera*: This is used to capture the image of the person accessing the lock. The camera is activated with the help of sensors, when someone comes close to the windows or doors.

- *Motor*: This is a device that can control the latch to open and close.

- *Fingerprint sensor*: This type of sensor is used to validate the person and offer a protected environment. The use of a fingerprint sensor also presents an organized method of unlocking a door.

- *Motion sensor*: This type of sensor monitors movement near the doors and windows that can offer access into home. If there is movement in front of these spaces, the camera is activated so that the person can be observed.

– Smart home component:

- *Relay*: This module becomes a part of the hardware device used to support the remote device knobbing. Through this module, the user is able to automatically control the devices using remote access. Appliances can be organized as remote power-driven with on or off commands.

- *Gas or smoke sensor*: This type of sensor is used to activate an alarm to inform the customer if there is a gas leak in the home.

- *Light sensor*: This sensor can help in the management of the lighting in the house. For examples, the lights are switched on when the user enters the house (if artificial lighting is required) and they are automatically switched off when the user leaves the home.

– Smart attentive components:

- *Alarm*: This is used to alert the nearby environment in case some urgent attention is required for a fire, gas leak or any other kind of unauthorized access.

- *GSM module*: This module is a kind of device that can send messages to the customer in any emergency situation. It can make the customer attentive and can provide an exclusive Internet link to access the house remotely.

Along with these components, the system software is designed to include an immediate database that can take care of these different devices. An Android operating system also becomes essential for the development of applications involving XML, Python, JAVA, etc.

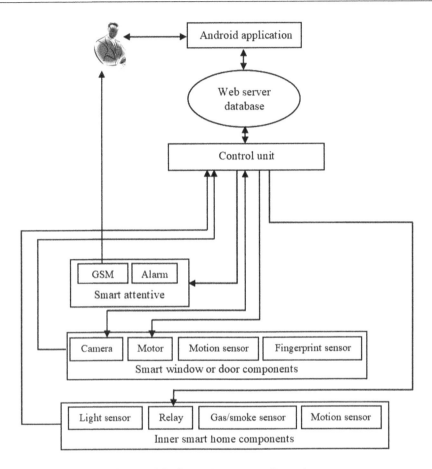

Figure 4.2. *Smart home security system*

4.3. IoT network security

Network security continues to be a substantial concern within the smart home community. In order to combat the network attacks, a number of security improvement strategies have been created and distributed within the Internet community. Surprisingly, these attacks are frequently either customized to run off detection or completely new ones to forfeit the plans. Although it may not be possible for the average user to understand, the attacker's attempt to infiltrate Internet related systems presents the most common and recurrent problem. For this reason, different levels of network security have been established in IoT on the basis of network levels. Customers are obtaining IoT devices for smart homes on the assumption that the producer has embedded suitable security in the devices.

Therefore, in a fundamental approach, the common security threats are identified and resolved at the network level (Sivaraman *et al.* 2015; Ray *et al.* 2020).

The concerns over network security have become more complicated as the range of devices has increased past computers such as desktops or laptops. These systems use operating systems (MacOS, Linux, and Windows) with small memories and protection mechanisms. Commonly, these devices are able to connect via peer devices or networks, using similar protocols to that of wireless networks, such as BLE, Bluetooth, NFC, ZigBee, Wi-Fi, LoRaWan, Thread etc. (Gomez and Paradells 2010). The Internet Engineering Task Force (IETF) has put in a strong effort during the establishment of required light weight communication protocols in support of controlled environments, in addition to the existing IP network (Lin and Bergmann, 2016). This contains the IPv6 in excess of Low Power Wireless Personal Area Networks (6LoWPAN: RFC 6282) (Hui and Thubert 2011), the IPv6 Routing Protocol for Low power and Lossy Networks (RPL: RFC 6550) (Winter *et al.* 2012), along with the Constrained Application Protocol (CoAP: RFC 7252) (Castellani *et al.* 2017).

The modest instance contains the suitable access control procedures that safeguard the particular IoT device. Whereas a typical instance may engage energetic procedures that modify the access control derived from the situation (for example, the members of family that are present or absent from home). Complicated security similar to those that need a mixture of network management and data analytics becomes absent right now, and is able to satisfy network level security. The network level security has been described in Figure 4.3, where the security management provider interconnects with the Internet service provider or the tools of home router from one side, using dynamic application programming interfaces (APIs), and with home customers using a user-friendly graphical interface from the other side. The purpose of the SMP is to implement the control of configuration in excess of the Internet service provider (ISP) network, as well as the home router for the customer (Dahiya 2017; Lin and Bergmann 2016).

SMP procedures and benefits: The security management provider offers apps or portals of customization interfaces to customers, translating these into network level functions summoned by application programming interfaces (APIs). This purposely decouples the security management provider from the infrastructure based dealer or operator, so that multiple objectives are able to compete on behalf of the procedure. The vendor of a home router or ISP could potentially develop SMP abilities in the home, increasing maintenance costs and thus income. A content provider (for example, Netflix or Google) or cloud service provider (for example, Apple or Amazon) may also have an interest in the procedure, in order to develop its individual services. Otherwise, an innovative competitor could adopt a similar procedure with better analytics and visibility of home network systems. The ease with which SMP procedures can be implemented is a potential asset to business organizations that can help to overcome the existing stagnation in home Internet contributions (Lin and Bergmann 2016).

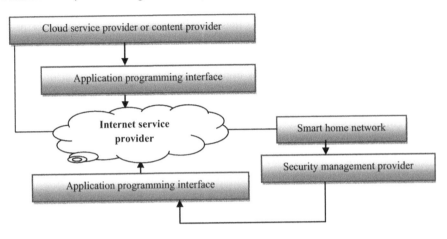

Figure 4.3. *Network level security*

Internet service provider and home router vendor procedures and benefits: Nowadays, home routers (like commercial routers) are included in the network and may have various management interfaces; they may have come from different vendors. These vendors may give up user interface improvement, as well as consent to an outdoor unit of SMP to organize network behavior (the prototype controls open source platforms, for instance OpenWRT). This decreases the growth related problem for vendors, permitting them to concentrate on viable improvement, whereas the model of cloud based control is able to provide the best response to the aspect of device usage. A corresponding argument affects the ISP, which offers Internet connectivity at low-margins. ISPs may monetize the large level of marketplace service customization, and they can also decrease the load of consumer management. The configuration of network APIs can be computerized using software defined network (SDN) technology and consequently, the ISP is able to sustain them at a small price (Lin and Bergmann 2016).

Embedded devices procedure and benefit: This system of embedded devices produces and runs a control system to secure the IoT-based smart home. Embedded systems and devices include a wide range of appliances contained by the inhabitant, business, healthcare, automotive, and other types of users. Usually, embedded systems include firmware or operating systems in support of designed, managed and controlled security related issues in IoT related smart home applications. These devices become smaller in size due to low power consumption, as well as low computing power, such as when monitoring the sensitivity rate. The embedded monitor inside of a timepiece can be attached to an Android device or Smartphone to demonstrate the status of the heart in real time. Automatic Teller Machines (ATM) and Point of Sale (POS) also become models of embedded systems or devices. These numerous features contact the procedures that desire the most excellent control system, together with outlay and complication of system installation toward the greatest technological outcomes (Gann *et al.* 1999).

Virtual or cyber security procedures and benefits: security is the major concern in positioning IoT-based smart homes. IoT systems make use of wireless communication protocols to provide customers and devices with the ability to drive and take delivery of information involving each other with control and secure IoT-based home appliances. This can build up a complete system that is extremely susceptible toward the attacks of hackers. Consequently, the systems and devices must be installed into the smart home within the security mode, ensuring that these are not observable toward any intruder. A protocol of Near Field Communication (NFC) can also be applied, and this enables the related devices to use peer-to-peer to set-up the communication (Song *et al.* 2008). Accordingly, they are allowed to transmit data with everyone within extremely close proximity. The mechanism will not disclose the related ID and match up through any Smartphone in anticipation of the customer obtaining the related devices and passing it on the control or knob; then the knob discloses the ID related information and pairs with the customer's receiver. Though, immediately after the customer has set-up the communication via the system, the customer's device ID is screened toward the intruders or hackers, consequently increasing security related concerns. This complexity deals with encrypted data on the dispatcher device after decrypting it on the target device and vice versa. The procedure of encryption is utilized based on the communication protocol of machine-to-machine (M2M).

Customer procedure and benefits: Customers require the security in support for smart homes to be enhanced further than through the ISP or router vendor only. The main concern of the customer is learned and stored within the cloud, and re-established though the subscriber, which modifies the home router or ISP. The customer should be able to adapt security from the cloud, with the opportunity to modernize the configuration as a tool. ISPs offer management and control of the home gateway, also providing the physical home gateway subscriber or a virtual instance through the cloud (for example, vCPE). This theory becomes important and the resolution is given towards tasks pessimistic of inheritance through the network address translator (NAT), allowing smart home gateways (Lin and Bergmann 2016; Dahiya 2017).

Network controller of the ISP: The Floodlight (v0.9) OpenFlow controller is used to support the ISP network and improved Java modules are used with RESTful APIs (Lin and Bergmann 2016). The innovative modules connected to FloodLight execute the API to support access control, so that access control procedures (derived from a remote IP) can be pushed via the outdoor SMP unit to support a particular home device.

SMP Security composer: A security composer or Ruby-on-Rails is executed, and seizes the position and logic required by the SMP to deal with security in support of the subscriber. The ISP using the aforesaid APIs interrelates with the front-end gateway, as well as customer apps, using RESTful APIs. This is performed on the REST rules or commands from the customer apps or portal. This can recover the suitable state information subsequent toward the command of the subscriber, with the proper series of ISP and APIs toward the attainment of the functionality (Lin and Bergmann 2016).

Web-based app: Front-end support is made available to the customers to modify services, as well as execute them in HTML or JavaScript. The customer is able to see and manage it through a web-based app. Customers can see the smart home devices scheduled to work and they can access any support of security locations. The SMP seizes the information depending on the suitable techniques toward securing that exact device, and is able to insert correct access control procedures using the API network, possibly with the perspective of information from the home.

Therefore, the service of enclosing the SMP on condition of the IoT security becomes an added value service with the help of other supporting devices and mechanisms. The Nestsmoke-alarm and Philips Hue lightbulb are good examples of the support devices. The smart light bulb connects to the Internet via Wi-Fi, and iOS or Android apps propel the most wanted commands to regulate the settings of smart bulb. Nowadays, customers would nearly all be aware of this attack, and would know how to block it. The SMP appeals to the API network in the direction of insert suitable access control procedures that enable only identified users to access the smart bulb (Lin *et al.* 2016; Dahiya 2017). In terms of roaming, there may be a mobile app, installed on the customer's phone, that propels heartbeat messages toward the SMP through the communal IP address. This is then actively programmed into the access control list of the home router or the edge router. This technique may offer protected access to the smart bulb at the network level, along with a variety of IoT devices. A technique to improve the security of the Nest smoke alarm installed in smart homes and organizations can also be applied. This device is connected via a Wi-Fi network to cloud-based servers offering real time emergency alerts to the customer app. As the device holds the light and motion sensors, this becomes a valid anxiety that the device is able to track customers within the smart home and provide these details to Nest. There has been enhanced functionality that obstructs the Dropcam from uploading or recording video to the cloud when the customer is at home. It is amazing that this can be done automatically each time via the security alert. Therefore, certain suppliers provide IoT security as a service and energetically control the firewall procedures in support of the customer (with access switch of ISP or at the home gateway) that observes and controls the network level functions in support of every IoT device. Usually, by assessing IoT devices several at a time, all-purpose procedures can be implemented for all IoT devices, so that the improved security assertions can then be made available to the device manufacturer.

4.4. Prevailing standards and initiatives

With the increase in Internet access, the adoption of IoT in smart homes is also increasing. Correspondingly, IoT security concerns are also increasing. The market size of European smart home security is estimated to reach 7.95 billion USD by 2024 (Sovacool *et al.* 2020). The smart home security marketplace can also be attributed to the growing crime rate around the world. Due to the growing crime rate, customers are gradually paying more attention to security and safety systems, particularly in the housing sector. In order to combat the challenges, a number of home security standards have been developed to offer interoperability among the large range of associated products and services (Khoa *et al.* 2020; Sovacool *et al.* 2020; Sowah *et al.* 2020). The most important organizations involved in the development of the significant standards include:

Open Connecivity Foundation (OCF): In the smart home space, OCF became the biggest traverse business association in 2016, and its contribution in the amalgamation of the two most important proposals in support of interoperability is really remarkable. AllJoyn and IoTivity are the open source frameworks, which have been sponsored by OCF. Both of these standards work towards communication and encourage interoperability in technologies within the IoT. The recent creature is also functioning on an integrated IoT standard sustaining OCF stipulation.

Zigbee Alliance: Fundamentally amalgamated in smart home systems, Zigbee technology is implemented through the leading global service installers, suppliers and dealers. Supported by more than 400 associates, the ZigBee home automation standard is devoted to interoperability between an array of products irrespective of the producer. In 2017, the CES alliance completed a considerable move to advance interoperability with the creation of Dotdot, which is predicted to be a worldwide language in support of IoT. Dotdot is derived from the improvement of the widespread applicative upper level, which allows interconnection between Zigbee products and other products using Bluetooth and WiFi protocols. The ZigBee Alliance is approaching the standard in support of home devices, from lighting systems and temperature control to smoke detectors and security monitors. The ZigBee requirement is well-matched to smart home systems due to its consistency, low power consumption, and interoperability.

Bluetooth Low Energy: Marketed as Bluetooth Smart, Bluetooth Low Energy has been promoted by the Bluetooth Special Interest Group (SIG) as a smart, power friendly adaptation of wireless technology, in support of dot to dot contacts. Bluetooth provides the framework for direct connection from a tablet or smartphone, enabling customers to manage their smart home devices from a portable device. The Bluetooth SIG suggests that the Bluetooth mesh protocol should be favored. A mesh protocol would enhance the physical variety of devices via the Bluetooth network and it may possibly drop the power utilization.

IFTTT ("If This Then That"): This is a web tool that enables numerous applications and services to be linked using commands that trigger and automate actions. Within the smart home region (Sovacool *et al.* 2020), IFTTT enables devices to communicate with each other openly, without performing as a hub to exclude a channel. For example, if thermostat X's temperature reaches 90°, the system Y must activate an alarm. IFTTT is implemented and utilized through several considerable performers within the smart home. IFTTT perform operations through Samsung's SmartThings, LIFXlight bulbs, Nest thermostats or within Google Home.

Open APIs: Several industries have improved platforms to create devices that work together using Samsung's SmartThings or Apple's HomeKit. Accordingly, developers of related inventions are able to execute SmartThings as well as Homekit using similar software, or in a few cases, with hardware growth. The most recent competitor is Amazon with its smart voice sponsor Alexa within the Echo device, which provides an innovative and easy method to interrelate products. Amazon has unconfined the smart home skill API with the Alexa Skills Kit (ASK), which allows innovators to provide Alexa with skills or abilities, allowing Alexa to communicate with the related inventions. Eventually, these platforms could possibly be converted into de facto standards, the same as the system device. The creator would profit from the improved visibility while customers would be able to attach and utilize them without difficulty (see: https://ec.europa.eu/growth/tools-databases/dem/).

Thread: Thread is an innovative low power wireless network standard for smart home security. The standard protocol sustains IPv6 by 6LoWPAN (Sovacool *et al.* 2020). The proposal behind Thread is the resolution of consistency, safety, power, and similarity concerns that regularly occur within smart home products. Thread is put on the physical layer that becomes the source of ZigBee devices, where an OEM is able to simply renew its ZigBee devices to sustain Thread through the development of software. Thread is very useful and provides an extra inclusive solution than earlier low-power wireless standards.

Constrained Application Protocol (COAP): This is a standard communication protocol for resource restrained devices in IoT. Several IoT deployments need proxies for asynchronous communication involving edge devices. This actually enables the proxies to access the vulnerable parts of CoAP messages (Gunnarsson *et al.* 2021). The latest standard protocol Object Security for Constrained Restful Environments (OSCORE) offers back-to-back security in support of CoAP messages by third party proxies. It executes the predictable services, through the improvements of significant security and privacy. OSCORE resourcefully offers sensitive trustworthy security and encryption on the dissimilar parts of CoAP messages (Gunnarsson *et al.* 2021). To evaluate whether the related security aspects consume a large amount of the limited resources that exist on a restricted device, OSCORE is implemented as an open-source protocol and its effectiveness is evaluated. OSCORE has been standardized to a large extent under the Internet Engineering Task Force (IETF) (Selander *et al.* 2019).

Datagram Transport Layer Security (DTLS): This is an Internet standard based security channel providing the transport layer that secures communications in excess of untrustworthy datagram protocols (e.g. UDP). Security is ensured by using two nodes that become the adjoining transport layer hops. DTLS is a secure reproduction of the TLS protocol (Dierks *et al.* 2008) with corresponding security assurances. For example, it prevents eavesdropping, interfering, tampering and message imitation. DTLS, in particular, is modified to support the use of UDP rather than the transmission control protocol (TCP). The innovative CoAP requirement (Shelby 2014) specified DTLS as a single security method to secure the CoAP exchange messages. There are two communicating devices, which primarily use the DTLS handshake protocol to swap cryptographic key material and network information to support message security. Specifically, one device performs like a client, while another performs like a server. The defaulting handshake relies on documentation, excluding annexes derived from symmetric pre-shared keys (Eronen 2005), or on raw public keys (Wouters *et al.* 2014). A comprehensive handshake determines a protected session, wherein the client and server are able to start swapping data secured by considered key material. Secure communication is subsequently accomplished through the use of the DTLS record protocol, which ensures the consistency and security of message transfers.

4.5. Conclusion

The IoT is not a perfect application in a smart home as the security is always very critical. Even though the overall nature of security threats is also related to other domains such as confidentiality, authentication, and access threats, the vulnerability is still high considering the sensitivity of home-based applications. In addition, because the networked system is user-friendly, the physical accessibility of the systems leads to another big threat. The heterogeneity of the different devices and the fixed firmware further contributes to the system complexity. A number of solutions have been proposed that recognize and block the related threats at the network level and can contribute to the security of IoT-based smart homes. However, there is still a big gap to be bridged to offer seamless network security across all usable devices in IoT-based smart homes.

4.6. References

Ahmed, M.S., Hoque, M.A., Khattak, A.J. (2016). Real-time vehicle movement tracking on Android devices through Bluetooth communication with DSRE devices. *2016 IEEE Vehicular Networking Conference (VNC)*, 1–2.

Alaa, M., Zaidan, A.A., Zaidan, B.B., Talal, M., Kiah, M.L.M. (2017). A review of smart home applications based on Internet of Things. *Journal of Network and Computer Applications*, 97, 48–65

Almusaylim, Z.A. and Zaman, N. (2019). A review on smart home present state and challenges: Linked to context-awareness Internet of Things (IoT). *Wireless Networks*, 25(6), 3193–3204.

Atzori, L., Iera, A., Morabito, G. (2010). The Internet of Things: A survey. *Computer Networks*, 54(15), 2787–2805.

Balte, A., Kashid, A., Patil, B. (2015). Security issues in Internet of Things (IoT): A survey. *International Journal of Advanced Research in Computer Science and Software Engineering*, 5(4), 450–455.

Brass, I., Tanczer, L., Carr, M., Elsden, M., Blackstock, J. (2018). Standardising a moving target: The development and evolution of IoT security standards. In *Living in the Internet of Things: Cybersecurity of the IoT – 2018*, IEEE (ed.). IET, London.

Broll, G., Rukzio, E., Paolucci, M., Wagner, M., Schmidt, A., Hussmann, H. (2009). Perci: Pervasive service interaction with the Internet of Things. *Journal of Internet Computing*, 13(6), 74–81.

Castellani, A., Loreto, S., Rahman, A., Fossati, T., Dijk, E. (2017). Guidelines for mapping implementations: HTTP to the constrained application protocol (CoAP). *Internet Engineering Task Force (IETF): Fremont*, CA, 2070–1721.

Cousin, P., Maló, P., Pham, C., Yu, X., Li, J., Song, J., Thiare, O., Daffe, A., Kofuju, S., Marão, G., Amazonas, J., Gürgen, L., Yonezawa, T., Akiyama, T., Maggio, M., Moessner, K., Miyake, Y., Vermesan, O., Le Gall, F., Almeida, B. (2011). European IoT international cooperation in research and innovation. In *Digitising the Industry: Internet of Things Connecting the Physical, Digital and Virtual Worlds*, Vermesan, C. and Friess, P. (eds). River Publishers, Aalborg [Online]. Available at: https://www.riverpublishers.com/pdf/ebook/chapter/RP_9788793379824C10.pdf.

Dahiya, M. (2017). Issues and countermeasures for smart home security. *International Journal of Innovative and Emerging Research in Engineering*, 4, 124–126.

Davidson, C., Rezwana, T., Hoque, M.A. (2018). Smart home security application enabled by IoT. *International Conference on Smart Grid and Internet of Things*, Springer, Cham, 46–56.

Dierks, T. and Rescorla, E. (2008). The transport layer security (TLS) protocol version 1.2. Memo, RFC, RFC Editor, Fremont, CA.

Domb, M. (2019). Smart home systems based on Internet of Things. *Internet of Things (IoT) for Automated and Smart Applications*, IntechOpen, 1–14. DOI: http://dx.doi.org/10.5772/intechopen.84894.

Drahansky, M., Paridah, M., Moradbak, A., Mohamed, A., Owolabi, F., Asniza, M. (2016). We are IntechOpen, the world's leading publisher of Open Access books built by scientists, for scientists TOP 1%. *Intech 1(Tourism)*, 13.

D'Ulizia, A., Ferri, F., Grifoni, P., Guzzo, T. (2010). Smart homes to support elderly people: Innovative technologies and social impacts. *Pervasive and Smart Technologies for Healthcare: Ubiquitous Methodologies and Tools*, IGI Global, 25–38.

Dutton, W.H. (2014). Putting things to work: Social and policy challenges for the Internet of Things. *Info*, 16(3), 1–21.

ENISA (2017). Baseline security recommendations for IoT in the context of critical information infrastructures [Online]. Available at: https://op.europa.eu/en/publication-detail/-/publication/c37f8196-d96f-11e7-a506-01aa75ed71a1.

Eronen, P. and Tschofenig, H. (2005). Pre-shared key ciphersuites for transport layer security (TLS). RFC 4279. Memo, The Internet Society, December.

Froiz-Míguez, I., Fernández-Caramés, T.M., Fraga-Lamas, P., Castedo, L. (2018). Design, implementation and practical evaluation of an IoT home automation system for fog computing applications based on MQTT and ZigBee-WiFi sensor nodes. *Sensors*, 18(8), 2660.

Gann, D., Barlow, J., Venables, T. (1999). *Digital Futures: Making Homes Smarter.* Chartered Institute of Housing, Coventry.

Gomez, C. and Paradells, J. (2010). Wireless home automation networks: A survey of architectures and technologies. *IEEE Communications Magazine*, 48(6), 92–101.

Gubbi, J., Buyya, R., Marusic, S., Palaniswami, M. (2013). Internet of Things (IoT): A vision, architectural elements, and future directions. *Future Generation Computer Systems*, 29(7), 1645–1660.

Guillemin, P., Berens, F., Carugi, M., Arndt, M., Ladid, L., Percivall, G., Thubert, P. (2013). Internet of Things standardisation – Status, requirements, initiatives and organisations. In *Internet of Things: Converging Technologies for Smart Environments and Integrated Ecosystems*, Vermesan, O. and Friess, P. (eds). River Publishers, Aalborg.

Gunnarsson, M., Brorsson, J., Palombini, F., Seitz, L., Tiloca, M. (2021). Evaluating the performance of the OSCORE security protocol in constrained IoT environments. *Internet of Things*, 13, 100333.

Gyarmathy, K. (2020). Comprehensive guide to IoT statistics you need to know in 2020 [Online]. Available at: https://www.vxchnge.com/blog/iot-statistics.

Hoque, M.A. and Davidson, C. (2019). Design and implementation of an IoT-based smart home security system. *International Journal of Networked and Distributed Computing*, 7(2), 85–92.

Hui, J. and Thubert, P. (2011). Compression format for IPv6 datagrams over IEEE 802.15.4-based networks. Document, IETF.

James, M., Chui, M., Bisson, P., Woetzel, J., Dobbs, R., Bughin, J., Aharon, D. (2015). The Internet of Things: Mapping the value beyond the hype. *McKinsey Global Institute*, 3, 1–24.

Jian, M.S., Wu, J.Y., Chen, J.Y., Li, Y.J., Wang, Y.C., Xu, H.Y. (2017). IoT base smart home appliances by using Cloud Intelligent Tetris Switch. *2017 19th International Conference on Advanced Communication Technology (ICACT)*, 589–592.

Joo, I.Y. and Choi, D.H. (2017). Distributed optimization framework for energy management of multiple smart homes with distributed energy resources. *IEEE Access*, 5, 15551–15560.

Khoa, T.A., Nhu, L.M.B., Son, H.H., Trong, N.M., Phuc, C.H., Phuong, N.T.H., Duc, D.N.M. (2020). Designing efficient smart home management with IoT smart lighting: A case study. *Wireless Communications and Mobile Computing*, 1–18.

Kraemer, M.J. and Flechais, I. (2018). Researching privacy in smart homes: A roadmap of future directions and research methods. In *Living in the Internet of Things: Cybersecurity of the IoT – 2018*, IEEE (ed.). IET, London.

Li, B. and Yu, J. (2011). Research and application on the smart home based on component technologies and Internet of Things. *Procedia Engineering*, 15, 2087–2092.

Li, X., Yoshie, O., Huang, D. (2017). A passive method for privacy protection in the perceptual layer of IoTs. *International Journal of Pervasive Computing and Communications*, 13(2), 194–210.

Lin, H. and Bergmann, N.W. (2016). IoT privacy and security challenges for smart home environments. *Information*, 7(3), 44.

Manyika, J., Chui, M., Bughin, J., Dobbs, R., Bisson, P., Marrs, A. (2013). *Disruptive Technologies: Advances that will Transform Life, Business, and the Global Economy*. McKinsey Global Institute, San Francisco, CA.

Mao, J., Lin, Q., Bian, J. (2018), Application of learning algorithms in smart home IoT system security. *Mathematical Foundations of Computing*, 1(1), 63.

Miorandi, D., Sicari, S., De Pellegrini, F., Chlamtac, I. (2012). Internet of Things: Vision, applications and research challenges. *Ad Hoc Networks*, 10(7), 1497–1516.

Morris, M.E., Adair, B., Miller, K., Ozanne, E., Hansen, R., Pearce, A.J., Said, C.M. (2013). Smart-home technologies to assist older people to live well at home. *Journal of Aging Science*, 1(1), 1–9.

Padyab, A. and Stahlbrost, A. (2018). Exploring the dimensions of individual privacy concerns in relation to the Internet of Things use situations. *Digital Policy, Regulation and Governance*, 20(6), 528–544.

Perrig, A., Szewczyk, R., Tygar, J.D., Wen, V., Culler, D.E. (2002). SPINS: Security protocols for sensor networks. *International Conference on Mobile Computing and Networking*, 8, 189–199.

Pillitteri, V.Y. and Brewer, T.L. (2014). Guidelines for smart grid cyber security. NISTIR 7628 Revision 1.

Ray, A.K. and Bagwari, A. (2020). IoT based smart home: Security aspects and security architecture. *2020 IEEE 9th International Conference on Communication Systems and Network Technologies (CSNT)*, 218–222.

Selander, G., Mattsson, J., Palombini, F., Seitz, L. (2019). Object security for constrained restful environments (oscore). RFC8613 (Proposed Standard). Internet Engineering Task Force, RFC Editor, Work in Progress.

Shelby, Z., Hartke, K., Bormann, C. (2014). The constrained application protocol (CoAP). Document, RFC, RFC Editor, Fremont, CA, DOI: 10.17487/RFC7252.

Sivaraman, V., Gharakheili, H.H., Vishwanath, A., Boreli, R., Mehani, O. (2015). Network-level security and privacy control for smart-home IoT devices. *2015 IEEE 11th International Conference on Wireless and Mobile Computing, Networking and Communications (WiMob)*, 163–167.

Song, G., Ding, F., Zhang, W., Song, A. (2008). A wireless power outlet system for smart homes. *IEEE Transactions on Consumer Electronics*, 54(4), 1688–1691.

Sovacool, B.K. and Del Rio, D.D.F. (2020). Smart home technologies in Europe: A critical review of concepts, benefits, risks and policies. *Renewable and Sustainable Energy Reviews*, 120, 109663.

Sowah, R.A., Boahene, D.E., Owoh, D.C., Addo, R., Mills, G.A., Owusu-Banahene, W., Sarkodie-Mensah, B. (2020). Design of a secure wireless home automation system with an open home automation bus (OpenHAB 2) framework. *Journal of Sensors*, 1–22.

Vinodhan, D. and Vinnarasi, A. (2016). IoT based smart home. *International Journal of Engineering and Innovative Technology (IJEIT)*, 5(10), 35–38.

Winter, T., Thubert, P., Brandt, A., Hui, J.W., Kelsey, R., Levis, P., Alexander, R.K. (2012). RPL: IPv6 routing protocol for low-power and lossy networks. *RFC*, 6550, 1–157.

Wouters, P., Tschofenig, H., Gilmore, J., Weiler, S., Kivinen, T. (2014). Using raw public keys in transport layer security (TLS) and datagram transport layer security (DTLS). Document, Internet Engineering Task Force (IETF), Fremont, CA, 2070–1721.

Yang, Y., Wu, L., Yin, G., Li, L., Zhao, H. (2017). A survey on security and privacy issues in Internet of Things. *IEEE Internet of Things Journal*, 4(5), 1250–1258.

Yang, H., Lee, W., Lee, H. (2018). IoT smart home adoption: The importance of proper level automation. *Journal of Sensors*, Hindawi Article ID 6464036, 1–12.

Yashwant, S.K., Krishna, P.V., Kumar, B.B., Chandan, G., Prasad, J.V.D. (2020). iLock: State-of-the-art sophisticated door lock for wireless devices. *2020 2nd International Conference on Innovative Mechanisms for Industry Applications (ICIMIA)*, 718–721.

Yim, S.J. and Choi, Y.H. (2012). Neighbor-based malicious node detection in wireless sensor networks. *Journal of Wireless Sensor Network*, 4(9), 219–225

Yousuf, O. and Mir, R.N. (2019). A survey on the Internet of Things security. *Information & Computer Security*, 2056–4961, 27(2), 292–323.

5

IoT in a New Age of Unified and Zero-Trust Networks and Increased Privacy Protection

Sava Zxivanovich[1], Branislav Todorovic[2],
Jean Pierre Lorré[3], Darko Trifunovic[2], Adrian Kotelba[4],
Ramin Sadre[5] and Axel Legay[5]

[1]Technology Partnership, Belgrade, Serbia
[2]Institute for National and International Security (INIS), Belgrade, Serbia
[3]Linagora Grand Sud Ouest, Toulouse, France
[4]VTT Technical Research Centre of Finland Ltd, Espoo, Finland
[5]UCLouvain, Ottignies-Louvain-la-Neuve, Belgium

In a new age of integration of many different services and zero-trust networks, the IoT has to overcome hardware limitations and provide adequate security. Our goal is to provide methods and effective tools to help build a network that is both easy to use and secure. It is based on Pi Platform for Unified Secure Communications, Services and Web-Applications, providing a foundation for home/small/medium office hubs. IoT security is based on the zero-trust philosophy – all communications are encrypted, no unidentifiable device is accepted on the network, each device has to provide its passport with a description of its network behavior and better encryption key generation. This IoT solution also addresses potential configuration problems by allowing trusted third-party providers to remotely access and correctly configure home/small/medium office hubs as well as informing users about any potentially harmful behavior or external access to their equipment.

Cybersecurity in Smart Homes,
coordinated by Rida Khatoun. © ISTE Ltd 2022.

5.1. Introduction

With the advancement of new technologies and the rapid proliferation of devices at home and in cities, users are now faced with a myriad of possible security vulnerabilities. The risk is particularly large, especially with IoT environments that increasingly integrate the devices of our daily lives at home and in the city, including electrical and gas appliances. In this context, any stolen private data can be used to manipulate sensitive information that endangers the personal, social and financial lives of citizens.

Privacy and data protection are fundamental human rights that are strictly established within the United Nations (UN). A prerequisite for this is building strong rules and technology frameworks to empower citizens and protect personal data and privacy. However, some members of the digital society are more vulnerable as they are less prepared to confront cyber-attacks and personal data breaches, such as biometric data breaches, resulting from a lost or stolen fingerprint and facial recognition data or through malicious mobile apps; or data breaches in the gaming industry, compromising million of accounts containing usernames, email addresses, IP addresses and hashed passwords. The scale, value and sensitivity of personal data in the cyberspace domain, in particular, the IoT domain, are significantly on the rise and citizens are typically uncertain about who monitors, accesses and modifies their personal data. Personal data breaches may facilitate abuse by third parties, including cyber-threats such as coercion, extortion and corruption.

One of the fundamental privacy challenges is the possibility that, in systems that depend on user settings, a large number of options may not be adopted by the general public due to the difficulty in their use. In addition to this, for the most part, service providers still rely on the traditional limited consent-based model, fostering binary ("allow/deny") systems that do not easily allow the management of large quantities of data. On the other hand, full granularity of choice for each data set, authorised party and purpose may engender "consent fatigue" and alienate users. This reflects a tension between granularity and usability, both of which need to be taken into account during the design of the cloud and mobile services (Hansen and Limniotis 2018). From the point of view of security, the main challenges are related to the lack of adoption of client side encryption or layered encryption. On related security challenges, stronger authentication measures are needed, as well as more transparent procedures for dealing with data breaches and other incidents. In addition to this, due to the diversity of the IoT domain, it seems necessary to have different levels of security and privacy protection.

The history of the IoT also reflects its weaknesses, in relation to data privacy protection in particular. Increased data flow through all local networks on a daily basis renders every attempt by individuals, companies and institutions to follow and control it impossible, except for those who are highly specialized. Network traffic also usually contains a certain amount of sensitive data, often digitally manipulated in some way (e.g. a variety of formats and data structures required by different applications). Such a situation makes a network breach or misuse of information even simpler during the course of an ordinary IoT operation.

There still a need for novel solutions to better protect users' personal data, to ensure that data usage remains consistent with laws and legality and to help citizens to better monitor and audit their security, privacy and personal data protection, enabling them to become more engaged and active in the fight against cyber-risks. These innovative solutions can benefit from a self-sovereign identity, distributed ledger technologies and federated data processing to accomplish these needs.

This chapter outlines a first attempt to provide a solution to security and privacy challenges of the Internet of Things. The main contributions are as follows:

– To introduce the zero-trust philosophy and architecture for improved overall network security and better encryption.

– To define the use of Unified Secure Communications, Services and Web-Applications as a foundation for home/small/medium network hubs based on existing, tested and verified solutions (e.g. Pi Platform).

– To discuss methods and effective tools that could assist in creating networks that are both easy to use and secure not only for network members, but for trusted third-party providers and other remote users.

The next section presents a brief overview of the IoT with particular attention paid to security and data privacy. Section 5.3 highlights security and privacy challenges in order to clarify this issue and lay the foundation for the solution that will be proposed later in this chapter. In section 5.4 the authors have tried, within the chapter's limits, to draw the outline of the current state of the art in the field of IoT security. Its purpose is twofold, to assist the reader in understanding the relation the proposed solution has with the current competitive solutions and to underline the main streams of the current work on the global level in order to emphasize differences with the new solution. Section 5.5 presents a zero-trust approach for security and privacy protection. This section provides all answers to problems listed previously, defines capabilities for applications, including compatibility and interoperability, and sets grounds for a practical example. In combination with the specific use case, section 5.6 demonstrates the applicability of this zero-trust approach in the form of a secure and private interactive intelligent conversational system and paves the way to the final sections on discussion and conclusions.

5.2. Internet of Things

The term Internet of Things (IoT for short) is neither precisely defined nor is its history exactly known. It is likely that it was first used in a presentation by Kevin

Ashton in 1999 who, at the time, worked for Procter and Gamble (Ashton 2009). In that presentation he presented his reflections on using new technologies such as RFID to track a large number of physical objects and collect information from them without human involvement.

Today, the IoT has become an umbrella term for technologies enabling the communication, acquisition and processing of information from various kinds of networked devices. There is however no strong agreement on what types of devices and communication exactly belong to the IoT. Some authors, especially those in the tradition of Wireless Sensor Networks, consider only small resource-constrained devices that use low-power and/or long-range communication to send sensor data to central data collection and processing points to be IoT devices. Others extend the definition to all sorts of devices with specific purposes that are deployed on a large scale, such as home routers, smart home equipment and mobile phones.

The development of the concept of the IoT has been enabled by progress in several fields in recent decades. The field of Wireless Sensor Networks has driven the mass production of low-power embedded systems with radio interfaces. The work on Wireless Adhoc Networks has contributed new network protocols that allow an efficient and robust exchange of information in unreliable networks. Thanks to Cloud computing, the large amount of data produced by an Internet of Things deployment can be processed in an adaptive and flexible way without requiring its users to acquire and manage their own server infrastructure. Finally, Machine-to-Machine application protocols, such as CoAP (Shelby *et al.* 2014) or MQTT[1], are used to exchange information between the various components without the need for human intervention.

Zhao and Ge (2013) introduced a widely accepted general model of the IoT with three layers which we present here in a slightly extended version that allows for IoT devices with actuator capabilities:

– The *perception layer* consists of the IoT devices, i.e. field devices with sensor or actuator functions. For cost reasons and convenience (changing batteries), these devices are often resource-constrained in terms of computation, memory and energy and are based on embedded hardware platforms, running small optimized operating systems such as RIOT[2] or Contiki[3].

– The *network layer* is responsible for the collection, aggregation and transmission of the data sent or received by the devices in the perception layer. In modern IoT deployments, this layer not only comprises the communication networks and their protocols, but also the necessary infrastructure (often in the cloud) for storing and processing the data.

---

1. https://mqtt.org/.
2. https://www.riot-os.org/.
3. http://www.contiki-os.org/.

– The *application layer* contains all the applications and solutions driven by the sensory data. Various free and commercial frameworks exist to support the design and implementation of IoT applications. The larger vendors, such as Amazon[4] and Google[5], also provide management, storage and data processing services located in the network layer. Some vendors offer solutions that target specific use cases, most notably the smart home market, for example Samsung's SmartThings platform[6], and industrial applications[7], the latter called the *Industrial IoT*.

The fulfillment of this model required a small embedded operating system (OS) that would be capable of enabling data transfer from IoT devices to the Internet. Due to a variety of IoT applications with specific functions and inputs/outputs, there are quite a few IoT operating systems in use to cover different requirements and demands. Almost every manufacturer and developer has their own preferences and ranking of IoT OSs. Therefore the list of IoT OSs in Table 5.1 is just an indication with regard to variety. To the best of our knowledge not one of the listed IoT platforms provides complete transparency on what data can be collected or means for users to select and define which data can be processed. The documentation also does not specify ways to recover from a cyber attack nor tools to protect hidden data that could be exploited by third parties. It was felt that more responsibility is put on the developers who use these solutions. However, there is an increasing awareness among platform vendors of the necessity of providing online management services, performing regular OS patch updates and scrutinizing all incoming and outgoing network traffic.

Furthermore, the significant growth in IoT deployment has led to the emergence of IoT platforms that provide users with the ability to quickly build, test, deploy and iterate on IoT-specific applications, supporting (Hammi 2018):

1) Easy integration of new devices and services.

2) Communication between devices (objects and servers).

3) The management of different devices and communication protocols.

4) The transmission of data flows and the creation of new applications.

5) Interoperability among components, objects, gateways, cloud data and software applications.

6) Scalability of the IoT infrastructure.

---

4. https://aws.amazon.com/de/iot/.

5. https://cloud.google.com/solutions/iot.

6. https://www.samsung.com/smartthings/.

7. https://siemens.mindsphere.io.

Name	Core language	Security Support	Privacy Support	Other features
Contiki	C language	WolfSSL	N/A	SSH Access
Android Things	Android	HTTPS and SSL	N/A	Developer kit
Riot	C or C++ language.	WolfSSL	N/A	Remote update
Apache Mynewt	Command-line interface (CLI).	WolfSSL	N/A	Remote monitoring and upgrade
Huawei LightOS	SDKs: Java, Python, NET, Node.js, Go	Encrypted transmission	N/A	Remote upgrade
Zephyr	Zephir language for PHP developer	WolfSSL	N/A	Development kit, Threat modeling
Snappy	Snappy Ubuntu Core	SSL-Certificate	N/A	Automatic upgrade
TinyOS	nesC	TinySec, WolfSSL	N/A	Remote reprogramming
Fuchsia	Dart, Go, Rust, C, C++	SSL	N/A	Remote control service

Table 5.1. *Overview of selected IoT operating Systems (OS)*

According to the level of services provided, IoT platforms can be divided into (Hammi 2018):

– Infrastructure-as-a-service backends: They provide a hosting space and processing power for applications and services, e.g. IBM Bluemix[8].

– M2M connectivity platforms: They focus on only the connectivity of IoT objects through telecommunication networks and protocols, e.g. Comarch[9] and AirVantage[10].

– Hardware-specific software platforms: Numerous companies sell their proprietary technology which includes the hardware and the software backend, e.g Google Nest[11].

– Enterprise software extensions: Some software and operating system companies, such as Windows and Apple, increasingly allow the integration of IoT devices such as smartphones, connected watches and home devices.

5.3. IoT security and privacy challenges

In this section, we will present challenges in IoT security that have been identified by experts, followed by an analysis of the risk situation related to the manipulation and treatment of privacy-sensitive data in IoT environments.

---

8. https://www.ibm.com/cloud-computing/bluemix/fr.

9. http://www.comarch.com/telecommunications/solutions/m2m-platform.

10. https://airvantage.net.

11. https://nest.com/.

5.3.1. *Security challenges*

The increasing growth of the Internet of Things, either by putting new devices on the market or by developing new applications based on those devices, has raised many questions about the secure use of IoT platforms and associated services as well as the protection of users' privacy. Sadique *et al.* (2018) discussed the current state of security in IoT and its challenges and identified issues such as device identity, firmware updating and installation if new patches are available, implementation of security algorithms knowing that IoT devices are often resource-constrained, with limited power, and finally, trust between different components in the IoT paradigm. However, IoT security is not only limited to the IoT devices themselves. For binti Mohamad Noor and Hassan (2019), the objective of IoT security is privacy protection, confidentiality and the security of the users, infrastructures, data and devices, as well as the guarantee of the availability of services offered by an IoT ecosystem. In this context, Ogonji *et al.* (2020) propose a privacy and security taxonomy which highlights threats, attack surfaces, vulnerabilities and countermeasures.

That the concerns of experts about the security of the IoT are not unfounded has been demonstrated in many recent incidents of security exploits and data breaches, such as the hacking of smart home devices (Marotti 2019) or home security cameras (Vigdor 2019). Systematic studies by researchers have revealed numerous vulnerabilities in products and services targeting the smart home market (Fernandes *et al.* 2016; Kafle *et al.* 2019). Even if an IoT device and its communication are secured, the complexity of the involved interactions among participating entities (devices, cloud services, mobile apps) results in security hazards that significantly increase the size of the attack surface (Zhou *et al.* 2019). Sometimes, the hazard is not accidental and/or is exploited by the device manufacturer or the service provider themselves (McGregor 2019; Osborne 2019; Thapliyal 2019).

To date, the issues identified are still topical, as no consensus has yet been reached to regulate this area. Attempts to arrive at standards are still ongoing. It should be noted that there are several links in the IoT chain, such as communication protocols, data formats, etc., which require hard exchanges among many actors. While some authors (e.g. in Hassan *et al.* 2020) argue that new developments such as the Narrowband-Internet of Things (NB-IoT)[12] improve privacy and reliability of transmission, it seems that existing standards for secure communication are not sufficient. When comparing security architectures, Ammar *et al.* (2018) show that different methodologies are followed by individual actors to provide other security properties in addition to the standards used for securing communications.

---

12. NB-IoT is a standard-based low-power wide-area network (LPWAN) technology developed to connect a wide range of new IoT devices and services.

The observations above are also valid for the so-called Industrial Internet of Things (IIoT). According to Liberg *et al.* (2020), the IIoT is part of critical system operation in many industrial use cases. Consequences of faulty operation can be disastrous. This is even truer when considering the pharma industry where IoT sensors and detectors can be used to supervise different styles of biomaterials and chemicals, detect tool flaws, and can be also used to assist in the prevention of fraudulent drug activities (Deepak *et al.* 2020). Munirathinam (Munirathinam 2020) considers security and privacy to be the number one challenge faced by the Industrial IoT.

As we have said, due to the diversity of the IoT domain, it seems necessary to have different levels of security and privacy protection. The control of a street lamp does not have the same security and privacy requirements as a portable health gadget. Once identified, these levels can be used to automate and personalize security and privacy services. The rapid evolution of the IoT domain and the emergence of new IoT products of all kinds lead the way towards reuse and adaptation strategies for security and privacy in order to avoid compromising platforms that are already operational.

Before continuing, it is necessary to clarify some very important concepts used in the rest of this chapter.

DEFINITION 5.1.– *Cyber security risk* *is the possibility of losing data or/to take control of your system, letting your private data be exposed or cyber-bulling, leading to financial or physical harm.*

DEFINITION 5.2.– *Cyber-bullying*[13] *is often based on altered information, helping to propagate false ideals and news. Cyber-bullying is defined as using electronic technologies in order to bully another person through the Internet. Unfortunately, cyber-bullying very often stays unreported.*

5.3.2. *Privacy challenges*

In the past, user data were limited to a few pieces of profile information, and the risk of exploiting this information was minimal. Today, the risk is great because more and more systems are tracking and storing even the smallest amount of user usage data, known as data analytics. Advances in artificial intelligence and communications networks such as 4G and 5G have also expanded the scope of data that can be exploited to include voice, video and image. As a result, the user has lost any possibility of preserving their privacy. With the increase in attacks against systems for data theft and malicious use, prices for security services will rise sharply. The result is that normal users and small businesses will be the most exposed and affected by the manipulation of their private data.

---

13. https://www.coe.int/en/web/children/bullying.

Practical applications of solutions that handle privacy issues in the EU in general follow the guidance of corresponding institutions on the European level. The latest corresponding initiatives in the EU are related to the European Self-Sovereign Identity Framework (ESSIF), as part of the European Blockchain Service Infrastructure (EBSI). The EBSI is a joint initiative from the European Commission and the European Blockchain Partnership (EBP). EBSI provides a common, shared and open infrastructure based on blockchain technologies aimed at providing a secure and interoperable ecosystem that will enable the development of EU-wide cross-border digital services in the public sector. The driving concept of the EBSI, according to the EBP mission and vision, is to

> enhance efficiency, security, transparency and engagement, providing an interoperable framework for data and services that from one side enables the key EU visions (Once Only, Single Digital Gateway, ...) and at the same time allows each participating entity to run cross-border or internal services with secure access to needed information while maintaining autonomy running its own processes with its own technology stacks, regardless of the processes and technologies of any other entity[14].

In this sense, the implementation of decentralized biometric credential storage options in the EU is often proposed via blockchains using DIDs and DID documents within the IEEE 2410-2017 Biometric Open Protocol Standard (BOPS). Decentralized identifiers (DID) are a type of identifier that enables a verifiable, decentralized digital identity. They are an important component of decentralized web applications[15].

Also worth mentioning is eIDAS (electronic IDentification, Authentication and trust Services), EU regulation no. 910/2014 on electronic identification and trust services for electronic transactions in the internal market. Adopted on 23 July 2014, it provides a predictable regulatory environment to enable secure and seamless electronic interactions between businesses, citizens and public authorities. From September 29, 2018[16], all organizations delivering public digital services in an EU member state must recognize electronic identification from all EU member states.

When developing tools for IoT, data subjects may have or may not have particular rights depending on the legal basis that the data controller uses. Specifically, as you can see for the right to be forgotten (the right to deletion), the data subject may not have the right of erasure if the legal basis used by the data controller is a legal obligation (e.g. data relating to criminal proceedings) or public interest (e.g. information processed by a public authority in line with a public task). Figure 5.1

---

14. https://ec.europa.eu/cefdigital/wiki/display/CEFDIGITALEBSI/Mapping+of+Vision%2C+Mission%2C+and+Goals.

15. https://en.wikipedia.org/wiki/Decentralized_identifiers.

16. https://ec.europa.eu/futurium/en/content/eidas-regulation-regulation-eu-ndeg9102014.

is a very useful table which summarizes data subjects' rights as conceived by the French Data Protection Authority.

	Right of access to data	Right to rectification of errors	Right to deletion/right to be forgotten	Right to restrict processing	Right to data portability	Right to object
Consent	✓	✓	✓	✓	✓	Withdrawal of consent
Contract	✓	✓	✓	✓	✓	✗
Legitimate interest	✓	✓	✓	✓	✗	✓
Legal obligation	✓	✓	✗	✓	✗	✗
Public interest	✓	✓	✗	✓	✗	✓
Protection of vital interests	✓	✓	✓	✓	✗	✗

Figure 5.1. *Data subjects' rights*

Particularly, the following specifications should be considered when dealing with data subjects' rights.

– The data controller may have other procedures in place for enabling a data subject to request the deletion of their data (e.g. by filling in an online form or sending an email to a particular email address) and might not wish to comply with the search and destroy program. In that case, there should be a way to indicate to the data subject the way to request the erasure, without necessarily having to notify the data protection authorities.

– Locating and erasing personal data is also processing, thus this will be processing personal data and will need a legal basis, which most likely will be consent or a contract. This will also need an additional legal basis for processing sensitive personal data (when applicable), which most likely would be explicit consent.

– When trawling publicly available registries and databases, some datasets may be protected under trade secrets and other confidentiality rules. However, inferred or derived data which occurred after processing the original data lose their protection because it will be easy to find subject's initially provided data, e.g. sexual orientation based on postal code.

– Notifying the data protection authority should occur only if the data subject has exhausted all other means of trying to exercise their right to deletion (right to be forgotten) for instance, by contacting the data controller and the relevant deadline for action has passed, otherwise the authorities may dismiss the claim as invalid.

This extensive introduction to data privacy takes the formal form defined below:

DEFINITION 5.3.– *Privacy protection is about control of access to personal or Small and Midsize Business (SMBs) data that is, by law, private or that is assumed to be private by individuals. Privacy protection is about protection of personal information that is a term that may be used in a slightly different manner by different people. In this document, personal information denotes privacy sensitive information that includes the following:*

– Personal data is consistent with Article 4 of General Data Protection Regulation (GDPR)[17]: Any information relating to an identified or identifiable natural person. An identifiable natural person is one who can be identified, directly or indirectly, in particular by reference to an identifier such as a name, an identification number, location data, an online identifier or to one or more factors specific to the physical, physiological, genetic, mental, economic, cultural or social identity of that natural person.

– Sensitive data are in line with Article 9 of GDPR[18] personal data revealing racial or ethnic origin, political opinions, religious or philosophical beliefs or trade union membership, and the processing of genetic data or biometric data for the purpose of uniquely identifying a natural person or data concerning health or data concerning a natural person's sex life or sexual orientation.

– Usage data: Data collected from computer devices such as printers; behavioral information such as viewing habits for digital content, users' recently visited websites or product usage history.

– Unique device identities: Other types of information that might be uniquely traceable to a user device, e.g. IP addresses, Radio Frequency Identity (RFID) tags, unique hardware ID ties.

5.4. Literature review

The aforementioned privacy and security challenges are typically addressed by technical mechanisms, most prominently tools known as privacy-enhancing technologies (PET), e.g. encryption, protocols for anonymous communications, attribute-based credentials, trusted computing, multi-party computation, homomorphic encryption, data obfuscation, privacy infomediaries, and private search of databases (Mowbray and Pearson 2012; Encinas *et al.* 2015; Guasconi *et al.* 2018). The effectiveness of those privacy-enhancing technologies has already been demonstrated by researchers and in pilot implementations. However, apart from a few exceptions, for example, encryption for data in transit and in rest became widely

---

17. https://gdpr-info.eu/art-4-gdpr/.
18. https://gdpr-info.eu/art-9-gdpr/.

used, privacy-enhancing technologies have not become a widely-used component in system design according to the European Union Agency for Network and Information Security (ENISA 2018a, 2018b).

Starting with IoT security issues in general, it can be noted as the general observation that

> Today's IoT devices are insecure and incapable of defending themselves. This is due to mainly the constrained resources in IoT devices, immature standards, and the absence of secure hardware and software design, development, and deployment. The efforts of defining a robust global mechanism for securing the IoT layers are also being hampered due to diversity of resources in IoT (Khan and Salah 2018).

A number of authors analyze various aspects of IoT security, e.g.

> The Internet of Things (IoT) envisions pervasive, connected, and smart nodes interacting autonomously while offering all sorts of services. Wide distribution, openness and relatively high processing power of IoT objects made them an ideal target for cyber attacks. Moreover, as many of IoT nodes are collecting and processing private information, they are becoming a goldmine of data for malicious actors. Therefore, security and specifically the ability to detect compromised nodes, together with collecting and preserving evidences of an attack or malicious activities emerge as a priority in successful deployment of IoT networks (Conti *et al.* 2018).

In this case authors also list the existing major security and forensics challenges within the IoT domain and briefly discuss some aspects of targeting identified challenges.

Wide application of the IoT heavily influences the complexity of the problem, in particular due to fast technological advance in the field. For that reason some authors restrict their research of trends and open issues in IoT security to recent years, in order to provide a valid overview of the current state of IoT security research, the relevant tools, IoT modelers and simulators. binti Mohamad Noor and Hassan (2019) explain that

> the results of IoT failures can be severe, therefore, the study and research in security issues in the IoT is of extreme significance. The main objective of IoT security is to preserve privacy, confidentiality, ensure the security of the users, infrastructures, data, and devices of the IoT, and guarantee the availability of the services offered by an IoT ecosystem. Thus, research in IoT security has recently been gaining much momentum with the help of the available simulation tools, modelers, and computational and analysis platforms.

In addition to individual attempts in analyzing and publishing topics related to IoT security, there are conferences, webinars and similar activities that gather experts in the field in search for common solutions to the problem. One such example related to multidisciplinary approach emphasizes that "as Internet of Things (IoT) devices and systems become more tightly integrated with our society (e.g., smart city and smart nation) and the citizens (e.g., implantable and insertable medical IoT devices), the need to understand, manage and mitigate cybersecurity risks becomes more pronounced" (Choo *et al.* 2021). In their special issue of the journal, Choo *et al.* try to cover topics of problem classification, detection, analysis, privacy issues and protection. Despite their efforts, in the conclusion they state that a number of challenges still remain to be addressed. Nevertheless, we present below the abstract of one paper from the special issue that deals with similar topics as this chapter. In "Proof of X-repute blockchain consensus protocol for IoT systems", researchers from the Harbin Institute of Technology in China, Shandong University of Science and Technology in China, Tencent Research Institute in China, Ch. Charan Singh University in India and King Saud University in Saudi Arabia designed a reputation-based consensus protocol for blockchain-enabled IoT systems (Choo *et al.* 2021).

One result of various initiatives and works, seriously motivated by the real need to find a practical solution to IoT security issues, is the "zero-trust".

> The Internet of Things (IoT) connects billions of devices to the Internet and the number is still increasing, which makes it very challenging to secure the applications, data, users, and devices in the complicated system. The zero-trust security has shown great potentials for IoTs which follows the "never trust, always verify" principle. In the past few years, the zero-trust security has attracted attentions from both industry and academics. The zero-trust holds the principle that every attempt to access the resources in IoT should be verified before granting the access (Li 2019).

Due to its importance, zero-trust philosophy and networks have also caught the attention of large companies and institutions up to the governmental level. The USA, as often taking leadership in topics about technology, have published some guidelines regarding Zero-Trust Architecture.

> Zero-trust (ZT) is the term for an evolving set of cyber-security paradigms that move defenses from static, network-based perimeters to focus on users, assets, and resources. A zero-trust architecture (ZTA) uses zero-trust principles to plan industrial and enterprise infrastructure and workflows. Zero-trust assumes there is no implicit trust granted to assets or user accounts based solely on their physical or network location (i.e., local area networks versus the Internet) or based on asset ownership (enterprise or personally owned). Authentication and

authorization (both subject and device) are discrete functions performed before a session to an enterprise resource is established. Zero-trust is a response to enterprise network trends that include remote users, bring your own device (BYOD), and cloud-based assets that are not located within an enterprise-owned network boundary. Zero-trust focuses on protecting resources (assets, services, workflows, network accounts, etc.), not network segments, as the network location is no longer seen as the prime component to the security posture of the resource. This document contains an abstract definition of zero-trust architecture (ZTA) and gives general deployment models and use cases where zero-trust could improve an enterprise's overall information technology security posture (Rose *et al.* 2020).

Previously in this chapter we mentioned that the innovative approach might include Self-Sovereign Identity (SSI), though with the original use, not relying on solutions which are already available.

In the age of increasing digital interactions and analysis of user data, the concept of Self-Sovereign Identities has gained a large amount of interest. It promises its users more control and a more user-centric experience that, in contrast to previous user-centric efforts, does not have to rely on any centralised entities. The concept of verifiable claims has been extended by the Identity Registry Model as well as the Claim Registry Model. These decentralized registries were enabled by blockchain technology and although not a necessity the storage can be decentralised too. This only leaves the claim-issuers and their position of trust as centralised entities in the system (Mühle *et al.* 2018).

Some SSI solutions are built upon blockchain technology as this already provides decentralized persistent data and consensus, but joining these two is not a must, as shown in some research. Both blockchain-based and other Self-Sovereign Identity solutions show to fulfill most of the evaluation criteria. The importance lies in the differences between solutions in both variants. Blockchain-based solutions definitely meet more properties on average than the others. The scheme by van Bokkem *et al.* (2019) shows that it is possible to create an SSI solution without blockchain technology.

5.5. Security and privacy protection with a zero-trust approach

A zero-trust approach aims to provide a framework for a network of home hubs, mobile phones, cloud services and edge devices with advanced encryption and blockchain. The reference architecture is based on Pi Platform. Its design is recommended for private individuals and SMEs. With intrusion detection and a notification system, it will provide herd notification like with meerkats and herd immunity that will significantly increase Internet security. It provides communication infrastructure for users, services and IoT-enabled devices. The main objectives addressed by this approach are listed below:

– Security and privacy management for a big and heterogeneous volume of data: The nature and amount of data generated by users' devices need new processing mechanisms in order to achieve better security and data privacy, for example, selecting better encryption mechanisms for more sensitive user data. We need security and privacy management methods that can be rapidly deployed and do not rely on instantaneous data access and availability.

– Real-time and adaptive mechanisms for data protection: Real-time monitoring is a big challenge and an important factor to detect and react to any data security and privacy violation. The goal is put in practice by handling priorities and adaptive security mechanisms that are able to manage high data volumes, such as those produced by IoT devices.

– Inter-site network security and data privacy management: User data are actually generated and available in different environments, such as at home when using a game console, mobile when connecting to their home manager, in the city when tracked by a security camera, at work when calling their meal provider, etc. Facilitating efficient collaboration between multiple secure platforms deployed in different places and in the cloud, gathering, protecting and securing data related to the same user will be a large challenge that needs to be investigated.

– Intrusion detection and proactive defence strategies techniques and tools: Novel intrusion detection mechanisms and defence strategies, mainly those based on artificial intelligence, should be included to produce a more robust platform against attacks.

As shown in Figure 5.2, the ZTA will base its approach on SSI and Pi Platform[19].

SSI means that the user IoT device will directly manage its personal information and control access over it. With SSI, the power to control personal data resides in the user and not in any third party granting or tracking access to these credentials. SSI is based on credentials: users have verifiable credentials of different personal information (information certified by trusted issuers, for instance, a manufacturer could provide a credential of production date for an IoT device so anyone could trust that credential as it was directly provided by the manufacturer). Users will own several credentials for different personal information. They could limit and share just the required personal information for the required recipient. Users use the credentials in a privacy-preserving manner whenever and wherever they want. No prior agreement is needed, and no intermediaries are needed: devices will securely exchange personal information directly between them. The result is a more flexible, more secure and more private personal information management.

---

19. Developed by Tehnolosko Partnerstvo Doo Beograd (Stari Grad).

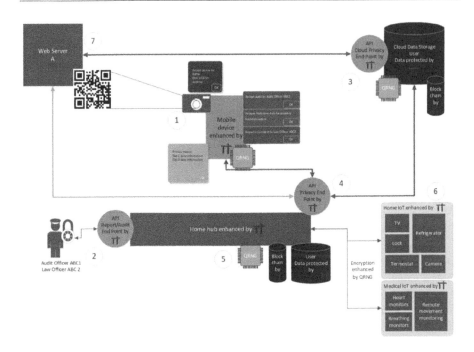

Figure 5.2. *Zero-trust framework. For a color version of this figure, see www.iste.co.uk/khatoun/cybersecurity.zip*

Pi Platform provides several services presented below:

1) **Verified by Pi-based service**: An efficient blockchain implementation that can be used to verify images and documents. For example, it helps to distinguish between altered images and new and original ones and provide needed accuracy. Such an approach allows easy object verification. In addition, Pi Platform provides communication infrastructure for users, services and IoT-enabled devices. All calls/messages/services are encrypted using TLS 1.2 + AES 128/256. The intention is to improve it using quantum RNG using QRNG (Figure 5.2, point 5) chipset like SKT IDQ S2Q000 that will enhance the security of the users' data by using quantum encryption technology to generate random numbers and create unpredictable secure keys and provide the QRNG cloud service as infrastructure.

2) **Vault by Pi service**: Uses QR code (Figure 5.2, point 1 and 7) as a part procedure, making human interaction and decision mandatory. QR codes could be generated by the Vault by Pi service and signed using Verified by Pi, limiting the number of bits in the QR code and making easier to read from a computer screen. Using the Verified by Pi signing service, an application on a mobile phone that reads data, will be able to verify that the content provided in the QR code is created by a particular website and limit the possibility of hijacking the QR code. To help organisations boost transparency concerning data processing operations and enable

data subjects to receive essential information in order to make informed decisions reducing the time and effort needed, compared to the current practices generated QR codes, will contain information about: which organisation is accessing data, for what kind of purpose, the data to be accessed, for how long they would like to access data and for how long they would like to keep data but limited to the Vault by Pi setting controlled by the user.

3) **Trusted Third Party service**: Provides privacy as a service (Figure 5.2, point 3). PasS will be based on encrypted non-complete data requiring additional data to be provided to decrypt the data. PasS could be hardware as well as a software-based system. Such a system would provide trust by design. Accessing PasS will be allowed via the Vault by Pi application on a mobile phone. Providing PasS cloud-based and private cloud-based services will increase the speed of implementation as users will not need to purchase additional devices.

4) **Family Hubs service**: Allows all communication to go through Family Hubs by Pi (Figure 5.2, point 4), parents will be able to set up rules against cyber-bulling or introducing new rules of Internet engagement for their children without a need to monitor all communications.

5) **Analyse trustworthiness of data sources and risk assessment service**: Aims to enable enhanced security for the emerging IoT market. Security of IoT devices is very often overlooked in favour of the price of the equipment. Enhancing security for the IoT (Figure 5.2, point 6) is based on sharing better generated keys for secure communications as well as on AI analysing the traffic patterns inside networks, allowing faster responses to potential threats. Each IoT device will have its passport that will describe its credentials and traffic requirements. To expand potential threat analysis, we would use federate learning about all devices to be able to recognise trends and more subtle hacks.

6) **Audit interface service**: This is used by certified organisations to check edge devices (Figure 5.2, point 2), to provide secure configurations and help users as needed.

5.6. Case study: secure and private interactive intelligent conversational systems

Artificial intelligence (AI) has opened new horizons for IoT applications benefitting from the huge amount of data produced by IoT devices. However, software design has not yet evolved in order to propose new methods and measures that bring security and privacy to these new AI-based technologies. In this chapter, we are particularly interested in the user's interaction in the intelligent environment. We will focus on interactive intelligent conversational systems because they concern a large part of futuristic IoT applications and products, such as home assistants, robots and driving assistants.

Interactive intelligent conversational systems leverage a number of heterogeneous components which are supposed to work seamlessly while maintaining a high level of responsiveness, robustness, accountability and data integrity. The simplest user case, consisting of asking "what is the weather doing today" implies a pipeline consisting of a DSP-based microphone array processor, a phonetic processing unit, a speech to text module, a natural language processor, a SAAS (Software As A Service) client capable of gathering the weather information, a natural language generator, a text to speech engine, and a behavior and animation controller capable of synchronising the movement of the GUI avatar with the output speech. On top of that, one needs to account for the fact that the speech to text and text to speech module might be deployed on the cloud and subject to potential data losses as well as malevolent data compromising. All these heterogeneous modules might be written in different languages and operate on different architectures and hardware, on desktop computers, embedded appliances or cloud-based servers.

The paragraph above suggests an obvious first challenge: the heterogeneous nature of interactive dialog-based applications increases the complexity of deployment, testing and security assessment. The current chapter aims at answering these challenges by designing and proposing a set of relevant components and tools by means of security and data privacy according to the architecture presented in section 5.5. To that end the following specific goals are set: (i) Establish measures for secure conversational systems in IoT, assuring the privacy of data from user interaction to the accomplishment of user request, (ii) Establish privacy procedures for the exchanged data, (iii) Formally specify modules and their composition to guarantee the functioning of a compound system, and finally, (iv) Show, via a scenario, how it works.

We will use LinTO[20] infrastructure as our primary field of study on interactive conversational systems for the case studies. LinTO is part of an industrial initiative to design a smart conversational assistant for companies. It includes a set of innovative features for individual or collective use. It is based on the French speech recognition engine in the advancement development phase at LINAGORA[21]. Some use cases include: hands-free processes for better productivity, facility management using vocal control in the office and voice integration to end-users applications.

5.6.1. *LinTO technical characteristics*

LinTO is an open-source client-server system that enables the conception, deployment and maintenance of complete software and hardware clients that uses voice as a natural user interface. LinTO includes transcription services for simple commands and a large vocabulary. The standalone version is an embedded board with limited resources, a touch screen, speakers, a matrix of microphones and,

---

20. https://linto.ai/fr/.
21. https://www.linagora.com/fr/.

according to the configuration, a panoramic camera can be plugged into the board. It is complemented by a software platform for conversational assistance that supports intelligent interaction modalities.

More advanced deployment uses a functional LinTO platform stack running on a server and a LinTO client running on a device. The messages coming from the device are addressed to the platform using MQTT topics. The client could for example send an audio voice request to the server for further processing or stream an audio flux for live transcription. In contrast, server to client messages are used to control device behaviors such as speech synthesis and command execution. Currently, LinTO client is available for Raspberry Pi and Android. In addition, LinTO provides a user block programming interface where it is possible to create different applications through the combination of different components and services.

Given the potential usage permitted by LinTO, such as voice control of remote devices, it becomes important to secure the data flows, including privacy data such as user identities and locations. This is also taking into account the performance issues that may arise due to the complexity and size of the audio data. The zero-trust architecture presented above is used to provide that protection. A running example is presented in the following to show how this is being implemented.

5.6.2. *Use case*

Lisa is an elderly woman who lives alone but finds it difficult to move easily around her apartment to carry out even the simplest daily activities. An association offers her the secure LinTO device to control her most commonly used devices such as TV, heating, the front door and her medical bracelet. An example of the dialogues are shown below:

```
[case 1]
Lisa: LinTO
LinTO: Yes, ma'am
Lisa: Turn the heat up to 22 degrees
LinTO: Action executed, do you want something else?
Lisa: No
LinTO: (standby)


[case 2]
Lisa: LinTO
LinTO: Yes, ma'am
Lisa: Turn on the TV
LinTO: Action executed, do you want something else?
Lisa: Activate the series -Call the Midwife- on Netflix.
LinTO: Started in progress, please wait!
```

```
LinTO: Action executed, do you want something else?
Lisa: No
LinTO: (standby)


[case 3]
<Mobile device rings>
<Lisa picks up the device>.
LinTO: Ma'am, your heartbeat is not regular.
Lisa: Contact the doctor
LinTO: Yes, ma'am
LinTO: Hello doctor, I'm the intelligent assistant,
       madam has an irregular heartbeat.
Doctor: Send me all the data of last 3 days
LinTO: Data being transmitted, do you want something else?
Doctor: No
LinTO: (standby)
```

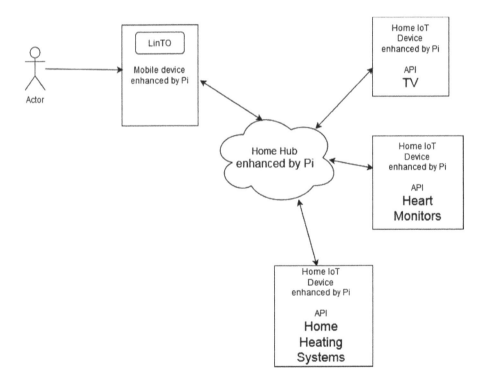

Figure 5.3. *Zero-trust framework mapped on LinTO use case*

5.6.3. *Use case mapping on the reference architecture*

Three types of components, presented by Figure 5.3, are used to develop the above scenarios: a mobile device where the LinTO conversational application is configured into command mode and is running, a home network gateway connecting all smart home devices to the network, and finally the client specific application providing a specific API (Application Programming Interface) that depends on the type of smart device functionalities. Each component is protected by the security and privacy features provided by the Pi Platform, detailed in section 5.5; this way all communications are protected from intrusion and personal injury.

The enhancement by Pi at all levels of IoT system deployment ensures consistency of inter-component exchanges and continuous verification at each entity of zero-trust architecture against any hacking attempt from outside parties.

5.7. Discussion

No system is really perfect, therefore the proposed IoT solution will also need to pass the tests of operability and usability, extended practical application, endurance to hacker attacks and various other misuses, and acceptance by the large number of users. Such proper testing in the field would require a period of commercial use, besides case studies and pilots. Furthermore, a complex solution like this IoT system requires well-organized handling of the feedback from users in order to perform debugging, fine-tuning and possible updates.

Some of the additional topics either directly connected to the proposed IoT solution or related to it in some way, might include:

– further enhancement of IoT data privacy, including accountability, verification of secure data origin and transparency of data;

– IoT secure information integrity;

– IoT emerging threats and risk management;

– IoT cybersecurity incident prevention, response and mitigation;

– physical security handling in IoT systems;

– enhancement of the system for IIoT (industrial Internet of Things) and Industry 4.0;

– IoT surveillance issues, including legal aspects.

The proposed IoT solution seems very promising so far and advanced encryption, SSI and block-chain have the power to overcome the limitations of the IoT with regard to data protection and privacy. At the same time, one must not forget that the very same advanced technology and block-chain have high computation requirements, restricted scalability, high bandwidth overhead and latency, making them overall unsuitable to the concept of IoT in their basic form. The Pi-based service provides an efficient block-chain implementation, but the optimization of processes in order to run efficiently in the IoT might show some tradeoff of which we are not aware at the present stage.

Another aspect which cannot be predicted with certainty is the behavior and the acceptance of the proposed IoT solution by people. Besides the subjective attitude towards security (e.g. "it will not happen to me" behavior) and potential issues with SSI that in essence passes the management of personal information to the user's IoT-device, there is also the problem of efficient standard testing and the presentation of results regarding the stability, performance, and security of the application. It is mandatory that a large number of people understand, accept and agree with the defined criteria. In this way, verification would be valid and users would have the motivation to use such block-chain based products.

5.8. Conclusion

Big enterprises and cloud service providers are collecting data about their users and limiting users' options and limiting the functionality of systems that their users use. Such huge data gatherings are an enviable target and hackers are gathering data as they break into systems built by companies that are collecting data with users' consent. A personal data breach may facilitate abuse by third parties, including cyber-threats such as coercion, extortion and corruption. According to the most recent IBM Security report, the average cost of a single data breach amounts to approximately 3.86 million dollars. Customers' personally-identifiable information is the most frequently comprised type of record (80 per-cent of all breaches).

In this work, we recommend the use of the zero-trust approach at all layers of the IoT infrastructure. In particular, we recommend to perform a centralized configuration and management of devices, to access the health of IoT devices in a continuous manner, monitor IoT devices for anomalous behaviors, protect privileged identities, and slice networks into segments to minimize the impact of a potential intrusion. We also stress the need for automation and artificial intelligence-based methods to detect and quickly respond to a possibly ongoing attack.

The architecture presented in this chapter, advances the state of the art of usable security and privacy by proposing an application of self-sovereign identity (SSI) technology. With SSI, the power to control personal data resides with the user and not with any third party granting or tracking access to these credentials. Users can freely limit and share only the required personal information and for the required recipient. No prior agreement is needed and no intermediaries are needed: devices will securely exchange personal information directly between them. The result is more flexible, more secure, and more private personal information management.

5.9. Acknowledgements

This work was part of an initial project involving the following institutions and companies: VTT Technical Research Centre of Finland Ltd., Tehnolosko Partnerstvo Doo Beograd (Stari Grad), Huawei Technologies Oy (Finland) Co Ltd, Fundacion Tecnalia Research & Innovation, Hypertech (Chaipertek) Anonymos Viomichaniki Emporiki Etaireia Pliroforikis Kai Neon Technologion, Institutt For Energiteknikk, Software Imagination & Vision Srl, Universite Catholique de Louvain, Vrije Universiteit Brussel, Linagora Grand Sud Ouest Sa, Institut Za Nacionalnu I Medjunarodnu Bezbednost, Halden Kommune, Centrul National De Raspuns La Incidente De Securitate Cibernetica, Nixu Oyj, City of Novi Sad.

5.10. References

Ammar, M., Russello, G., Crispo, B. (2018). Internet of things: A survey on the security of IoT frameworks. *Journal of Information Security and Applications*, 38, 8–27 [Online]. Available at: https://www.sciencedirect.com/science/article/pii/S2214212617302934.

Ashton, K. (2009). That 'Internet of Things' thing. *RFID Journal*, 22(7), 97–114.

van Bokkem, D., Hageman, R., Koning, G., Nguyen, L., Zarin, N. (2019). Self-sovereign identity solutions: The necessity of blockchain technology. *CoRR*, abs/1904.12816 [Online]. Available at: http://arxiv.org/abs/1904.12816.

Choo, K.-K.R., Gai, K., Chiaraviglio, L., Yang, Q. (2021). A multidisciplinary approach to Internet of Things (IoT) cybersecurity and risk management. *Computers & Security*, 102, 102136 [Online]. Available at: https://www.sciencedirect.com/science/article/pii/S0167404820304090.

Conti, M., Dehghantanha, A., Franke, K., Watson, S. (2018). Internet of Things security and forensics: Challenges and opportunities. *Future Generation Computer Systems*, 78, 544–546 [Online]. Available at: https://www.sciencedirect.com/science/article/pii/S0167739X17316667.

Encinas, L.H., Muñoz, A.M., Martínez, V.G., Espigares, J.N., Sánchez García, J.I., Castelluccia, C., Bourka, A. (2015). Online privacy tools for the general public: Towards a methodology for the evaluation of pets for internet and mobile users. Technical report, European Union Agency for Network and Information Security.

Fernandes, E., Jung, J., Prakash, A. (2016). Security analysis of emerging smart home applications. *Proceedings of IEEE S&P*, IEEE.

Guasconi, F., Panagopoulou, G., D'Acquisto, G., Bourka, A., Drogkaris, P. (2018). Reinforcing trust and security in the area of electronic communications and online services: Sketching the notion of state-of-the-art for SMES in security of personal data processing. Technical report, European Union Agency for Network and Information Security.

Hammi, B., Khatoun, R., Zeadally, S., Fayad, A., Khoukhi, L. (2018). IoT technologies for smart cities. *IET Networks*, 7, 1–13.

Hansen, M. and Limniotis, K. (2018). Recommendations on shaping technology according to GDPR provisions: Exploring the notion of data protection by default. Technical report, European Union Agency for Network and Information Security.

Hassan, M.B., Ali, E.S., Mokhtar, R.A., Saeed, R.A., Chaudhari, B.S. (2020). 6 - NB-IoT: Concepts, applications, and deployment challenges. In *LPWAN Technologies for IoT and M2M Applications*, Chaudhari, B.S. and Zennaro, M. (eds). Academic Press, London [Online]. Available at: https://www.sciencedirect.com/science/article/pii/ B9780128188804000065.

Kafle, K., Moran, K., Manandhar, S., Nadkarni, A., Poshyvanyk, D. (2019). A study of data store-based home automation. *Proceedings of the Ninth ACM Conference on Data and Application Security and Privacy*, 73–84.

Khan, M.A. and Salah, K. (2018). IoT security: Review, blockchain solutions, and open challenges. *Future Generation Computer Systems*, 82, 395–411 [Online]. Available at: https://www.sciencedirect.com/science/article/pii/S0167739X17315765.

Li, S. (2019). Editorial: Zero trust based Internet of Things. *EAI Endorsed Transactions on Internet of Things*, 5(20), 1–2.

Liberg, O., Sundberg, M., Wang, E., Bergman, J., Sachs, J., Wikström, G. (eds) (2020). Technical enablers for the IoT. *Cellular Internet of Things*, 2nd edition. Academic Press, London.

Marotti, A. (2019). Smart devices hacked in digital home invasions [Online]. Available at: https://eu.detroitnews.com/story/business/2019/02/12/smart-home-devices-like-nest-thermostat-hacked/39049903/ [Accessed December 2020].

McGregor, J. (2019). Here's how Amazon's ring doorbell police partnership affects you [Online]. Available at: https://www.forbes.com/sites/jaymcgregor/2019/08/06/heres-how-amazons-ring-doorbell-police-partnership-affects-you [Accessed May 2021].

binti Mohamad Noor, M. and Hassan, W.H. (2019). Current research on Internet of Things (IoT) security: A survey. *Computer Networks*, 148, 283–294 [Online]. Available at: https://www.sciencedirect.com/science/article/pii/S1389128618307035.

Mowbray, M. and Pearson, S. (2012). Protecting personal information in cloud computing. In *On the Move to Meaningful Internet Systems: OTM 2012*, Meersman, R., Panetto, H., Dillon, T., Rinderle-Ma, S., Dadam, P., Zhou, X., Pearson, S., Ferscha, A., Bergamaschi, S., Cruz, I.F. (eds). Springer, Berlin Heidelberg.

Mühle, A., Grüner, A., Gayvoronskaya, T., Meinel, C. (2018). A survey on essential components of a self-sovereign identity. *Computer Science Review*, 30, 80–86 [Online]. Available at: https://doi.org/10.1016/j.cosrev.2018.10.002.

Munirathinam, S. (2020). Industry 4.0: Industrial Internet of Things (IIOT). In *The Digital Twin Paradigm for Smarter Systems and Environments: The Industry Use Cases*, Raj, P. and Evangeline, P. (eds). Elsevier, Cambridge, MA.

Ogonji, M.M., Okeyo, G., Wafula, J.M. (2020). A survey on privacy and security of Internet of Things. *Computer Science Review*, 38, 100312 [Online]. Available at: https://www.sciencedirect.com/science/article/pii/S1574013720304123.

Osborne, C. (2019). Amazon employees listen in to your conversations with Alexa [Online]. Available at: https://www.zdnet.com/article/amazon-employees-are-listening-in-to-your-conversations-with-alexa/ [Accessed May 2021].

Rose, S., Borchert, O., Mitchell, S., Connelly, S. (2020). Zero trust architecture, National Institute of Standards and Technology (NIST). Technical report, Special Publication 800-207, U.S. Department of Commerce.

Sadique, K.M., Rahmani, R., Johannesson, P. (2018). Towards security on Internet of Things: Applications and challenges in technology. *Procedia Computer Science*, 141, 199–206 [Online]. Available at: https://www.sciencedirect.com/science/article/pii/S1877050918318180.

Sharma, D.K., Bhargava, S., Singhal, K. (2020). Internet of Things applications in the pharmaceutical industry. In *An Industrial IoT Approach for Pharmaceutical Industry Growth*, Balas, V.E., Solanki, V.K., Kumar, R. (eds). Academic Press, London.

Shelby, Z., Hartke, K., Bormann, C. (2014). The constrained application protocol (CoAP). RFC 7252 [Online]. Available at: https://rfc-editor.org/rfc/rfc7252.txt.

Thapliyal, S. (2019). A leak suggests that Google employees may be listening in on your conversations with Google Home [Online]. Available at: https://www.pastemagazine.com/articles/2019/07/a-leak-proves-google-is-listening-in-on-your-conve.html [Accessed May 2021].

Vigdor, N. (2019). Somebody's watching: Hackers breach Ring home security cameras [Online]. Available at: https://www.nytimes.com/2019/12/15/us/Hacked-ring-home-security-cameras.html [Accessed December 2020].

Zhao, K. and Ge, L. (2013). A survey on the Internet of Things security. *2013 Ninth International Conference on Computational Intelligence and Security*, IEEE.

Zhou, W., Jia, Y., Yao, Y., Zhu, L., Guan, L., Mao Y., Liu, P., Zhang, Y. (2019). Discovering and understanding the security hazards in the interactions between IoT devices, mobile apps, and clouds on smart home platforms. *28th USENIX Security Symposium (USENIX Security 19)*, Santa Clara, CA [Online]. Available at: https://www.usenix.org/conference/usenixsecurity19/presentation/zhou.

6

IOT, Deep Learning and Cybersecurity in Smart Homes: A Survey

Mirna Atieh[1], Omar Mohammad[2], Ali Sabra[3] and Nehme Rmayti[3]

[1] Computer Science Department, Lebanese University, Beirut, Lebanon
[2] Department of Computer Science, Lebanese International University, Bekaa, Lebanon
[3] Computer Science Department, Varna Free University, Bulgaria

6.1. Introduction

Home automation implementation relies on a medium that supports communication and cooperation between devices. To achieve the desired objectives, it is necessary to adopt an approach that guides the implementation and design of such a home.

Smart home developers have solved many problems and addressed numerous issues to make the life easier through automation, or to help people (the elderly, children, people with disabilities) live a safe, independent life when necessary. However, many problems do not yet have solutions.

Cyber technology is now unavoidable in everyday life; note that wearable IoT devices, in relation to smart homes, have played a pioneering role in this technological revolution.

The more people rely on this technology, the greater the risk of infiltration and data leakage. Thus, the greater the need to develop a cybersecurity infrastructure that

Cybersecurity in Smart Homes,
coordinated by Rida Khatoun. © ISTE Ltd 2022.

protects these systems and their users, keeping in mind that it has now become clear that the IoT is vulnerable to many security breaches.

Additionally, IoT devices produce huge volumes and assortments of data, with varying degrees of veracity. Accordingly, when big data innovations are introduced, better and better information processing can be achieved.

Furthermore, as more devices become integrated into smart home solutions, the risk of attack increases, while securing smart home solutions becomes more challenging.

It is well known that IoT and smart home devices have low computing power, custom architectures and very little memory and storage while security solutions require a certain level of performance to operate. It is hard to port to custom architectures and requires a considerable amount of memory and storage for databases.

Cybersecurity experts have noticed an increasing trend towards machine learning-based solutions and most of them revolve around machine learning and deep learning techniques, especially if big data management is involved. This is because machine learning in cybersecurity looks for patterns in given data and requires very little computing power, memory and storage, it is easy to port to unknown architectures and it has the ability to send data to the cloud to analyze.

This chapter consists of seven parts. In the first part we present the problems related to the security of the various devices connected in smart homes. In the second part, we present the state of the art on smart homes and connected objects. The third part explains the IoT architecture and its different layers. IoT security is presented in part four and, in part five, we look at artificial intelligence, machine learning and deep learning, and the difference between them. We also define deep learning and the importance of its application to cyber security in Smart Homes. Part six is devoted to human activity recognition in smart homes, using neural networks and deep learning. To conclude, we present several methods for detecting anomalies and attacks in smart homes.

It is important to note that, when considering smart home network and device security for people with disabilities, we are dealing with a particularly sensitive topic in that it is related to human life and survival, and is not only about securing comfort and wellbeing.

6.2. Problems encountered

Gartner[1] predicted that more than 20 billion IoT connected devices would exist by the end of 2020. These devices are not general purpose devices, such as smart phones and PCs, but dedicated function devices, such as retail vending machines, aircraft engines, smart cars, thermostats, wearable gadgets and a wide range of other examples (Hung 2017).

Gartner also stated that, by 2020, more than 25% of identified attacks in enterprises would involve the IoT, and yet the IoT would account for less than 10% of IT security budgets (Panetta 2016).

According to Kaspersky Labs, the number of malware samples for IoT devices has been increasing rapidly, from 3,219 samples in 2016 to 121,588 samples in 2018. It was made evident that there are a huge number of vulnerabilities within IoT devices (Kuzin *et al.* 2018).

In 2016, a distributed denial of service (DDoS) cyber attack was launched, causing major disruption to Internet services that affected some of the most technologically important companies, including Amazon and Twitter.

The cybercriminals behind the attack exploited the security weaknesses of thousands of IoT devices, allowing them to be hijacked and turned to be the sources of domain name system (DNS) requests that flooded traffic to the DNS hosting provider Dyn. It is worth bearing in mind that Dyn had DDoS countermeasures in place.

The DNS provider, Dyn, stores log data that has been efficiently processed by big data technologies and analyzed using deep learning algorithms, to determine any type of anomalous behavior. With over 20 billion connected things expected to be in use by the end of 2020, it is highly likely that this kind of DDoS attack is just the beginning (Gassais *et al.* 2020).

The increase in and spread of IoT devices has led to cyber security experts having to deal with new challenges, and it has widened the area of attack, starting with the smart home platforms themselves to the operating systems, communication media and the whole system in which it operates. This can lead to new types of attacks, such as denial-of-sleep attacks that drain the batteries of devices. These

---

1. Gartner is the world's leading research and advisory company that equip business leaders with indispensable insights, advice and tools to achieve their mission-critical priorities. http://www.gartner.com/.

challenges are very real as many manufacturers of smart home appliances are solely focused on functionality; security is a much lower priority for them and some are not equipped to secure their devices against cyber threats. In addition, many IoT devices do not have the supporting infrastructure to run security solutions or even have updating mechanisms and, most dangerous of all is consumer negligence[2].

Furthermore, smart home solutions consist of tens or hundreds of IoT devices on the same network (in most cases these are wireless). Rather alarmingly, most of these devices have little or no protection at the software and infrastructure levels. The technology that was the science fiction of yesterday has become the reality of today yet, at the same time, it is making us more vulnerable to attacks. We do not wish to demonize these solutions, but we believe that smart home and IoT security must be taken more seriously.

On the other hand, smart home systems typically generate huge amounts of data from a wide range of sources and devices; these include sensors, situational data such as object locations, forecast data such as the weather, contextual data such as number of residents in the home, and operational data to manage the whole IoT system. These data must be converted into decisions and actions by suitable data science tools that are designed to work on big data.

Big data is high-volume, high-velocity and high-variety information that requires innovative forms of information processing for decision-making. Traditionally, big data is characterized by six basic characteristics, commonly known as the 6Vs. In general, data is classified as big data if it fulfills the first 3Vs: volume, velocity and variety. Big data technologies are the tools that are used to efficiently process big data.

Therefore, because the goal is to protect and secure substantial, high-value systems, and because the risks are high and multiple, and because huge amounts of data have to be handled by the network, the weekly or monthly security analytics reports would not be sufficient to detect and mitigate the cyber attacks in real time. Defensive tools that are efficient and advanced to the same degree as the systems and the attacks are needed.

In the recent past, most of us were used to having a laptop and a smartphone, each requiring the installation and maintenance of security solutions to protect them against attacks. Nowadays, some smart homes have more intelligent and interconnected devices than most medium-sized companies had some years ago.

---

2. https://www.iotsecurityfoundation.org/machine-learning-will-be-key-to-securing-iot-in-smart-homes/.

It becomes difficult to handle updates, passwords, settings, etc. for each of these devices. For this reason, we consider the importance of adopting deep learning technology to secure each smart home solution, which in turn secures the whole system.

6.3. State of the art

Smart technology has been evolving for decades and, from time to time, a new concept appears. The smart home is one such concept and is the subject of several recent research works. Previous technologies include artificial intelligence, connected objects and cyber security. The concept of connected objects (Internet of Things, IoT) appears to have a promising future and will make life easier. In this chapter, we provide a clear idea of the IoT technology in smart homes by presenting the history, advantages and disadvantages, as well as the challenges of each.

6.3.1. *IoT overview*

IoT is a network of interconnected devices and tools with advanced capabilities to interact with other devices and also with humans and their environment to perform a set of tasks (Bari *et al.* 2013). To do this, we use sensors with a transparent connection between devices and the physical world. The new IoT devices have a wide range of sensors (microphones, light sensors, gas detectors, etc.) thus enabling more efficient applications (Lane *et al.* 2010). IoT devices can detect any change in their environment using sensors and take action to improve their operation (Suo *et al.* 2012); this has made it possible to make effective decisions. Communication between devices and the physical world has also made IoT devices operational in several fields of application (health, industry, household appliances, etc.). Indeed, the evolution of IoT tools has ensured the growth and development of the industry.

To guarantee the success of IoT technology, security should be guaranteed and vulnerabilities should be resolved. As mentioned previously, IoT consists of four layers; guaranteeing security at each of these layers means we can achieve complete security in IoT (Li *et al.* 2016). IoT depends on collecting information from physical objects and presenting them to the user through services and applications. Healthcare is an example of IoT technology that collects personal information about a patient's health and transmits this to a healthcare system. Since a lot of personal information is collected, this information should be protected from unauthorized users to maintain people's privacy. The transportation of information should be protected from the sensor (source) to the application (destination) (Bertino 2016; Vyas *et al.* 2016).

IoT connects millions of devices in order to collect information. As the number of devices increases, the amount of information collected increases, thus privacy threats increase (Abomhara and Koien 2015).

To secure IoT, attacks should be prevented and security methods should be applied to prevent the vulnerabilities. Attackers will always target systems that have vulnerabilities, thus securing systems against attackers is the main goal because attackers are ever-present (Li *et al.* 2016) (Abomhara and Koien 2015).

6.3.2. *History*

IoT has been through several important development stages (Ibarra-Esquer *et al.* 2017):

– 1969: the Internet was born out of the ARPANET project;

– 1971: the first embedded systems[3] appeared with the Intel 4004;

– early '90s: the concept of ubiquitous computing was proposed by Mark Weiser;

– mid '90s: the development of sensor nodes, wireless communication and digital electronics began;

– 1999: the term IoT was first used.

6.3.3. *Literature review*

Suo *et al.* (2012) refer to the challenges associated with the Internet of Things which stem from the following:

– IoT extends the "Internet" through traditional Internet, mobile networks, sensor networks and so on;

---

3 http://www-igm.univmlv. fr/~dr/XPOSE2002/SE/accueil.html.

– every "thing" will be connected to this "Internet";

– these "things" will communicate with each other.

Subsequently, Roman *et al.* (2013) focus on the distributed approach for IoT and the challenges related to the security of this architecture.

In 2014, an approach that describes challenges related to the security and privacy of IoT was presented. These challenges still need to be overcome in the coming years for maximum buy-in from all IoT stakeholders involved. Furthermore, a distributed capability-based access control mechanism was proposed, which is built on public key cryptography in order to cope with some of these challenges (Skarmeta *et al.* 2014).

Nobakht *et al.* (2016) focus on an intrusion detection and a mitigation framework called IoT-IDM to provide network-level security. They used machine learning to create patterns for some known network-level attacks and demonstrated this with a real IoT device: the "smart light bulb".

Aly *et al.* (2019) present an extensive description of security threats and challenges across the different layers of the architecture of IoT systems. In addition, they focus on the solutions and countermeasures proposed in the literature to address these security issues.

Ahmad *et al.* (2019) focus on the modeling of the fog computing architecture and compare its performance to the traditional model. They present a comparative study with a traditional IoT architecture based on classifying applications, define a priority for each application, and use the cell operator as the main fog center to store data. Then, they give a solution to decrease data transmission time, reduce routing processes, increase response speed, reduce Internet usage and enhance the overall performance of IoT systems.

6.3.4. *Advantages, disadvantages and challenges*

Each piece of technology has its advantages, disadvantages and must overcome challenges in order to be usable, adaptable and secure for human use. The same goes for IoT (Yaakoub *et al.* 2019).

6.3.4.1. *Advantages*

The most important advantages of IOT are (Cognizant 2015; Sarmah *et al.* 2017; Soumyalatha 2019):

– *communication*: IoT provides machine-to-machine (M2M) communication through which devices can stay connected, allowing full transparency and better performance and quality;

– *automation and control*: by using IoT, a huge amount of data can be automated and controlled by machines without the need for human intervention. This produces faster and more timely results;

– *saving time and money*: money and time are saved by monitoring different aspects of life using sensors;

– *new profit resource for businesses*: the sale of connected devices and related services exceeded $200 trillion in revenue through 2020. In addition, the value of IoT for organizations across industries is estimated to be $14 trillion in the next few years, which will likely lead to a 21% increase in global corporate profits by 2022;

– *improving productivity*: through JIT[4] training and better labor efficiency;

– *improved quality of living*: IoT applications aim to make life easier and more comfortable;

– *new professions*: as new technological advances emerge, the opportunity for creating new jobs increases and therefore economic growth increases;

– *decision-making support*: vast amounts of information gathered by sensors and monitoring can aid better decision-making.

6.3.4.2. *Disadvantages*

Several disadvantages are noted in the literature (Arpita *et al.* 2015; Banafa 2017; Soumyalatha 2019):

– *compatibility*: no international standardization of M2M protocols, variety of devices, firmware and operating systems used by IoT, non-consolidated cloud services;

---

4. Just In Time inventory system.

– *complexity*: IoT architectures and networks are complex, thus hardware or software issues could lead to serious repercussions. Power failures may also cause disruption;

– *privacy*: an enormous amount of data is exchanged between devices and is monitored by various companies, making privacy breaches more likely;

– *unemployment*: humans are replaced by automated systems that are capable of performing many activities, which could result in increased unemployment rates;

– *controlling life*: the purpose of IoT is to automate activities and control various environments; as devices become more prevalent, humans will become more reliant on them;

– *possibility of malware spread*: the interconnectedness of devices imposes a risk of malware spreading throughout the home system, with consequences ranging from minor to very severe (Soumyalatha 2019).

6.3.4.3. Challenges

Despite the fact that connected objects do actually facilitate life, organizations face different challenges that represent barriers to growth. These challenges include (Cognizant 2015; Soumyalatha 2019):

– *scalability*: smart devices are connected to the network automatically, thus IoT should be capable of handling information management and service management issues across a wide range of environments;

– *self-configuration*: IoT devices should be automatically configured to be suitable for certain environments;

– *interoperability and lack of standards*: the various number of companies, technologies and protocols smart devices use, prevents interoperability where "connected systems should be able to talk the same language of protocols and encodings" (Zain *et al.* 2016). The lack of standards that allow smart devices to connect and communicate as desired makes it difficult for organizations to integrate applications and devices;

– *software complexity*: software infrastructure is required to support the network that smart devices connect to, since the latter operate with minimal resources;

– *storage*: smart devices collect enormous amounts of data that require scalable data storage to be allocated;

– *data interpretation*: context interpretation is important to generate useful information, and to draw conclusions from the data sent by the sensor;

– *security and privacy*: protecting data collected by smart devices from unauthorized use or attack is a major concern. Privacy concerns also arise from the massive amount of information supplied by users who are unaware that this information is being captured. Other challenges include hacking, criminal abuse and security breaches;

– *energy optimization*: a significant amount of energy is needed to operate several devices on the network, hence energy optimization is crucial to prevent shutdown;

– *communication means*: the networks used for connection and data exchange impose challenges such as availability, congestion and delays;

– *data and information management*: traditional infrastructure is not suitable for the sheer amount of data collected by smart devices, rather more advanced algorithms and systems are required to mine, analyze and derive value.

6.4. IoT architecture

The IoT architecture is composed of elements that fall into three categories:

– IoT hardware is composed of devices such as sensors;

– IoT middleware is composed of tools used for data storage and analytics;

– IoT presentation which is composed of tools used for data interception and visualization to keep track of various events occurring.

These elements are represented as four main layers which are: the sensing layer, the network layer, the service layer and the application–interface layer (Leloglu 2017) (Table 6.1.).

Sensing layer	Radio frequency identification reader, sensors, gateway, GPS
Network layer	2G/3G communications network, Internet, mobile network, broad television network
Service layer	Information processing, cloud computing, data analytics, data storage
Application– interface layer	Medical applications, entreprise computing, transportation applications, mobile applications

Table 6.1. *Layers of IoT*

6.4.1. *Sensing layer*

The sensing layer is the layer between connected devices and the network layer. It collects information from the devices and passes this to the network layer. In the sensing layer, we have the IoT connected devices. Let us consider the four communication models for these IoT devices. First, there is the device-to-device communication model where devices communicate directly with one another using different types of networks. An example of this model is the smart home. Second, there is the device-to-cloud communication model where devices communicate with a cloud service using a wired or Wi-Fi connection. An example of this model is the smart TV. Third is the device-to-gateway communication model where devices communicate with the cloud service through the gateway. Finally, there is the back-end data sharing model where data is combined from different devices through multiple cloud services.

6.4.2. *Network layer*

The network layer is between the sensing layer and the service layer. It defines the communication between the connected devices to transfer collected information to the service layer to be processed.

6.4.3. *Service layer*

The service layer is between the network layer and the application–interface layer. It processes the information collected and saves it in the database for later use by the services that the user requires.

6.4.4. *Application–interface layer*

The application–interface layer is between the service layer and the users. It is developed based on user requirements or industry specifications.

At each layer there are multiple and various security risks that must be resolved. Therefore, each layer may have a different security solution for the information being collected from the devices before it reaches the application–interface layer, in order to achieve a totally secure system.

6.5. IoT security

Security is an important aspect of IoT to ensure the reliability, confidentiality and availability of the system. Imagine working with sensitive data on a system with weak security where anyone can intercept, read or modify this data. We treat security as a high priority when considering the development of the system. First, we consider the vulnerabilities and the risks found at each of the four layers in the IoT architecture. (Abomhara and Køien 2015).

6.5.1. *Security in the sensing layer*

The first layer is the sensing layer which gathers and exchanges information using sensors connected to the physical world (Li *et al.* 2014). The main concerns in this layer are:

– cost, energy consumption, and resources for the IoT devices such as sensors and RFID tags;

– deploying IoT devices at one time or at several times according to the requirements;

– using the hybrid network to connect IoT devices such as mobile networks and wireless networks;

– heterogeneity of IoT devices due to the huge amount of devices.

In this layer, security challenges and requirements are divided into two parts, one for the sensing layer and the other for the end devices connected in IoT. The security requirements for the sensing layer include device authentication, user authentication, confidentiality, integrity, non-repudiation, availability, access control, privacy and physical security protection. Device authentication is verifying the devices are trusted while user authentication is verifying user credentials in order to access the system. The security requirements for the end devices are data source authentication, device authentication, confidentiality, integrity, availability and timelessness. Examples of threats in this layer are: spoofing attacks, where the attacker masquerades as an IoT device and sends fake data; DoS attacks where the resource becomes unavailable to the users (Li *et al.* 2016).

6.5.2. *Security in the network layer*

The second layer is the network layer which describes how IoT devices are connected and specifies the medium used. The network layer includes communication technology like ZigBee (Ning *et al.* 2013) and 3G/4G/5G wireless communications (Ejaz *et al.* 2016). The main concerns in this layer are:

– QoS of data being transmitted;

– network management according to the type of network;

– confidentiality of information;

– privacy and security of user sensitive data.

The security requirements in this layer relate to overall security requirements, privacy leaks, communication security, fake network messages, overconnected devices, denial of service (DoS) and man-in-the-middle attacks. Many attacks can target the IoT communication protocols, such as eavesdropping against Bluetooth, NFC, Wi-Fi, etc. (Bapat *et al.* 2017). Eavesdropping and replay attacks are other common attacks in this layer (Vafaei 2014). Examples of threats in this layer include data breaches, where secure information is released to an untrusted environment, malicious code such as viruses, malware and Trojans.

6.5.3. *Security in the service layer*

The third layer is the service layer which stores data needed by the user for the applications. The main concerns in this layer are:

– the APIs of the service;

– management should be trustworthy;

– service discovery and composition to find the suitable service required by the user (Choi *et al.* 2012).

The security requirements in this layer are authorization, service authentication, group authentication, privacy protection and privacy leaks. Examples of threats in this layer are DoS attacks, unauthorized access to data, tampering with data, etc. (Atzori *et al.* 2010).

6.5.4. Security in the application–interface layer

The fourth layer is the application layer where various applications are presented to the users. The main concerns in this layer are:

– confidentiality, authentication, authorization and integrity between layers;

– safe software downloading, secure remote management and isolation of sensitive data (Gu *et al.* 2014).

The security requirements in this layer include sensitive information isolation, safe remote configuration, software downloading and updating, administrator authentication, a unified security platform, security patches, integrity and confidentiality for transmission between layers, cross-layer authentication and authorization, etc. Authorization is verifying the user has permission to access a resource. Examples of threats in this layer are: social engineering a very popular technique where an attacker obtains information from the users by tricking them, injection attacks, where an attacker executes the code on the server directly which causes data loss or data modification, distributed DoS, etc. (Ning *et al.* 2013).

This four-layer infrastructure maintains total security for IoT to avoid connecting fake devices, capturing data generated by attackers, as well as other risks. If we compare the risks at each layer, we find that the common risks are DoS attacks, lack of authentication, authorization, data confidentiality and privacy

6.5.5. Cross-layer threats

Information exchanged between the layers may be vulnerable to threats such as:

– sensitive information being transmitted from one layer to another;

– leakage of sensitive information at the boundaries of the layers;

– misconfiguration.

The security requirements in this layer are security protection, privacy protection and trust (Li *et al.* 2016).

6.5.6. Security attacks

Since IoT is susceptible to many threats and vulnerabilities, attacks occur in different layers and typically concern four aspects of security: secrecy, authentication, integrity and availability (Li and Da Xu 2017). Some examples of different attacks are presented below.

6.5.6.1. DoS attack

In this type of attack, an attacker tries to deny access to the resources and services which affect the availability of the services. DoS attacks involve requests and messages being sent to consume the resources of a certain device (Saadeh *et al.* 2016).

6.5.6.2. Replay attack

In this type of attack, an attacker intercepts the communication, copies the message, and sends it again impersonating the real sender. This leads to the theft or modification of messages being transmitted (Mahalle *et al.* 2013).

6.5.6.3. Eavesdropping

In this type of attack, an attacker only listens to the communication of data being transmitted between two parties but does not modify data, thus affecting the privacy of the data only (Saadeh *et al.* 2016).

6.5.6.4. Physical attacks

In this type of attack, the hardware components of IoT devices are attacked through configuration modifications (Abomhara and Køien 2015).

6.5.6.5. Man-in-the-middle attack

In this type of attack, an attacker takes the advantage of threats and vulnerabilities to intercept the communication of the data being transmitted between the two parties, to read or modify the data.

6.5.6.6. Data modification

In this type of attack, an attacker gains access to the data transmitted between parties so they can read or change the format of the data, affecting the confidentiality of the data received.

6.5.6.7. Spoofing

In this type of attack, an attacker sends a malicious tag to a sensor and this sensor treats it as a valid tag; this approach can result in full control over the system.

6.5.6.8. *Sniffing attack*

In this type of attack, an attacker can gain access to information by sniffing or monitoring network traffic using sniffing applications (Abdul-Ghani *et al.* 2018).

6.5.7. *Security requirements in IOT*

As fog computing is still in its infancy, there is a limited amount of work dedicated to certain security/privacy issues. While using the fog network at this stage, new problems and concerns will arise as a result of the properties of the fog computing network. For instance, fog network heterogeneity, the diversity of fog network framework, the need for low power connected end devices, and mobility holdup are some resulting problems of fog network. The research will focus on a systemic review of fog networks and platforms, determine the possible security gaps, analyze existing security solutions and list comprehensive solutions that can eliminate many potential security flaws within fog systems.

Since each layer has different features and roles, each layer also has different security requirements (Figure 6.1).

Figure 6.2 shows the six aspects of security requirements for the IoT framework which are: confidentiality, availability, privacy, authenticity, integrity and non-repudiation. Confidentiality is needed to secure the data; availability ensures that the resources and data are accessible; privacy is needed to protect customer data; authenticity components ensure proof of identity; integrity is to guarantee the data is accurate and trusted; and finally, non-repudiation is needed to provide a trusted audit trail. All of these security challenges make the data vulnerable and exposed to an attacker (Li *et al.* 2016; Pal *et al.* 2020). To ensure security across the system, we work on a solution in each layer.

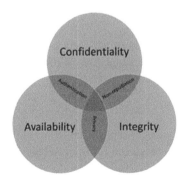

Figure 6.1. *Security requirements in IoT*

6.5.8. *Security solutions for IOT*

Having discussed the security problems in IoT, we now consider recommended security solutions at each layer (Li *et al.* 2016).

6.5.8.1. *Security solutions in sensing layer*

To resolve the security problems and avoid attacks on IoT devices, four actions should be done:

– implement specific security standards for all IoT devices so all devices apply the same standards, in order to avoid loss of data in the event a device is replaced;

– build a trusted data sensing system to continue receiving data from trusted devices only;

– trace and identify the source of a user to ensure validity.

These actions can be applied in two steps at the sensing layer. The first step is to ensure that the users are authorized and authenticated before accessing sensitive data. The second step is to apply security methods for IoT devices to ensure the data is collected and transmitted securely. To ensure the privacy of the data, there are multiple techniques applied according to the type of the data. For example, encryption, decryption and hashing techniques are applied on text data while a CRC (cyclic redundancy check) and image compression techniques are applied on images. For RFID devices, multiple techniques are applied such as cryptography, AES (advanced encryption standard) and hashing algorithms. For the integration of RFID devices and WSN nodes, new challenges arise such as user authentication, communication security, privacy and others. These techniques are applied when the devices are manufactured. Basic security protocols for communication are authentication, availability, confidentiality and integrity (Li *et al.* 2014; Pal *et al.* 2020).

6.5.8.2. *Security solutions at the network layer*

To resolve these problems and avoid any attack on the network, two actions should be done:

– authentication and authorization to avoid any attack and validate the identities of the users;

– secure transport protocols to maintain secure transmission of the data through the network.

Security in this layer is divided into two sub-layers according to the medium: the wireless sub-layer and the wired sub-layer. Security solutions for the wireless sub-layer are concerned with developing protocols while security solutions for the wired sub-layer are concerned with securing connected devices (Li *et al.* 2016).

6.5.8.3. *Security solution at the service layer*

To resolve these problems and avoid service attacks, two actions should be done:

– secure transmission between the service and the other layers;

– secure service management to maintain secure service identification and secure access control.

In this layer, each service requires a particular method according to the features of the service. Examples of the methods applied are authentication, access control, privacy and information integrity (Choi *et al.* 2012).

6.5.8.4. *Security solutions at the application–interface layer*

Several actions should be taken on IoT devices to keep them secure and safe such as:

– design the cluster for the IoT devices based on an efficient energy solution;

– use lightweight security solutions for different IoT devices;

– focus on the safety of IoT devices.

In this layer, security solutions are applied according to the application being used. For example, local applications require encryption and steganography, while global applications (applications from an external network) require additional methods such as authorization, authentication, antivirus, as well as others. An example of an application is the SCADA (supervisory control and data acquisition) system which presents technical solutions to monitor processes in the industrial environment. In the SCADA system, some security methods are authentication, physical security, system recovery and backup.

The success of IoT depends on the guarantee of security at all layers of the infrastructure.

6.6. Artificial intelligence, machine learning and deep learning

Artificial intelligence (AI), machine learning (ML) and deep learning (DL) are three separate terms, however there is some crossover between them. Artificial intelligence encompasses both machine learning and deep learning. Machine learning, in turn, encompasses deep learning, as shown in Figure 6.2.

In the field of artificial intelligence, not all that is machine learning will be deep learning (Wasicek 2018; Oppermann 2019).

– *Artificial intelligence* is the science and engineering behind intelligent machines and programs.

– *Machine learning* means computers can learn without being explicitly programed.

– *Deep learning* is learning based on deep neural networks.

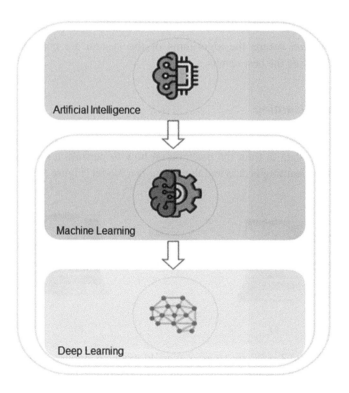

Figure 6.2. *AI, ML and DL. For a color version of this figure, see www.iste.co.uk/khatoun/cybersecurity.zip*

6.6.1. *Artificial intelligence*

Artificial intelligence (AI) is a concept that has theoretically been around for a hundred years. The first intelligent machines were developed in the 1950s. These work and react like humans. Artificial intelligence is any system, program or machine that can think, analyze, learn, make decisions and develop like a human. In other words, it is "the simulation of human intelligence processes by machines"[5]. Nowadays, AI applications include a vision and/or speech recognition system, an expert system, and natural language processing (NLP).

Intelligence programming is based on three essential elements: learning, reasoning and the process of self-correction (Burns *et al.* 2021):

– *Learning* means collecting data and formulating rules to turn data into actionable information.

– *Reasoning* is a cognitive skill that allows the appropriate algorithm to be chosen in order for the system to achieve a desired result.

– *Self-correction* means the algorithms of the system are continuously being developed to provide the best results.

6.6.2. *Machine learning*

Machine learning differs from traditional programming which requires manual coding. ML uses data to train the machine on how to perform a specific task. The input of machine learning is data and the output is a model (Figure 6.3).

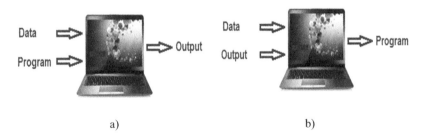

a)   b)

Figure 6.3. *a) Traditional programming; b) machine learning. For a color version of this figure, see www.iste.co.uk/khatoun/cybersecurity.zip*

---

5 Formica (2021) "Which AI learns on its own?" [Online]. Available at: https://www.formica.ai/blog/which-ai-is-learn-by-its-own.

Through machine learning, a system can perform a learning function with the data it ingests and thus it becomes progressively better. This learning is possible through the use of examples to improve some aspects of performance. The data is considered to be a set of training examples. The algorithms parse the training data, and use the individual training examples to see how well they can answer the question related to their goal. That answer is then analyzed and used to improve the algorithm's ability to give better answers in the future.

This learning process is repeated for each example. In this way, each training example contributes a little bit to the accuracy or predictive power of the algorithm. If the learning process works, we say that the learning algorithm generalizes, meaning that its predictions are useful beyond the training examples (Wasicek 2018).

Like any other technology, machine learning excels at solving certain types of problems or tasks, whereas other technologies are more suitable for solving other problems. Below are three general problem settings that are well suited to a machine learning approach:

– *Classification*: sorting individual items into a set of classes, like recognizing anomalies in unusual sequences of credit card transactions.

– *Regression*: predicting outcomes based on historical records, like predicting the future of stock prices or currency exchange rates or which movies a person will like according to the historical records of the problem.

– *Clustering*: finding items similar to one another, like recognizing patterns in objects in real scenes, facial identities or facial expressions and/or spoken words.

Many machine learning techniques can be categorized into one of the four following types:

– *supervised learning* deals with labeled data and direct feedback. It can predict an outcome or future trends;

– *unsupervised learning* deals with unlabeled data and works without feedback. It is good at finding the hidden structures or patterns in data;

– *semi-supervised learning* falls in-between supervised and unsupervised learning and works well with partially labeled data;

– *reinforcement learning* focuses on decision processes and reward systems during progress. It can learn a series of actions.

6.6.3. *Deep learning*

Over the last few years, deep learning has become a prominent arrangement of machine learning techniques dependent on learning data representation. It has become apparent that deep learning algorithms can beat best-in-class approaches in conventional AI issues such as picture and sound classification (Dean *et al.* 2012). Furthermore, it has been expressed that they may outperform human-level abilities in classifying these sorts of information (Sparks *et al.* 2013).

Deep learning is a subsection of machine learning (and therefore of artificial intelligence) that is based on artificial neural network (ANN) models. The artificial neural network is an important programming paradigm. Previously, to make things easier for the computer, we split the big problems into small tasks. But, with neural networks, the computer has the ability to learn from training data in order to find the best solution. Since 2006, machine learning and deep neural networks have enabled deep learning. Deep learning provides better performance for certain problems like speech recognition and computer vision.

Neural networks are clustering and classification tools of data that we store and manage, according to their similarities or their labeling. In addition, artificial neural networks have the possibility to make a predictive analysis to establish correlations between items.

The word deep refers to the number of layers in neural networks. Deep learning currently plays a critical role in the development of highly automated systems.

The notable advancement of deep learning is the result of three fundamental elements:

– the collection of huge amounts of data;

– the turn of events and openness of new AI structures and machine learning platforms (Abadi *et al.* 2016, pp. 265–283) and algorithms (Niu *et al.* 2011) because of advances in equivalent (Raina *et al.* 2009) and adaptable programming frameworks (Gonzalez *et al.* 2012);

– storage costs have been quickly decreasing (Komorowski 2015) and mobile applications, IoT and the significance of information as an asset (Parkins 2017) have all prompted further interest in innovative work using deep learning technology (Press 2016).

Deep learning is based on a deep neural network. It is a subset of machine learning which is the ability to learn without being explicitly programmed, and it is a part of artificial intelligence, which is the engineering of intelligent machines and programs.

Deep learning involves learning data representations by utilizing a network of multiple layers of nonlinear preparing units for different sorts of highlight extraction and change. Each layer's output is the successive layer's input. Generally, deep learning models and techniques endeavor to copy the movement in layers of neurons in the neocortex, for example, an artificial neural network. It learns, like other machine learning strategies, by iteratively grouping a preparation informational collection, and refreshing its boundaries marginally into the correct bearing each time a characterization error happens. Eventually, the tweaked boundaries of the algorithm are tried on an assessment informational collection to quantify the algorithm's performance. Such an algorithm works with the programmed classification of information which, when conveyed, eliminates the requirement for an individual to classify the information physically (Domingos 2012).

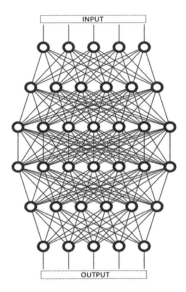

Figure 6.4. *Structure of the deep learning network*

6.6.4. *Deep learning vs. machine learning*

Deep learning has proved to be more successful than machine learning because deep neural networks (DNNs) have significant capacity for storing information

(Figure 6.5.); on the other hand, DNNs do not need feature extraction which requires experts in the field of the problem to be solved.

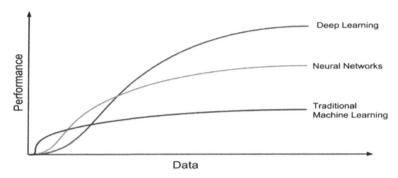

Figure 6.5. *Deep learning vs machine learning (Wasicek 2018). For a color version of this figure, see www.iste.co.uk/khatoun/cybersecurity.zip*

Flat algorithms (in traditional machine learning) such as decision trees, SVM, or others require feature extraction before applying them to raw data. This step will be adapted and tested for a given task over several iterations to achieve the optimal result, using classic machine learning algorithms (Alabs 2019) (Figure 6.6).

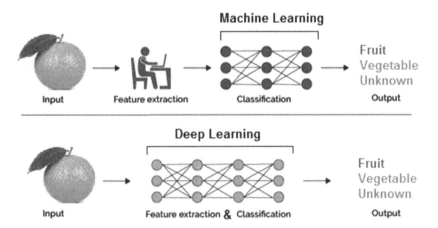

Figure 6.6. *Deep learning has no feature extraction step. For a color version of this figure, see www.iste.co.uk/khatoun/cybersecurity.zip*

6.7. Smart homes

A smart home can be characterized as a home equipped with sensors and a middleware framework, as well as communication interfaces that anticipate and react to the needs of the inhabitants to improve their comfort, enjoyment and security through the use of technology inside the home (Aldrish 2003). A smart home can support a variety of services and automated tasks from temperature control and smart climate control system to more complex requests such as monitoring the surroundings of an inhabitant or tracking their behavior or wellbeing in the home (Liu *et al.* 2016).

6.7.1. *Human activity recognition in smart homes*

Human activity recognition (HAR) is a unique and challenging research topic (Ranasinghe *et al.* 2016). The purpose of HAR is to determine activities performed by one inhabitant or numerous inhabitants depending on various sensors that are prearranged and configured to notice and detect many events, for example movement sensors, pressure identifiers, RFID tags, electrical power analyzers (Belley *et al.* 2015), and more. The HAR cycle includes a few stages. The four primary stages are as follows (Figure 6.7):

– *Pre-processing*: separating raw data from sensor streams to deal with inadequacy, remove noise and repetition, and perform data standardization and labeling.

– *Feature extraction*: separating features from raw data to utilize it as input to machine learning.

– *Feature selection*: reducing the number of features to improve their quality and lessen the computational effort required for classification.

– *Classification*: identifying the given activity using AI and machine learning.

The general objective of the HAR framework is to replace all – or almost all – of the human tasks inside the home, either by predicting these activities and acknowledging them when important or by meeting the necessities and requirements predefined by the residents. For instance, with the assistance of sensory devices, a HAR framework can monitor the medical issues of an inhabitant and alert healthcare services in the event of an emergency. (Rashidi and Mihailidis 2013; Zhao *et al.* 2019).

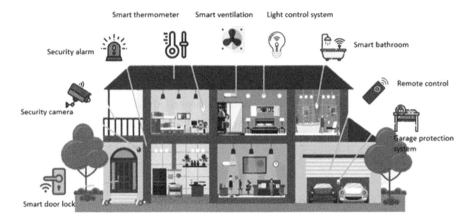

Figure 6.7. *Smart home applications and systems. For a color version of this figure, see www.iste.co.uk/khatoun/cybersecurity.zip*

6.7.2. *Neural network algorithm for human activity recognition*

In the field of human activity recognition, neural networks have recently demonstrated a decent level of proficiency and precision in comparison to other machine learning algorithms.

The first application using ANNs in a smart home environment was developed by Mozer (1998). This application, named ACHE (Adaptive Control of Home Environments) was able to adapt the environmental conditions (heating, lighting, ventilation and water heating) to the needs of residents and their level of comfort (Kasabov 2002).

Jorge and Goncalves (2001) worked on automated monitoring of the health of the elderly using artificial intelligence tools. They collected data from the elderly regarding neurological disorders (loss of motor, sensory and cognitive abilities) via computer devices, with the aim of predicting the next activity (Elman 1990).

Pigot *et al.* (2003) tried to minimize the risks resulting from actions taken by elderly people in a physical environment, both at a theoretical and practical level. The authors applied ANNs with other mathematical models to aid in the detection of models associated with risk (Pigot *et al.* 2003; Stefanov *et al.* 2004).

Rivera-Illingworth *et al.* (2005) developed new connectionist architecture to recognize the behaviors of daily life (sleeping, eating, etc.), using simple sensors and an intelligent algorithm (Augusto and Nugent 2006; Montana and Davis 2006).

Three kinds of learning algorithms are required (Hiregoudar *et al.* 2014): supervised neural networks, unsupervised neural networks and semi-supervised neural networks. A brief description of each of the three calculations is given in Table 6.2. A typical neural network structure is shown in Figure 6.8.

ANNs can be categorized as either feed-forward networks or feedback networks, as shown in Figure 6.5. Each learning algorithm is intended for preparing a particular architecture. Consequently, when we examine a learning algorithm, a specific network architecture affiliation is implied (Jain *et al.* 1996). In Fang *et al.* (2014) back-propagation (BP) is utilized to prepare the feed-forward neural network for human activity recognition. This algorithm was compared with another probabilistic algorithm: the Naïve Bayes (NB) classifier and Hidden Markov Model (HMM). The outcomes show that neural networks that make use of BP calculation generally have better human movement acknowledgment exhibitions than the NB classifier and the HMM.

In Mehr *et al.* (2016), quick propagation (QP), the Levenberg–Marquardt (LM) algorithm and batch back propagation (BBP) have been used for human action recognition and compared alongside execution on the Massachusetts Institute of Technology (MIT) smart home dataset. The accomplished outcomes showed that the LM algorithm has better human activity recognition execution (92.81% accuracy) than QP and BBP algorithms. This is performed as if for a single occupant home. In the event of various clients, more complex learning is needed, with feature selection and more refined sensors.

Lee *et al.* (2017) proposed a technique based on a one-dimensional (1D) convolutional neural network (CNN) to detect and follow the activity of the person living in the house. They used the data collected (walking, running and resting) of the triaxial accelerometer from smart mobile phones. The speed of the activity has three parameters x, y and z which are transformed into vector magnitude information. These contribute to the learning of the 1D CNN. This technique had 92.71% accuracy. The accuracy of a neural network is based on the nature of the different characteristics, supervised exercises and limitations.

Hussein *et al.* (2014) created a system that gives people with disabilities the option to control aspects of everyday life or allow the system to automatically provide what is necessary for them to live independently, without the help of others. Their system is designed to monitor the elderly and people with disabilities so as to bring them more security and safety without disrupting their lives. Their behavior and living habits are recorded using a multisensory system. Learning and adapting to the habits of this group of people is achieved by introducing artificial neural networks (ANNs) to the output of this system. Thus, any sudden change can be analyzed. The multisensory system along with the ANN methodology used for learning can secure all parts of a complete environment for people with disabilities.

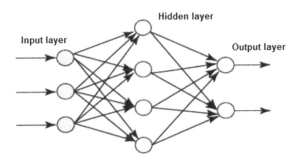

Figure 6.8. *Typical neural network structure*

Supervised neural network	– Attempts to predict a specific quantity – Has training examples with labels – Can measure accuracy directly
Unsupervised neural network	– Attempts to understand the data – Looks for structure or unusual patterns – Not looking for something specific – Does not require labeled data – Evaluation usually indirect or qualitative
Semi-supervised neural network	– Uses unsupervised methods to improve supervised algorithms – Usually few labeled examples and a lot of unlabelled data

Table 6.2. *Description of different neural network algorithms*

6.7.3. *Deep neural networks used in human activity recognition*

Lately, there has been developing revenue in deep learning techniques. It has become a basic exploration region in human activity recognition, natural language processing, machine interpretation and environmental monitoring (Guo *et al.* 2014).

Deep learning is an overall term for neural network methods which depend on taking in portrayals from raw data and contain more than one hidden layer.

The network has numerous layers of non-linear data processing for feature extraction and change. Each progressive layer utilizes the output from the previous layer as input.

Deep machine learning algorithms include restricted Boltzmann machines, auto-encoders, sparse coding, convolutional neural networks and recurrent neural networks (Figure 6.9). These deep learning strategies can be stacked into various layers to frame deep learning models that give improved framework execution, adaptability, robustness and eliminate the need to rely upon conventional handcrafted features (Nweke *et al.* 2018). These methods are applied to activity of daily living (ADL) (Hassan *et al.* 2018), like locating and detecting posture in Abdel-rahman *et al.* (2009), recognizing gestures activities of Alzheimer's, and diagnosis of emotional state for elderly people in Ravi *et al.* (2016). Deep learning methods are used also in automatic detection of activity of daily living (ADL) (Wang *et al.* 2016; Gu *et al.* 2018), health rate analysis during intensive sports activities and health monitoring (Jalal *et al.* 2017; Nweke *et al.* 2019), and representation of energy-related, health monitoring smart homes (Jianbo *et al.* 2015). Moreover, some methods go deeper to predict the relationship between exercises and sleep patterns, automatic pain recognition during strenuous sports activities, energy expenditure estimation, and tracking of personal activities (Hammerla *et al.* 2016). In addition, other applications used deep learning algorithms in HAR like: model temporal patterns in activity of daily living (ADL), progressive detection of activity levels, and falls and heart failure in the elderly (Ordóñez *et al.* 2016).

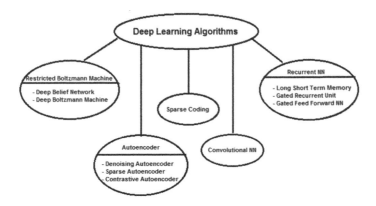

Figure 6.9. *Different deep learning algorithms*

Fang and Hu (2014) proposed a deep learning calculation to perceive human activity. They believed the deep belief networks (DBNs) worked using restricted

Boltzmann machines in the research. They additionally contrasted their outcomes and HMM and NBC.

Oniga and Suto (2014) interpreted the signs obtained from speed increase sensors utilizing a few artificial neural networks (ANN) algorithms. Zhang *et al.* (2015) combined HMM and DNN models to perceive activity. Be that as it may, there is at present no preferred deep learning method for human activity. This is likely because of the changeability of human practices, activities performed, types of sensors utilized and includes selection received.

The calculations of neural networks are based on modeling of the characteristics of the human brain. This leads to a relationship being formulated between the input and output variables on the basis of the observable data. The general model of the neural network consists of:

– examining a process in neurons;

– data interaction;

– multiplying the weights of connections for data transferred from one neuron to another to solve problems;

– calculating the output using the enable function at input.

The different categories of the neural network are shown in Figure 6.10.

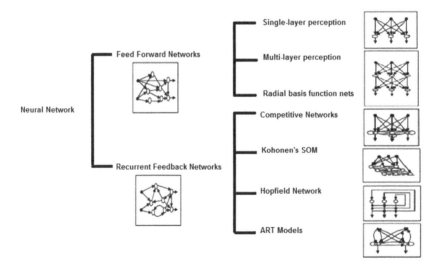

Figure 6.10. *Feed-forward and feedback network architectures*

6.8. Anomaly detection in smart homes

6.8.1. *What are anomalies?*

There are several definitions for the anomaly.

An anomaly refers to any phenomenon that deviates from what is considered normal[6].

Anomalies are data patterns that do not conform to a well defined notion of normal behavior (Chandola *et al.* 2007).

Anomaly detection or outlier detection is the identification of rare items, events or observations which raise suspicions by differing significantly from the majority of the data (Arthur and Erich 2017).

6.8.2. *Types of anomaly*

Anomalies are classified into three types.

Point anomalies: this is the case where an individual data instance is considered abnormal compared to the rest of the data.

Contextual anomalies: this is an anomalous data instance in a specific context; it is also called a conditional anomaly (Song *et al.* 2007).

Collective anomalies: when a collection of linked data instances is abnormal with respect to the dataset, this is the case of a collective anomaly.

6.8.3. *Categories of anomaly detection techniques*

An instance of data is said to be normal or abnormal according to the labels associated with this instance. Anomaly detection techniques operate in one of three modes, depending on the availability of labels.

Unsupervised anomaly: for an unlabeled dataset, unsupervised anomaly detection techniques assume that the majority of instances in the dataset are normal and look for instances that do not match the rest of the data.

---

6. https://www.futura-sciences.com/sante/definitions/medecine-anomalie-2982/.

Supervised anomaly: detects anomalies in a dataset that has been labeled as "normal" and "abnormal" and involves the training of a classifier.

Semi-supervised anomaly: this detection technique assumes that the training data has instances labeled only for the normal class. For this, these techniques are more widely applicable than the supervised techniques.

6.8.4. Related work of anomaly detection in smart homes

The detection of anomalies has been the subject of several studies in the last ten years. In what follows, we present some works that have dealt with the problems of anomaly detection.

In Stenudd (2010), the authors describe the concept of anomaly detection, used to monitor the behavior of the system to detect normal events from anomalies. It is very useful for security in smart systems, especially for intrusion detection. It is done by comparing the current behavior of the system with previously-stored normal behavior. The anomaly detection helps in detecting insider attacks, is difficult for an attacker to set an alarm off, able to detect known and unknown types of attacks and it fits all deployment environments. But, the authors suggested training the system before deployment to determine the normal behavior, the system generates a false alarm and sometimes users can gradually train the system to accept anomalous behavior as normal.

The research (Jakkula and Cook 2011) aims to detect anomalous events or actions in a smart home. The model starts with environmental sensing by collecting data from inhabitants and their environment to model it. The captured events are associated with timestamps, and then they used with the history of recognized sensor events to reveal patterns with frequent activity. The collected data contains five parameters: date, time, sensor ID, message and annotation. The system uses the one-class support vector machine (OCSVM) which is quite popular for anomaly detection problems. The authors proposed a solution for this problem by estimating a function f which is positive on S and negative on the complement S. The algorithm can be summarized as mapping the data into a feature space H using an appropriate kernel function and then trying to separate the mapped vectors from the origin with maximum margin. Once transformed to a different space, the data points which are closer to the origin are identified as an anomaly and reported (Figure 6.11). The research was the initial step in the anomaly detection system and used to start from a new perspective with advanced features.

In Ramapatruni *et al.* (2019) the authors work on a smart home equipped with many sensors. They presented some anomaly detection models for smart home security. The sensors are connected to the Internet through a wireless router and the data from the home. Data is sent to the gateway. The installation is modulated to add a data set collection machine, by configuring a port on the router dedicated to copying all the packets sent through the gateway to the data collection machine. The idea started by creating a model using hidden Markov models (HMMs) (Rabiner 1989) to learn common behavior in the smart home. The model takes into consideration many parameters like the number of the state as an N and the set of states represented by S corresponding to each sensor individually when used. Then, the different sensors are named with the capitalized first letter of each name like the min door sensor named as (MD). The value of sensors is on or off. Also, the M parameter is the number of unique observations possible for each state in S. The set V denotes the set of all possible observations in it. The model starts the observation under two conditions: the first one is evaluating through the general condition, the second is abnormal detection. The first condition is during the presence of an individual in the house who uses the sensor in real-time. The results show 96.8% of data values were stated as normal behavior. The net experiment performed using modified k-fold cross-validation to determine the efficacy of their approach in a general setting. The accuracy ranged from 95% to 98%. The second condition tested was where there is no user in the smart home. The HMM model detected 97% of the attack anomalies.

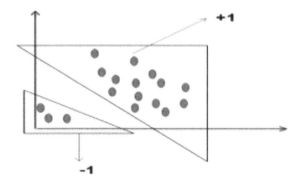

Figure 6.11. *Data points identified as anomaly detection*

In Yamauchi *et al.* (2020), they work on a new model of anomaly detection related to human behavior by focusing on a specific pattern of usage for users, in this research the work was done on smart home conditions. The anomaly detection learns from the repeated pattern, for example for a specific user on a cold day they turn the heater first then turn the humidifier then the model will detect another behavior if the order of action is changed. The model starts by learning events and then creates the sequence. After this, the model starts monitoring the sequence of events that happen and compares it to the learned one. The model learns through three phases: learning model, learning user behavior and detection. The learning model depends on the condition and user behavior. The first step is to define conditions, the sensor reading and place the condition in the table. In addition, for every condition, they stored the related human behavior. Now learning user behavior is done on the gateway by sorting sequences of events and differentiating between events from the users and events from guests that may be in the same house with the users. This is done by focusing on frequently repeated events that are most likely done by users. In the last phase, "detection", the gateway recognizes the executed operations and then compares them to the learning events. After the three phases, the model can detect whether the behavior or the events is normal behavior or an attack. The tested result shows a 90% pass in detecting the attack.

In Fu *et al.* (2021), the research focuses on appified smart homes, a term that refers to the smart home that uses many IoT devices and is connected to a different platform to control events in homes using smart applications. They proposed a Home Automation Watcher HAWatcher, which relies on semantic and logs events and then creates a hypothetical correlation according to semantic information and verifies them with events logs. For example, human activity changes device state then the device state also reflects human activities. The proposed model aims to determine the malfunctions in IoT devices if they are related to the network or technical part and is known as cyber, or physical which is related the device itself. Nevertheless, the model must detect whether it is a malfunction or an attack on the IoT devices. The model executes two steps: extract semantic from the smart app then converts it to correlation. They designed a shadow execution engine for anomaly detection. The role of this engine is to get access to internal device data and perform the tests on incoming events. The model faces some limitations such as deviation in human activity, false alarm rate and an attacker with knowledge of correlations, however it detected 62 real-world anomaly cases with high accuracy.

In Gassais *et al.* (2020), the authors propose a new framework for intrusion detection that combines machine learning, the space of the user and kernel to detect intrusion in smart devices. The framework installs a whole new infrastructure consisting of sensors, actuators and an analysis system. Smart devices running the tracers and the analysis system detect anomalies by aggregating the collected traces. The framework triggers an alarm when intrusion is detected. It also can be developed to correlate traces and take actions to prevent the intrusion. The framework was tested on many algorithms and the results show different efficiency on different algorithms. It is very useful, however for detecting attacks on the system especially in eavesdropping attacks which are very difficult to detect using network information only.

The Internet of Things allows devices and sensors in a smart environment (such as smart homes) to communicate with each other and share information between platforms. However, the IoT has proven to be susceptible to security vulnerabilities. It was therefore necessary to develop solutions capable of detecting anomalies and solving security problems. Because of this, in this section, we presented some studies that attempted to provide an overview of anomaly detection research.

6.9. Conclusion

In this chapter, we have highlighted the importance of cyber security in home automation using IoT devices, as well as the problems related to the security of the different devices connected in smart homes. The main challenge of smart home systems is the ability to adapt to the user by providing enhanced comfort, control and security.

One of the most commonly-used methods for learning in a smart home system is neural networks. These are enhanced by deep learning which allows the use of a vast amount of data with minimal storage cost and has the ability to learn without being explicitly programmed. In this chapter, we have also explained the relationship between artificial intelligence, machine learning and deep learning and how they differ. We have highlighted the importance of deep learning applications in cyber security and human activity recognition in smart homes using neural networks and deep learning.

In a smart home, many devices are connected to the Internet and therefore can experience problems and can be the target of cyber attacks. These attacks can cause serious problems and harm users. For this reason, we have presented several methods for detecting anomalies and attacks in smart homes.

6.10. References

Abadi, M., Barham, P., Chen, J., Chen, Z., Davis, A., Dean, J., Devin, M., Ghemawat, S., Irving, G., Isard, M. *et al.* (2016). TensorFlow: A system for large-scale machine learning. Paper, USENIX Association, Savannah, GA, USA.

Abdel-rahman, M., Dahl, G., Hinton, G. (2009). Deep belief networks for phone recognition. *Proceedings of the NIPS Workshop on Deep Learning for Speech Recognition and Related Applications*, 1–9.

Abdul-Ghani, H., Konstantas, D., Mahyoub, M. (2018). A comprehensive IoT attacks survey based on a building-blocked reference mode. *International Journal of Advanced Computer Science and Applications (IJACSA)*, 9(3), 355–373.

Abomhara, M. and Koien, G.M. (2015). Cyber security and the Internet of Things: Vulnerabilities, threats, intruders and attacks. *Journal of Cyber Security*, 4(1), 65–88 [Online]. Available at: https://doi.org/10.13052/jcsm2245-1439.414.

Ahmad, K., Mohammad, O., Atieh, M., Ramadan, H. (2019). IoT: Architecture, challenges, and solutions using fog network and application classification. *Proceedings of the 2018 International Arab Conference on Information Technology (ACIT)*, Werdanye, Lebanon, 1–7.

Alabs, T. (2019). How mastery of deep learning can trump machine learning expertise [Online]. Available at: https://www.analytixlabs.co.in/blog/how-mastery-of-deep-learning-can-trump-machine-learning-expertise/ [Accessed 1 October 2020].

Aldrish, F. (2003). *Smart Homes: Past, Present and Future*. Springer, London, UK.

Aly, M., Khomh, F., Haoues, M., Quintero, A., Yacout, S. (2019). Enforcing security in Internet of Things frameworks: A systematic literature review. *Internet of Things*, 6(4), 100050.

Arpita, R., Saxena, K., Bhadra, A. (2015). Internet of Things. *International Journal of Engineering Studies and Technical Approach*, 1(4), 37–42.

Arthur, Z. and Erich, S. (2017). *Outlier Detection. Encyclopedia of Database Systems*. Springer, New York, USA.

Atzori, L., Iera, A., Morabito, G. (2010). The Internet of Things: A survey. *Computer Networks*, 54(15), 2787–2805.

Augusto, J.C. and Nugent, C.D. (2006). *Designing Smart Homes: The Role of Artificial Intelligence*. Springer Verlag, Berlin, Heidelberg, Germany.

Banafa, A. (2017). Three major challenges facing IoT. *Internet of Things*, 33–44.

Bapat, C., Baleri, G., Inamdar, S., Nimkar, A. (2017). *Smart-Lock Security Re-engineered Using Cryptograpghy and Steganography*. Springer, Singapore.

Bari, N., Mani, G., Berkovich, S. (2013). Internet of Things as a methodological concept. *Proceedings of the Fourth International Conference on Computing for Geospatial Research and Application (COM. Geo)*, IEEE, San Jose, CA, USA.

Belley, C., Gaboury, S., Bouchard, B., Bouzouane, A. (2015). Nonintrusive system for assistance and guidance in smart homes based on electrical devices identification. *Expert System with Applications: An International Journal*, 42(19), 6552–6577.

Ben Aissi, A. (2013). Les systèmes embarqués [Online]. Available at: http://www-igm.univ-mlv.fr/~dr/XPOSE2002/SE/accueil.html.

Bertino, E. (2016). Data security and privacy in the IoT. *International Conference on Extending Database Technology (EDBT)*, Bordeaux, France.

Burns, E., Laskowski, N., Tucci, L. (2021). What is artificial intelligence (AI)? [Online]. Available at: https://searchenterpriseai.techtarget.com/definition/AI-Artificial-Intelligence [Accessed 2021].

Chandola, V., Banerjee, A., Kumar, V. (2007). Anomaly detection: A survey. *ACM Computing Surveys*, 41(3).

Choi, J., Li, S., Wang, X., Ha, J. (2012). A general distributed consensus algorithm for decision making in service-oriented Internet of Things. *Wireless Advanced*, 16–21.

Cognizant (2015). Reaping the benefits of the Internet of Things. Report [Online]. Available at: https://www.slideshare.net/cognizant/reaping-the-benefits-of-the-internet-of-things.

Dean, J., Corrado, G., Monga, R., Chen, K., Devin, M., Mao, M., Ranzato, M., Senior, A., Tucker, P., Yang, K. *et al.* (2012). Large scale distributed deep networks. *Proceedings of the 25th International Conference on Neural Information Processing Systems*, Toronto, Canada, 1223–1231.

Domingos, P. (2012). A few useful things to know about machine learning. *Communications of the ACM*, 55(10), 78–87.

Ejaz, W., Anpalagan, A., Imran, M.A., Minho, J., Naeem, M., Qaisar S.B., Wang, W. (2006). Internet of Things (IoT) in 5G wireless communications. *IEEE Access*, 4, 10310–10314.

Elman, J.L. (1990). Finding structure in time. *Cognitive Science*, 14(2), 179–211.

Fang, H. and Hu, C. (2014). Recognizing human activity in smart home using deep learning algorithm. *Proceedings of the 33rd Chinese Control Conference*, 4716–4720.

Fang, H., He, L., Si, H., Liu, P., Xie, X. (2014). Human activity recognition based on feature selection in smart home using back-propagation algorithm. *ISA Transactions*, 53(5), 1629–1638.

Gassais, R., Ezzati-Jivan, N., Fernandez, J.M., Aloise, D., Dagenais, M.R. (2020). Multi-level host-based intrusion detection system for the Internet of Things. *Journal of Cloud Computing: Advances, Systems and Applications*, 9(62), 1–16 [Online] Available at: https://link.springer.com/content/pdf/10.1186/s13677-020-00206-6.pdf.

Gonzalez, J., Low, Y., Gu, A. (2012). PowerGraph: Distributed graph-parallel computation on natural graphs. Paper, USENIX, Stanford, CA, USA.

Gu, L., Jingpei, W., Sun, B. (2014). Trust management mechanism for Internet of Things. *China Communications*, 11(2), 148–156.

Gu, F., Khoshelham, K., Valaee, S., Shang, J., Zhang, R. (2018). Locomotion activity recognition using stacked denoising autoencoders. *Internet of Things Journal*, 5(3), 2085–2093.

Guo, J., Xie, X., Bie, R., Sun, L. (2014). *Structural Health Monitoring by Using A Sparse Coding-based Deep Learning Algorithm with Wireless Sensor Networks.* Springer Verlag, London, UK.

Hammerla, N.Y., Halloran, S., Ploetz, T. (2016). Deep, convolutional, and recurrent models for human activity recognition using wearables [Online]. Available at: https://www.ijcai.org/Proceedings/16/Papers/220.pdf.

Hassan, M.M., Zia Uddin, M., Mohamed, A., Almogren, A. (2018). A robust human activity recognition system using smartphone sensors and deep learning. *Future Generation Computer Systems*, 81, 307–313.

Henglong, F., Qiang, Z., Xiaojiang, D. (2021). HAWatcher: Semantics-aware anomaly detection for appified smart homes [Online]. Available at: https://www. usenix.org/conference/usenixsecurity21/presentation/fu-chenglong.

Hiregoudar, S.B., Manjunath, K., Patil, K. (2014). A survey: Research summary on neural networks. *IJRET: International Journal of Research in Engineering and Technology*, 3(Special 3), 385–389.

Hung, M. (2017). Leading the IoT: Gartner insights on how to lead in a connected world [Online]. Available at: https://www.gartner.com/imagesrv/books/iot/iotEbook_digital.pdf.

Hussein, A., Adda, M., Atieh, M., Fahs, W. (2014). Smart home design for disabled people based on neural networks. *Procedia Computer Science*, 117–126 [Online]. Available at: doi: 10.1016/j.procs.2014.08.020.

Ibarra-Esquer, J.E., González-Navarro, F.F., Flores-Rios, B.L., Burtseva, L., Astorga-Vargas, M.A. (2017). Tracking the evolution of the Internet of Things concept across different application domains. *Sensors*, 17(6), 1379 [Online]. Available at: https://doi.org/10.3390/s17061379.

Jain, A.K., Mao, J., Mohiuddin, K.M. (1996). Artificial neural networks: A tutorial. *Computer*, 29(3), 31–44.

Jakkula, V.R. and Cook, D.J. (2011). Detecting anomalous sensor events in smart home data for enhancing the living experience. *Conference: Artificial Intelligence and Smarter Living: The Conquest of Complexity, Papers from the 2011 AAAI Workshop*, San Francisco, CA, USA.

Jalal, A., Kim, Y.-H., Kim, Y.-H., Kamal, S., Kim, D. (2017). Robust human activity recognition from depth video using spatiotemporal multi-fused features. *Pattern Recognition*, 61, 295–308.

Kasabov, N. (2002). *Evolving Connectionist Systems: Methods and Applications in Bioinformatics, Brain Study and Intelligent Machines.* Springer Verlag, London, UK.

Komorowski, M. (2014). A history of storage cost (update) [Online]. Available at: http://www.mkomo.com/cost-per-gigabyte-update [Accessed 11 February 2022].

Kuzin, M., Shmelev, Y., Kuskov, V. (2018). New trends in the world of IoT threats [Online] Available at: https://securelist.com/new-trends-in-the-world-of-iot-threats/87991/ [Accessed 10 May 2020].

Lane, N.D., Miluzzo, E., Lu, H., Peebles, D.,Choudhury, T., Campbell, A.T. (2010). A survey of mobile phone sensing. *IEEE Communications Magazine*, 48(9), 140–150.

Lee, S.-M., Yoon, S.M., Cho, H. (2017). Human activity recognition from accelerometer. *Proceedings of the IEEE International Conference on Big Data and Smart Computing (BigComp)*, Jeju, South Korea.

Leloglu, E. (2017). A review of security concerns in Internet of Things. *Journal of Computer and Communications*, 5, 121–136.

Li, S. and Da Xu, L. (2017). *Securing the Interent of Things*, 1st edition. Elsevier, Cambridge, UK.

Li, S., Xu, L.D., Zhao, S. (2014). The Internet of Things: A survey. *Information Systems Frontiers*, 17(2), 243–259.

Li, S., Tryfonas, T., Li, H. (2016). The Internet of Things: A security point of view. *Internet Research*, 26(2), 337–359.

Liu, L., Stroulia, E., Nikolaidis, I., Miguel-Cruz, A., Adriana, R.R. (2016). Smart homes and home health monitoring technologies for older adults: A systematic review. *International Journal of Medical Informatics*, 91, 44–59.

Mahalle, P., Anggorojati, B., Prasad, N., Prasad, R. (2013). Identity authentication and capability based access control (IACAC) for the Internet of Things. *Journal of Cyber Security and Mobility*, 1(4), 309–348.

Mehr, H.D., Polat, H., Cetin, A. (2016). Resident activity recognition in smart homes by using artificial neural networks. *Proceedings of the 2016 4th International Istanbul Smart Grid Congress and Fair (ICSG)*, Istanbul, Turkey.

Montana, D. and Davis, L. (2006). Training feedforward neural networks using genetic algorithms. *Machine Learning*, 762–767.

Mozer, M.C. (1998). The neural network house: An environment that adapts to its inhabitants [Online]. Available at: https://www.aaai.org/Papers/Symposia/Spring/1998/SS-98-02/SS98-02-017.pdf.

Ning, H., Liu, H., Yang, L.T. (2013). Cyberentity security in the Internet of Things. *Computer Science*, 46(4), 46–53.

Niu, F., Recht, B., Re, C., Wright, S.J. (2011). Hogwild!: A lock-free approach to parallelizing stochastic gradient descent [Online]. Available at: https://proceedings.neurips.cc/paper/2011/file/218a0aefd1d1a4be65601cc6ddc1520e-Paper.pdf.

Nobakht, M., Sivaraman, V., Boreli, R. (2016). A host-based intrusion detection and mitigation framework for Smart Home IoT using OpenFlow. *Proceedings of the 11th International Conference on Availability, Reliability And Security (ARES)*, Salzburg, Austria.

Nweke, H.F., Teh, Y.W., Al-garadi, M.A., Alo, U.R. (2018). Deep learning algorithms for human activity recognition using mobile and wearable sensor networks: State of the art and research challenges. *Expert Systems with Applications*, 105, 233–266.

Nweke, H.F., Teh, Y.W., Mujtaba, G., Al-garadi, M.A. (2019). Data fusion and multiple classifier systems for human activity detection and health monitoring: Review and open research directions. *Information Fusion*, 46, 147–170.

Oniga, S. and Suto, J. (2014). Human activity recognition using neural networks [Online]. Available at: https://www.researchgate.net/profile/Stefan-Oniga/publication/273257656_Poster_ICCC2014_Oniga_A4/links/54fc6fc80cf2c3f52422a7a6/Poster-ICCC2014-Oniga-A4.pdf?origin=publication_list.

Oppermann, A. (2019). Artificial intelligence vs. machine learning vs. deep learning [Online]. Available at: https://towardsdatascience.com/artificial-intelligence-vs-machine-learning-vs-deep-learning-2210ba8cc4ac [Accessed September 2021].

Ordóñez, F., Roggen, O., Ordóñez, F.J., Roggen, D. (2016). Deep convolutional and LSTM recurrent neural networks for multimodal wearable activity recognition. *Sensors*, 16(115), 1–25.

Pal, S., Hitchens, M., Rabehaja, T., Mukhopadhyay, S. (2020). Security requirements of the Internet of Things: A systematic approach. *Sensors*, 20, 1–35.

Panetta, K. (2016). Gartner's top 10 security predictions 2016 [Online]. Available at: https://www.gartner.com/smarterwithgartner/top-10-security-predictions-2016/ [Accessed 23 October 2020].

Parkins, D. (2017). The world's most valuable resource is no longer oil, but data. *The Economist*, May 6th [Online]. Available at: https://www.economist.com/leaders/2017/05/06/the-worlds-most-valuable-resource-is-no-longer-oil-but-data.

Pigot, H., Lefebvre, B., Meunier, J., Kerherve, B., Mayers, A., Giroux, S. (2003). The role of intelligent habitats in upholding elders in residence. *Proceedings of the 5th International Conference on Simulations in Biomedicine*, Slovenia, 497–506.

Press, G. (2016). Forrester predicts investment in artificial intelligence will grow 300% in 2017. *Forbes* [Online]. Available at: https://www.forbes.com/sites/gilpress/2016/11/01/forrester-predicts-investment-in-artificial-intelligence-will-grow-300-in-2017/?sh=3feff97f5509.

Rabiner, L.R. (1989). A tutorial on hidden Markov models and selected applications in speech recognition. *Proceedings of the IEEE*, 77(2), 257–286.

Raina, R., Madhavan, A., Ng, A. (2009). Large-scale deep unsupervised learning using graphics processors. *Proceedings of the International Conference on Machine Learning – ICML*, New York, USA, 873–880.

Ramapatruni, S., Narayanan, S.N., Mittal, S., Joshi, A., Joshi, K. (2019). *Anomaly Detection Models for Smart Home*. IEEE, Washington DC, USA.

Ranasinghe, S., Machot, F., Mayr, H. (2016). A review on applications of activity recognition systems with regard to performance and evaluation. *International Journal of Distributed Sensor Networks*, 12(8), 1–22.

Rashidi, P. and Mihailidis, A. (2013). A survey on ambient-assisted living tools. *Journal of Biomedical And Health Informatics*, 17(3), 579–590.

Ravi, D., Wong, C., Deligianni, F., Berthelot, M., Andreu-Perez, J., Lo, B., Yang, G.-Z. (2016). Deep learning for health informatics. *Journal of Biomedical Health Informatics*, 21(1), 4–21.

Rivera-Illingworth, F., Callaghan, V., Hagras, H. (2005). A neural network agent based approach to activity detection in AmI environments. *Proceedings of the IEE International Workshop on Intelligent Environments*, Colchester, UK.

Roman, R., Zhou, J., Lopez, J. (2013). On the features and challenges of security and privacy in distributed Internet of Things. *Computer Networks*, 57(10), 2266–2279 [Online]. Available at: https://doi.org/10.1016/j.comnet.2012.12.018.

Saadeh, M., Sleit, A., Qatawneh, M., Almobaideen, W. (2016). Authentication techniques for the internet of things: A survey [Online]. Available at: https://moam.info/authentication-techniques-for-the-internet-of-things-a-survey-pdf-_59a652a61723dd0b40ac9a2e.html.

Sarmah, A., Baruah, K., Baruah, A. (2017). A brief review on Internet of Things. *International Research Journal of Engineering and Technology*, 4(10), 879–883.

Skarmeta, A.F., Hernández-Ramos, J.L., Victoria Monero, M. (2014). Decentralized approach for security and privacy challenges in the internet of things. *Proceedings of the 2014 IEEE World Forum on Internet of Things (WF-IoT)*, Seoul, South Korea.

Song, X., Wu, M., Jermaine, C., Ranka, S. (2007). Conditional anomaly detection. *IEEE Transactions on Knowledge and Data Engineering*, 19(5), 631–645.

Soumyalatha, N. (2019). Study of IoT: Understanding IoT architecture, applications, issues and challenges. *International Journal of Advanced Networking and Applications*, 477–482.

Sparks, E., Talwalkar, A., Smith, V., Kottalam, J., Pan, X., Gonzalez, J., Franklin, M.J., Jordan, M.I., Krask, T. (2013). MLI: An API for distributed machine learning. Paper, IEEE, Dallas, TX, USA.

Stefanov, D., Bien, Z., Bang, W.-C. (2004). The smart house for older persons and persons with physical disabilities: Structure, technology arrangements, and perspectives. *Neural Systems and Rehabilitation Engineering*, 12(2), 228–250.

Stenudd, S. (2010). *Using Machine Learning in the Adaptive Control of a Smart Environement*. VTT Technical Research Center of Finland, Espoo, Finland.

Suo, H., Wan, J., Zou, C., Liu, J. (2012). Security in the Internet of Things: A review. *Proceedings of the IEEE International Conference on Computer Science and Electronics Engineering*, Hangzhou, China.

Vafaei, R. (2014). *Encryption of 4G Mobile Broadband Systems*. Academia, Stockholm, Sweden.

Vegas Goncalves, J.D. (2001). Ubiquitous computing and AI towards an inclusive society [Online]. Available at: https://doi.org/10.1145/564526.564538.

Vyas, D.A., Bhat, D., Jha, D. (2016). IoT: Trends, challenges and future scope. *IJCSC*, 7, 186–197.

Wang, A., Chen, G., Shang, C., Zhang, M., Liu, L. (2016). Human activity recognition in a smart home environment with stacked denoising autoencoders. *Proceedings of the International Conference on Web-Age Information Management*, 29–40.

Wasicek, A. (2018). Artificial intelligence vs. machine learning vs. deep learning: What's the difference? [Online]. Available at: https://www.sumologic.com/blog/machine-learning-deep-learning/ [Accessed 01 October 2020].

Yaakoub, R., Atieh, M., Kalakech, A., Sarji, M. (2019). Connected objects in smart house for disabled people. Report, Lebanese University, Beirut, Lebanon.

Yamauchi, M., Ohsita, Y., Murata, M., Kato, Y. (2020). Anomaly detection in smart home operation from user behaviors and home conditions. *IEEE Transactions on Consumer Electronics*, 66, 183–192.

Yang, J.B., Nguyen, M.N., San, P.P., Li, X.L., Krishnaswamy, S. (2015). Deep convolutional neural networks on multichannel time series for human activity recognition. *Proceedings of the 24th International Joint Conference on Artificial Intelligence*, Singapore, 3995–4001 [Online]. Available at: https://www.ijcai.org/Proceedings/15/Papers/561.pdf.

Zain, I., Rehan, A., Ashraf, J. (2016). Internet of Things. *International Journal of Engineering Development and Research*, 4(3), 1088–1092.

Zhang, L., Wu, X., Luo, D. (2015). Human activity recognition with HMM-DNN model. *Proceedings of the 2015 IEEE International Conference on Cognitive Informatics & Cognitive Computing*, 192–197.

Zhao, R., Yan, R., Chen, Z., Mao, K., Wang, P., Gao, R.X. (2019). Deep learning and its applications to machine health monitoring: A survey. *Mechanical Systems and Signal Processing*, 115, 213–237.

7

sTiki: A Mutual Authentication Protocol for Constrained Sensor Devices

Corinna SCHMITT[1], Severin SIFFERT[2] and Burkhard STILLER[2]

[1]*Research Insitute CODE, Universität der Bundeswehr München, Neubiberg, Germany*
[2]*Communication Systems Group (CSG), Department of Informatics IfI, University of Zürich UZH, Switzerland*

Today, a large number of use cases exist for the Internet-of-Things (IoT) and Wireless Sensor Networks (WSN), such as home automation, ambient assisted living, eHealth, and logistics (Romeo 2016). For certain use cases it is desirable to make sensitive data (e.g. medical information or personal address) globally accessible (a) to authorized users only and (b) to data processing units through the Internet. Even seemingly inconspicuous data, such as the energy consumption measured by a smart meter, can lead to potential infringements on the users' privacy, e.g. by allowing an eavesdropper to conclude whether or not a user is currently at home.

From an industry perspective, there is a pressing need for security solutions, especially for the transmission of sensitive data, and access to it has increased. Due to leaks of such information to the public, end-users in the private sector have also demanded security for their data and require privacy support and data ownership rights. From a legal perspective, this is addressed by the EU General Data Protection Regulation (GDPR; Regulation (EU) 2016/679) (European Parliament and Council of the European Union 2016). Regarding the infrastructure of the IoT, including devices with different amounts of resources, security risks are aggravated by the trend toward a separation of sensor network infrastructure and applications (ETSI 2010; Leontiadis *et al.* 2012). Therefore, a true end-to-end security solution is required to reach an adequate level of security for IoT. Protecting data once it leaves a local network is not sufficient, because it may reach the final destination after many jumps and via an uncontrollable network.

However, the IoT is no longer limited to servers, routers, and computers. The IoT also includes constrained (tiny) devices – sensor nodes – limited in memory (app. 10–50 kByte RAM and 100–256 kByte ROM), computational capacity and power (a few AAA batteries) (Bormann *et al.* 2020). Those limited resources still demand end-to-end security support as requested by data owners, including the mutual authentication of communication partners (source and destination – sensor node, gateway, aggregator), which requires individual key agreements and a secured communication solution to be built between them. When explicitly depending on the resources of these devices, performing authentication and key agreement is challenging, because memory, computational capacity and energy are scarce. Furthermore, a deployed network may be dynamic, such that nodes dynamically join or leave, and require updates in security. Thus, a light-weighted solution is required, as represented by the described solution "sTiki" working under Contiki 3.0.

7.1. Introduction

Due to the growth of the Internet and the diversity of devices now available, the Internet-of-Things (IoT) is gaining a lot of attention. The IoT used to be to limited to Peer-to-Peer (P2P) architectures (Gerke *et al.* 2003), networks, dedicated applications (Mischke and Stiller 2003) and devices, such as servers, computers, and routers. However, the IoT now includes wireless sensor devices that form an individual Wireless Sensor Network (WSN). Those devices present a challenge for developers, because they are limited in memory, energy and computational capacity. In order to connect them to the Internet, they must support IP (Internet Protocol), which is often provided by using an IPv6 implementation called 6LoWPAN (Shelby and Bormann 2011).

The topology of WSNs can range from star topologies to pure P2P topologies, but a combination of both is employed in WSN deployments. This means that the network consists of Full-Function Devices (FFD) and Reduced-Function Devices (RFD). Both of these types of devices can support different functionalities depending on their location within the WSN, ranging from simple data collection and forwarding to pre-processing. The communication between devices in a WSN is performed wirelessly, using the UDP (User Datagram Protocol). The transmitted packet size is limited (e.g. 127 Byte), however existing IPv6 implementations, like 6LoWPAN, support packet fragmentation and compression in order to connect such limited devices to the IoT (Karl and Willig 2007). While many use cases for the IoT involve the collection and transmission of sensitive data, many deployments currently do not protect this data through suitable security schemes (Sen 2009). Different end-to-end security schemes were built upon existing Internet standards, specifically the Datagram Transport Layer Security (DTLS) protocol, but are not applicable to WSNs due to the use of constrained devices with especially limited memory resources. By relying on an established standard, existing implementations, engineering techniques, and security infrastructures can be reused to enable a security uptake from application developers (Kothmayr *et al.* 2013).

The challenge is now to bring standards-compliant security to resource constrained sensor nodes in an end-to-end security architecture, fulfilling the request to be light-weight. While the intended solution must satisfy the paradigm of end-to-end security, it has to be based on standards and support mutual authentication (e.g. Luk *et al.* 2007; Kothmayr *et al.* 2013; Lowack 2013). It should be taken into account, that the new solution must be able to process the basic functionality of the existing implementation in parallel, especially when gathering data, transmitting it using the TinyIPFIX (Schmitt *et al.* 2017) format and supporting aggregation in the network (Sgier 2016, 2017). Furthermore, flexibility concerning network updates (e.g. node addition or deletion) is key in order to establish efficient and secure communication within the network.

Such a light-weight solution that has been developed is "sTiki", working under Contiki 3.0 as an operating system. A key server offers authentication and dynamic node management, which were integrated into the server component on the gateway. Symmetric encryption provides data integrity and a message counter guarantees the freshness of the messages received. For encryption, a multitude of algorithms were considered and compared, with AES-128 (Advanced Encryption Standard) coming out on the top. Finally, confidentiality is achieved by using a Message Authentication Code (MAC). The implementation performed consumes about 4.5 kB of ROM and around 400 B of RAM, which allows sTiki to run on very constrained devices. sTiki was demonstrated to work and was tested successfully in multiple setups, including scenarios where certain nodes could not support sTiki. Combining sTiki with unencrypting nodes does work, even in case of heterogeneous hardware. It is, obviously, not possible to move from encrypted nodes back to unencrypted ones.

The remainder of this chapter[1] is structured as follows: section 7.2 illustrates the Internet's history leading to the current connected world, while section 7.3 presents insights of security for the IoT, and section 7.4 paves the way toward the security protocol "sTiki", developed for constrained devices. Section 7.5 covers the constraints

---

1. This chapter is based on the Bachelor Thesis by Severin Siffert, University of Zürich UZH (Siffert 2018), who was part of the SecureWSN project (see: https://www.csg.uzh.ch/csg/en/research/SecureWSN.html) lead by Corinna Schmitt during her employment at the University of Zürich UZH and included in her Habilitation Thesis (Schmitt 2019).

of developing software for sensor networks, the architecture chosen, and the choice of AES. The implementation of sTiki is discussed in two environments. Finally, section 7.6 evaluates the implementation and compares it to existing implementations, before conclusions are drawn.

7.2. Definitions and history of IoT

During the late 1970's the idea emerged to interconnect different networks in order to enhance the communication between universities and research facilities. The purpose of this connection was two-fold: (1) a simple exchange of knowledge using file sharing and (2) using the computational capacity of computer centers worldwide. This approach resulted in the Arpanet. Over the next decades more networks were connected, building the Internet, which was commercialized in 1990. As described in Kurose and Ross (2016) the Internet is defined as a network of networks with a specific infrastructure. Many networks operate as Autonomous Systems (AS), with one or more edge devices (gateways, routers and access points) responsible for forwarding traffic between different ASes Kurose and Ross 2016). Compared to other network participants, such as computers or servers, only a reduced OSI (Open Systems Interconnection) protocol stack is supported. This stack enables the forwarding of messages within an AS and between different ASes, even translation between different communication standards used on the physical layer (PHY) are possible.

During the last few decades the connectivity of devices used increased, due to stakeholders' requests to be connected all over the world using manifold devices, and with them manifold communication technologies. This is referred to as the *Internet-of-Things* (IoT). The term IoT was first coined by Kevin Ashton at a presentation at Proctor & Gamble in 1999 (Ashton 2009). According to Ashton, the IoT is a network of connected physical and fingerprintable objects (things) with a virtual representation in an Internet-similar structure. This definition still holds today, with the only exception that the connected device characteristics have changed over time. In the beginning only routers, hat ways, servers, and PCs were intended to be part of IoT, but new devices with specific and different characteristics have since been added. These new devices show the following characteristics (Schmitt 2019): (a) device size ranging from coin size to commonly used notebooks over smart devices, smart phones, and tablets, (b) devices support communication standards such as 3G to 5G and wireless communication, (c) devices are resource-constrained concerning energy, memory, and computational capacity, and (d) devices potentially require application specific (e.g. sensor devices, navigation systems, or alarm system) implementations and deployments. The existing diversity of devices shows that establishing connectivity between them may be challenging due to their characteristics, and may become even more complex when data formats, data transmission frequency, and requested support by stakeholders in terms of security and privacy are needed.

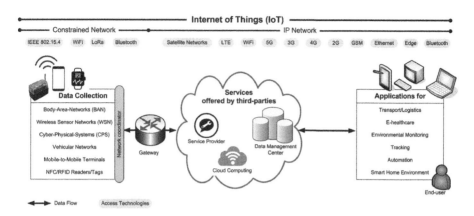

Figure 7.1. *Data flow within the IoT (Schmitt 2019). For a color version of this figure, see www.iste.co.uk/khatoun/cybersecurity.zip*

Similar to the aforementioned diversity in device characteristics common for IoT devices, is the diversity in terms of the definition of "IoT" itself. Research and industry refer to the aforementioned situation and the resulting network under the term IoT, as indicated in Figure 7.1. Deeper investigations show that no formal definition for the IoT exists overall, which makes discussions and comparisons of approaches and developments challenging. The following definitions exist:

International Telecommunication Union (ITU) Standard Y.4000 (ITU 2016):

Internet of Things (IoT): A global infrastructure for the information society, enabling advanced services by interconnecting (physical and virtual) things based on existing and evolving interoperable information and communication technologies. NOTE 1 – Through the exploitation of identification, data capture, processing and communication capabilities, the IoT makes full use of things to offer services to all kinds of applications, whilst ensuring that security and privacy requirements are fulfilled. NOTE 2 – From a broader perspective, the IoT can be perceived as a vision with technological and societal implications.

EU-Parliament Briefing (Davis 2016):

The Internet of Things (IoT) has been defined in a number of different ways. Generally speaking, it refers to a global, distributed network (or networks) of physical objects that are capable of sensing or acting on their environment, and able to communicate with each other, other machines or computers. Such "smart" objects come in a wide range of sizes and capacities, including simple objects with embedded sensors, household appliances, industrial robots, cars, trains, and wearable objects, such as watches, bracelets or shirts. Their value lies in the vast quantities of data they can capture and their capacity for communication, supporting real-time control or data analysis that reveals new insights and prompts new actions. As in the case of many emerging technologies, different experts may use different terms to refer to similar or overlapping concepts. Machine to machine (M2M) processing emphasizes the sharing of data and processing that takes place between these devices. On the other hand, the Internet of Everything explicitly includes people as participants in this global network. Ubiquitous computing emphasizes the fact that network and computing resources are available almost everywhere, whereas pervasive computing highlights the fact that processors are embedded in everyday objects all around us.

Internet Engineering Task Force (IETF) (Lee *et al.* 2010):

The basic idea is that the IoT will connect objects around us (electronic, electrical, non electrical) to provide seamless communication and contextual services provided by them. The development of RFID tags, sensors, actuators and mobile phones makes it possible to materialize things that interact and co-operate with each other to make the service better and accessible anytime, from anywhere.

Apart from these definitions, each developer, industry and service provider uses its own definition of the IoT depending on their specific settings, requirements, and views (International Data Corporation 2014; SAP 2014; 451 Research 2015). In general, those definitions focus on the stakeholders involved by grouping them by purpose (e.g. offered services, standardization organizations, service or platform providers, network infrastructure provides, protocol and device developers) (International Data Corporation 2014).

The cluster of European Research Projects on the Internet of Things (CERP-IoT) (Sundmaeker *et al.* 2010) states:

The Internet of Things (IoT) is an integrated part of the Future Internet and could be defined as a dynamic global network infrastructure with self configuring capabilities based on standard and interoperable communication protocols, where physical and virtual "things" have identities, physical attributes and virtual personalities, use intelligent interfaces, and are seamlessly integrated into the information network. In the IoT, the "things" are expected to become active participants in business, information and social processes, where they are enabled to interact and communicate among themselves and with the environment by exchanging data and information "sensed" about the environment, while reacting autonomously to "real/physical world" events and influencing them by running processes that trigger actions and create services with or without direct human intervention. Interfaces in the form of services facilitate interactions with these "smart things" over the Internet, and query and change their state and any information associated with them, taking into account security and privacy issues.

7.3. IoT-related security concerns

Due to the connectivity of devices in the IoT, the data amount continuously increases. A report by CISCO (Bhaiji 2008) stated that IP networks are growing exponentially and due to today's device manifoldness and application variety, networks are becoming more and more complex, with new challenges to run and manage them arising at the same time. This assessment has been confirmed by continuous statistics from various providers (e.g. statistica and CISCO (CISCO 2019)). Thus, the classic network infrastructure undergoes an evolution, introducing security concerns, which continuously result in changes in security paradigms (i.e. CIA triad – confidentiality, integrity, and availability (Andress and Winterfeld 2014; Summers and Tickner n.d.)) due to applications, environments and end-user requests linked with the resources of included devices in the network and the communication standards used.

These changes in security paradigms become obvious when extending common IP networks with constrained networks building the IoT today. Constrained networks show common characteristics with IP networks, especially in relation to security fundamentals (sometimes also named cryptographic properties), following the CIA triad – confidentiality, integrity, and availability – and enhancing it with data freshness and authentication (Boyd and Mathuria 2010). Whereas, *confidentiality* ensures that data is only available to those that are authorized to obtain it, *integrity* ensures that no message can be altered by an entity as it traverses from the sender to the recipient, and *availability* ensures that the service of a constrained network is always available, even in the presence of internal or external attacks (e.g. Denial-of-Service (DoS) attack). This triad is enhanced by *data freshness*, which implies that the data is recent and ensures that no adversary can replay old messages and *authentication*, which ensures the identity of the communication partners. Literature adds three additional security fundamentals (Boyd and Mathuria 2010; Eckert 2014): *data origin authentication* guarantees the origin of data, in order to archive entity authentication in protocols and establish keying material. *Non-repudiation* ensures that entities cannot deny sending data that they have committed to. Finally, *resilience* represents the ability to provide and maintain an acceptable level of service in the face of faults and challenges to normal operation.

In addition, further security fundamentals become essential for the assumed use case of constrained networks, due to their deployment options (random, fixed, partly fixed) (Karl and Willig 2007). *Self-organization* is required in a constrained network due to the dynamic nature of it, which makes it impossible to deploy any pre-installed shared key mechanism between several nodes. *Secure localization* is also necessary to locate each constrained device accurately and automatically if faults should be detected. Finally, *time synchronization* is needed for collaborative constrained networks or certain security mechanisms, such as periodic updates of keying material.

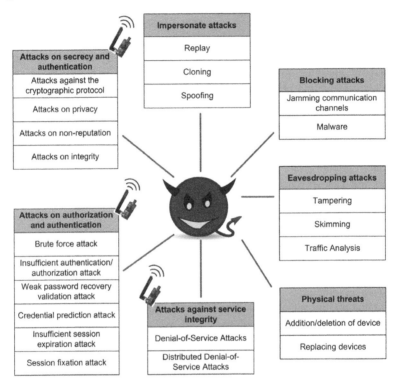

Figure 7.2. *Attack types in IP networks (Schmitt 2019)*

As constrained networks like Wireless Sensor Networks (WSN) are part of the Internet and are constructed out of constrained devices that usually have limited resources, they represent a criticality in the IoT. As highlighted in Figure 7.2, common attacks on constrained devices with a sensor device are (a) attacks against service integrity, (b) attacks on secrecy and authentication, and (c) attacks on authorization and authentication (i.e. Denial-of-Service (DoS) attacks) (Shi and Perrig 2004; Wang *et al.* 2006; Boyd and Mathuria 2010; Eckert 2014). Normal defense mechanisms against attacks can hardly work or not work at all for them due to the devices' constraints. Before addressing defense and prevention mechanisms, potential vulnerabilities must be determined. Hence, the following provides an overview of the most relevant security analysis guidelines, followed by the description of a threat modelling for the security analysis of solutions available. Based on this knowledge gained about the IoT, the security insights combined with security expectations lead to the definition of sTiki.

7.3.1. *Security analysis guidelines*

Before deploying protocols, algorithms, workflows, frameworks, and services or integrating them into commercial services and systems, they need to undergo a security analysis to check if they follow the security paradigms applied and requested by end users. For a security analysis, different guidelines apply to different application areas and developments (see section 7.3.1). For IoT networks and constrained networks especially, such analysis is essential to determine the specific service with respect to sensitive data from IoT devices.

The National Institute of Standards and Technology (NIST) published several recommendations, the most important of which are the "Information Security Handbook: A Guide for Managers" published 2006 and the "Technical Guide to Information Security Testing and Assessment" from 2008. The first recommendation provides:

> a broad overview of information security program elements to assist managers in understanding how to establish and implement an information security program. The topics within this document were selected based on the laws and regulations relevant to information security [. . .] The purpose of this publication is to inform members of the information security management team (agency heads; chief information officers (CIOs); senior agency information security officers (SAISOs), also commonly referred to as Chief Information Security Officers (CISOs); and security managers) about various aspects of information security that they will be expected to implement and oversee in their respective organizations. In addition, the handbook provides guidance for facilitating a more consistent approach to information security programs across the federal government. Even though the terminology in this document is geared toward the federal sector, the handbook can also be used to provide guidance on a variety of other governmental, organizational, or institutional security requirements (Bowen *et al.* 2006).

In comparison, the second recommendation offers:

> a guide to the basic technical aspects of conducting information security assessments. It presents technical testing and examination methods and

techniques that an organization might use as part of an assessment, and offers insights to assessors on their execution and the potential impact they may have on systems and networks. For an assessment to be successful and have a positive impact on the security posture of a system (and ultimately the entire organization), elements beyond the execution of testing and examination must support the technical process. [...] The information presented in this publication is intended to be used for a variety of assessment purposes. For example, some assessments focus on verifying that a particular security control (or controls) meets requirements, while others are intended to identify, validate, and assess a system's exploitable security weaknesses. Assessments are also performed to increase an organization's ability to maintain a proactive computer network defense. Assessments are not meant to take the place of implementing security controls and maintaining system security.

Following these recommendations, the target organizations of developments are requested (1) to establish an information security assessment policy, (2) implement a repeatable and documented assessment methodology, (3) determine the objectives of each security assessment, and (3) tailor the approach accordingly, analyze findings and develop risk mitigation techniques to address weaknesses (Scarfone *et al.* 2008).

Besides NIST, further investigations are ongoing to strengthen security analysis and establish standards. One of the most well known ones is the so-called "OWASP Application Security Assessment Standards Project". Its mission is:

to establish common, consistent methods for application security assessments standards that organizations can use as guidance on what tasks should be completed, how the tasks should be completed and what level of assessment is appropriate based on business requirement. [...] The final goal is to integrate a set of OWASP projects into an Application Security Assessment process in order to define a model which can be used by an organization to provide application security through OWASP standards. (OWASP Application Security Assessment Standards Project 2014)

Due to the continuous growth of technology and attack possibilities (see Web Application Security Consortium (2004) and The Open Web Application Security Project (2019)) the specification of security analysis is undergoing updates periodically, in order to recommend effective prevention and countermeasures. Currently, the following information security assessment types are commonly used and recommended to define and design appropriate solutions for applications:

– A *vulnerability assessment* counts towards the technical assessments. Its purpose is to yield as many vulnerabilities as possible in an environment, along with severity and remediation priority information.

– *Penetration tests* count towards the technical assessments as well and target a specific goal to identify vulnerabilities. Common target vectors are stealing customer data or gaining administrative access to an infrastructure.

– An *audit* can either be technical and/or document-based. It focuses on how an existing setup or configuration matches standards that need to be followed. Classic examples are who has access to a server, how often access rights are checked and if required revoked, and which backup procedure is implemented.

– A *risk assessment* is recommended to be performed periodically and aims to determine what the current level of acceptable risks is, measuring the current risk level, and then determining what can be done to bring these two in line where there are mismatches.

– A *threat assessment* focuses more on physical attacks than on the technology used. The main purpose is to determine whether a threat is credible or not and to identify how many resources are required to address the threat.

7.3.2. *Security analysis by threat models*

In addition to the aforementioned guidelines and recommendations mentioned it also became practice to discuss the security of protocols in the context of a threat model. The result of a threat model depends on the exact specification of the attacker analysis, and it is essential to be precise. The most used approach is the Dolev–Yao security model (Dolev and Yao 1983), which gives a formal definition of the strongest possible attacker. It is often used in the security evaluation of protocols and assumes that the attacker is in control of all of the communication channels. In particular, the attacker may carry out any of the following (Dolev and Yao 1983):

– *Eavesdropping* assumes that the attacker may eavesdrop on any communication in the network. Further it can be assumed that they have recorded all prior communication between any two nodes.

– *Message insertion* assumes that the attacker knows the protocol specifications and can create and insert new messages at will.

– *Message delay and delete* assumes that the attacker may delay any message in the network, or even delete it.

– *Message modification* assumes that attackers can modify intercepted messages.

– *Replays and out-of-order messages* assumes that the attacker can replay any previously sent messages, and they can also forward them out of order.

– *Attempt at impersonation* assumes that the attacker may attempt to act under the identity of another principal.

– *Old session keys* assume that the attacker is in possession of session keys from older protocol sessions.

– *Disabling the network* assumes that the attacker may flood the network with messages, or partially or completely disable it ("cut the wire") at any time. This is a capability against which a protocol cannot take measures. Protocols can only be designed to raise the barriers for the attacker as high as possible.

Note that the attacker may be a legitimate user of the network (i.e. they may act under their own identity). The attacker is, however, bounded by the strength of the cryptographic primitives' encryption and signatures. They cannot decrypt messages and they cannot forge signatures or message authentication codes without the knowledge of the corresponding key. This effectively results in secure channels on which the attacker cannot modify messages without tampering being detected, but they may still be able to suppress messages and interact with the normal protocol flow.

The rationale of using this model is as follows: first, it is one of the standard models in the security community, and is well understood. Second, it is reasonable to design a protocol that is secure against the strongest possible attacker because in many cases we cannot be entirely sure of the capabilities of an attacker. Third, current model checkers for cryptographic protocols, such as AVISPA or Scyther, use the Dolev–Yao model internally (Cremers *et al.* 2009). Model checkers have become an important method for evaluating the security of protocols and finding attack vectors. It is important to observe that the Dolev–Yao model is a model for the formal analysis of a given system. It restricts the attacker to attack vectors within the system. Therefore, it does not cover attacks outside of the system, like social engineering or errors in an implementation that lead to secret information being compromised.

The Dolev–Yao model was implemented into tools to automate the analysis of security protocols. The most common used tool nowadays is AVISPA[2] (Automated Validation of Internet Security Protocols and Applications). Its design is inspired by common software design following the push-botton strategy for the automated validation of Internet security sensitive protocols and applications. It gives the developers of protocols the possibility to specify their protocols and assumed security properties with the help of a modular and expressive formal language. The tool integrates different backends, allowing the implementation of a variety of state-of-the-art automatic analysis techniques, which are applied on the developer's input.

7.3.3. *sTiki's security expectations*

As depicted above, four security fundamentals exist, but not all may be needed or desired: (a) confidentiality, (b) integrity, (c) authentication, and (d) freshness. Authentication and integrity can both be achieved by using a cryptographic

---

2. See: http://www.avispa-project.org/.

checksum, commonly called a Message Authentication Code (MAC). Freshness is usually provided by timestamps, nonces or counters. Confidentiality is achieved by encryption. In order to achieve all four, decisions must be made: the first decision is made between symmetric and asymmetric encryption, as there are arguments in favour of both. As in many decisions with WSNs, this one too is between efficiency and security. Asymmetric ciphers win in security, but take significantly more resources (Mohd *et al.* 2015). For example, ECC (asymmetric) is about 100–1000x slower than AES (symmetric) (Potlapally *et al.* 2003; Eisenbarth *et al.* 2007). For the planned use cases, symmetric will be fine and will also allow a better comparison to Lowack (2013). The second decision is made between block and stream ciphers. Block ciphers encrypt blocks of a fixed size, whereas stream ciphers encrypt data of arbitrary length. Research about lightweight cryptography focuses mainly on block ciphers because they can also be used for computing MACs, and if necessary, can be turned into stream ciphers by using CBC (Chain-Block Chaining) or Counter mode (Mohd *et al.* 2015). As a result of this, the most high quality lightweight ciphers are block ciphers and when using one, the implementation of an additional cipher for computing MACs can be omitted, which is also why a block cipher is used here. Mohd *et al.* (2015) compared many lightweight symmetric block ciphers for various criteria. In addition to these ciphers compared, a new ultra lightweight block cipher called QTL (Li *et al.* 2016) was considered, but Çoban *et al.* (2017) and Sadeghi *et al.* (2017) have proven it to be insecure. Lightweight ciphers are a specialized category of encryption algorithms that try to find a good trade-off between resource consumption and security. They are commonly used in WSNs, Wireless Body Area Networks (WBAN), and other medical devices (Mohd *et al.* 2015). The power consumption is especially a concern. Because of the various security requirements of different applications (controlling a pacemaker vs. a home temperature monitoring system), different algorithms and variations exist.

Comparing different ciphers reveals that no universally accepted metric exists for measurements; security is not a well-defined term (Mohd *et al.* 2015). In addition, new and innovative ways of attacking highly rated algorithms may be discovered and render the ratings useless. Even a metric that does not consider security, like *efficiency* (e.g. defined as energy required per encrypted byte), fails at being a fair comparison, because it can be gamed in various ways (Badel *et al.* 2010). Instead, AES shows up close to the top for almost all metrics used in Mohd *et al.* (2015) and Potlapally *et al.* (2003), which makes it a relatively obvious choice. Its major problem is its relatively large memory footprint. But many hardware boards (including OpenMote) offer a hardware-implementation of AES, which requires almost no additional memory. The most popular implementation is AES-128. Based on the results as of Mohd *et al.* (2015), Tea/xTea would have been the second choice.

Even though the parameters of the hardware implementation of the OpenMote B platform selected (see section 7.4.1) cannot be changed, it is still required to understand the impact on energy consumption, in order to judge potential alternatives. The main parameters of block ciphers are key-size, block-size, and the number of rounds performed. The increase in energy consumption is roughly linear to key-size and the number of rounds (Potlapally *et al.* 2003). The main parameters, however, do not have the largest impact on energy consumption. Instead, the mode of operation has an impact that is two to three times larger (Potlapally *et al.* 2003). This is because the different modes run different procedures to determine the key for the next encryption step, which can be a substantial effort.

7.4. Background knowledge for sTiki

This section covers the most important technologies influencing the development of the proposed security protocol sTiki, which is designed for a subfield of IoT, namely WSNs. Such networks consist of just a few or up to thousands of small, very limited computers, normally called *nodes* or *constrained devices*. The nodes are usually battery powered and their memory is very limited, often measured in kB. Their purpose is to gather data, for example, about the temperature, humidity or movement of certain objects. Due to the limited memory and and the high probability of failure, the nodes usually send collected data to a device (or device combination) called a *sink* or *gateway*, which is more reliable and has more power and memory available (depicted in Figure 7.3). When a node is too far from the gateway, another node can forward the message to another node or to the sink. In certain use cases it is even feasible that a node processes the data (e.g. filtering out measurements that are not needed at the moment or computing an average value), in order to send less bytes or more useful data. The aggregators in Figure 7.3 do exactly that, whereas the collectors only produce measurements. Because the nodes are constrained in resources, they require specialized tools, such as the operating system or protocols shown in the following sections (Akyildiz *et al.* 2002; Yick *et al.* 2008; Siffert 2018).

As any protocol design is highly influenced by the hardware and operating system used, a brief overview for sTiki is presented in section 7.4.1. Some of the resources, especially memory, may already be consumed by existing application that need to be further supported by the new "add-on" protocol. This is also the case for sTiki, where a special TinyIPFIX application for data collection is required to be further supported, representing the individual payload that needs to be secured by sTiki. This is also briefly described in section 7.4.1. The identified security expectations for sTiki listed above influenced the selection of existing and light-weighted security protocols.

7.4.1. *Application dependencies for sTiki*

Here, OpenMotes were used as constrained devices to build the network. They are very small and are a combination of the OpenMote-CC2538 Rev.E and OpenUSB Rev.B parts. The OpenMote-CC2538 mainly consists of the CC2538 processor from Texas Instruments, which has an ARM Cortex-M3 microcontroller with 512 kB storage and 32 kB RAM. It also has hardware implementations for AES-128 and AES-256. The OpenUSB has a USB port, space for two AA batteries and sensors for light, temperature, humidity, and acceleration on three axes (Tex 2012; Vilajosana *et al.* 2015; Sgier 2017; Siffert 2018).

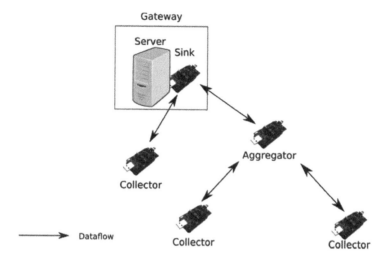

Figure 7.3. *Assumed WSN Setup for the sTiki Implementation (Siffert 2018)*

Specialized operating systems (e.g. Contiki (Dunkels *et al.* 2004), TinyOS (Levis *et al.* 2005), LiteOS (Cao *et al.* 2008) or MantisOS (Bhatti *et al.* 2005)) exist for WSNs, avoiding quick exhausting of the constrained devices in manifold angels, such as Random Access Memory (RAM), Read-Only Memory (ROM), and battery power. Therefore, it is not possible to run Windows or Linux on them. As Contiki is used in this setup, it is briefly characterized here. Contiki is an open source minimal OS written in C, that was created by Adam Dunkels in 2004. It has a modular architecture which is built on top of an event-driven kernel (Dunkels *et al.* 2004). Whenever an event is triggered, it runs to completion, but can be preempted if necessary. To keep the size as small as possible, threads are only implemented as a library that is included when needed (Farooq and Kunz 2011). In the spirit of saving resources, Contiki offers no way to synchronize the internal clocks, which makes it impossible to implement a multitude of protocols. Contiki can dynamically load and unload code, which allows the running code to be changed remotely and without recompiling (Dunkels *et al.* 2004). As Contiki is extremely resource efficient, there are only two ways to start code execution: either code can run once the node has powered up, or in reaction to an event happening like a timer running out or a packet arriving. In general, this event-driven nature of Contiki has a big impact on the coding of applications. But here, the impact is limited due to the fact that an encryption protocol mostly works in response to the requests – encrypt or decrypt a message – of the application it supports.

sTiki will secure the application's payload during transmission in the WSN. To understand the final design of sTiki it is essential to have basic knowledge of the important payload and its format. Thus, a short description is presented here. The payload follows the TinyIPFIX format representing an adaptation of the IP monitoring protocol IPFIX (Schmitt *et al.* 2016, 2017). The concept of IPFIX became interesting for WSNs as it also applied a push concept of messages in pre-defined intervals. Another advantage is the splitting of measurement and meta data into two small messages – *data records* and *template records* – using IDs for cross-referencing and limiting the transmission number of template records, as they stay unchanged during operation. This design leads to a reduction of traffic in the network. Comparing TinyIPFIX to IPFIX further, it can be observed that TinyIPDIX omits a lot of information that is not used in most WSN contexts, thereby reducing the size of these packets.

The implementation of the utilized TinyIPFIX also supports in-network data or message aggregation. Being able to aggregate the measurements is crucial to sending less data. This is important because sending data is one of the most power-intensive tasks a node can perform (Lowack 2013). Depending on the desired form of aggregation, it is possible to save a substantial amount of messages and energy by, for example, sending the average temperature of an entire room over two minutes instead of sending five nodes' measurements every ten seconds to a far away sink. If every measurement has to arrive at the sink, it is at least possible to perform message aggregation. Message aggregation works by combining multiple payloads into one, which works because TinyIPFIX has a constant overhead per message, regardless of payload size. Before implementing TinyIPFIX into an application it should be considered whether or not it actually makes sense to use TinyIPFIX. When it takes more power and time to aggregate the measurements than to simply forward them to the sink, then TinyIPFIX should only be deployed if network congestion is a bigger problem than the additional power requirements. Both forms of aggregation require that messages can be read by aggregators. If they cannot (i.e. due to encryption), aggregators are no longer able to take advantage of the aggregation. Being able to decrypt traffic on aggregator nodes is a key requirement for the encryption protocol discussed below.

7.4.2. *Inspiring resource-efficient security protocols*

The three protocols TinySAM (Lowack 2013), MiniSec (Luk *et al.* 2007), and TinyDTLS (Kothmayr *et al.* 2013) inspired the sTiki protocol. sTiki relies heavily on TinySAM and uses similar methods and mechanisms and, thus, it is described in more detail compared to the other two protocols.

TinySAM (Lowack 2013) is an application layer encryption protocol that uses any symmetric encryption (here and in Lowack (2013), AES-128 is used) and a key server. There are multiple reasons for those choices. It is implemented as an application, running below other applications, because this makes it as platform independent as possible. The protocol would support asymmetric cryptography with only minor adjustments, but asymmetric cryptography uses significantly more RAM and ROM than symmetric cryptography (Hummen *et al.* 2014), even though it would offer more security (Mohd *et al.* 2015). Using a key server is a tradeoff solution. Having a single key for the entire WSN is very susceptible to node capture and can compromise the network in its entirety. Because of that, every link should be encrypted with its own key. But storing the keys for interacting with every other node requires a lot of ROM, renders key distribution extremely complicated, and makes adding new nodes to the network very expensive (Khan *et al.* 2012). Using a key server is not without problems either, because it forms a single point of failure and is thus a weak point (Bechkit *et al.* 2012), but in the planned use cases with a single sink node, the same problems exist, even if the key server was not used.

Each TinySAM packet starts with a common header. The header may begin with a magic number, which serves to discriminate between packets that are encrypted with TinySAM from ones that are not. This is necessary in networks that have nodes that have no support for TinySAM. Also in the header is a number specifying the (TinySAM-internal) protocol (e.g. handshake, data transport, or alert) and sub-protocol (i.e. what type of alert) a packet should be forwarded to.

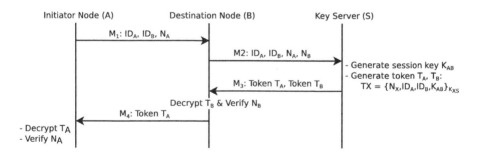

Figure 7.4. *Messages sent in the ANOR handshake (Lowack 2013)*

To establish the session key, the ANOR-protocol (see Figure 7.4) is used. ANOR (AN Otway-Rees) (Abadi and Needham 1994) is an improvement over the Otway-Rees key establishment protocol (Otway and Rees 1987). Each node has a key it uses to communicate with and authenticate itself with the key server. To begin the handshake, Node A sends the first message M_1 (containing ID_A and a nonce N_A) to B. B forwards this message, ID_B and nonce N_B to the key server in the second message, M_2. If both nodes belong to the network and may communicate with each other, the key server generates a session key K_{AB}. Then, the session key is encrypted once with A's initial key K_{AS} and once with B's initial key K_{BS}. Both versions are sent to B in M_3, which decrypts the session key with its own initial key. To conclude the handshake, B sends M_4 with the encrypted session key to A. By using B as an intermediate station to send the key to A, A only receives the session key *after* B has received the session key. This proves to A that the handshake was successfully completed and signals that buffered messages can be sent securely, using the just established session key. When working with static keys, sending the same data twice results in the same (encrypted) message being sent twice. This allows attackers to draw conclusions from repetition patterns. To protect against such an attack, a counter mode is used for encryption with a changing initialization vector (IV), resulting in a new key for every message. Because sending data draws a lot of power, the whole initialization vector is not transmitted with every message. Instead, certain bytes of it act as a message counter and only this counter is sent along with the payload. This counter can also be used to prevent replay attacks, where an attacker captures a message and later sends it again. This will be detected because the counter is not increasing from one message to the next. To ensure the data (for example the message counter) has not been tampered with, a MAC is added to almost all of the messages. To calculate the MAC, the session key has to be known and changing only one bit will result in a completely different MAC, making tampered or incorrectly transmitted data easy to detect.

The way TinySAM uses encryption results in all four properties being covered: using MACs produces authentication and data integrity, the counters offer freshness, and encrypting the data during transmission achieves confidentiality. TinySAM does not prescribe a specific cipher. With some minor modifications, even asymmetric ciphers would be feasible. In TinySAM, there are two common exceptional states. In the first case, a node has lost the initialization vector or has detected a packet with the wrong message counter. In that case, it instructs the other node to send a new initialization vector along with the next message. The other problem occurs when the session key was lost on a node, most likely because it lost power for a short amount of time, or because it crashed and had to reboot. If the node sending the message has lost the key, it will initiate a new handshake. The other node will simply overwrite the old session data. If the receiving node has lost the session key, it will relay the command to have the other node initiate a new handshake via the key server. This message is sent via the key server because the key server is the only node that has a key to communicate securely with the other node. If the instruction does not need to be secured, then a malicious node could permanently send 'missing session' alerts in the name of any node in the network, shutting down any communication.

MiniSec (Luk *et al.* 2007) is a security solution for WSNs with a version for unicasting and a version for broadcasting messages. Its main goal is low energy consumption, but with as little compromise in security as possible. In MiniSec, each node pair shares two encryption keys, one for each direction. This requires the network layout to be known in advance and does not allow new nodes to be added easily. The encryption is done with *Skipjack* in *Offset CodeBook* mode, which has the advantage of only requiring one pass over messages to produce the cipher text, as well as the integrity protection, thereby saving a lot of expensive encryption calculations. Message counters are included in the encryption keys to produce differing cipher texts, even when sending the same content repeatedly and to protect against replay attacks (Luk *et al.* 2007). MiniSec achieves all four security fundamentals listed in section 7.3.3. Confidentiality is provided by using encryption, authentication and data integrity are the result of integrity protection and freshness is achieved by using counters that alter encryption keys and initialization vectors. The main disadvantages of MiniSec are the pre-shared keys and its integration in the networking stack of the operating system. The pre-shared keys require a lot of planning before deployment and there is no easy way to switch out a single node in a network. The deep integration into the operating system makes it very convenient to use once it is set up, but the implementation is difficult and very hard to reuse in case it should be ported to a different operating system.

TinyDTLS (Kothmayr *et al.* 2013) is an implementation of the Datagram Transport Layer Security (DTLS) protocol on TinyOS for OPAL nodes with a Trusted Platform Module (TPM). The DTLS protocol is an adaption of SSL/TLS, altered to support unreliable communications, such as by UDP. In DTLS, the communication partners *can* authenticate each other, but do not have to. To do so, they present their X.509 certificates to each other, which will be verified by the certificate authority. Authenticity, therefore, is voluntary, but can be forced by the application. Confidentiality is provided by encrypting the payload and integrity is guaranteed through the use of MACs (Kothmayr *et al.* 2013; Siffert 2018).

The fact that DTLS is a standard protocol is a key advantage for interoperability with other systems. But this compatibility has a steep price: the overhead (compared to TinySAM (Lowack 2013) and MiniSec (Luk *et al.* 2007)) is large and messages are even padded, since DTLS only works with block ciphers. The code size and/or hardware support are also expensive: the handshake uses RSA encryption, the payload encryption AES-128 and the MAC computation SHA1, and to securely store the certificate, a TPM is required. Implementing and performing three different ciphers is expensive for sensor nodes, which only makes DTLS useful for nodes with spare resources. Finally, introducing a certificate authority adds a single point of failure to the system, which can be a high risk when working in harsh environments or with a severely limited power supply. The cost of generating, storing and distributing the certificates should also not be disregarded. The implementation of TinyDTLS uses about 20 kB of RAM and 67 kB of ROM, which is about ten times the amount TinySAM uses (RAM and ROM), or four times the amount of ROM and 25 times the amount of RAM used by MiniSec (Luk *et al.* 2007; Kothmayr *et al.* 2013; Lowack 2013).

7.5. The sTiki protocol

sTiki is designed in a similar way to TinySAM, which is an application layer encryption protocol using AES-128 for the symmetric encryption. As using a single key for the entire network deployment is very susceptible to node capture and can compromise the network in its entirety, a key server solution is combined with sTiki, and as a result, every link is encrypted with its own key. A drawback would be that storing keys for interactions with every node in the network would be memory consuming and make key distribution extremely complicated, especially when nodes are added to the network (Khan *et al.* 2012). Another drawback is that the key server solution would create a single point of failure in the network that is generally attractive for attackers (Bechkit *et al.* 2012). But this last drawback already exists, as in the existing network a single-point of failure is in place. This point is represented by the last node in the network, called a sink, which communicates with the server and together with it, represents the gateway (see Figure 7.3).

A sTiki packet always starts with a common header, including the following (Siffert 2018): (a) a magic number, which allows encrypted and unencrypted packets to be distinguished, as some devices (i.e. TelosB) may not have sufficient resources to encrypt data due to very limited resources and (b) a number specifying the sTiki-internal protocol (e.g. handshake, data transport, or alert) and sub-protocol (i.e. type of alert) used, a packet should be forwarded to.

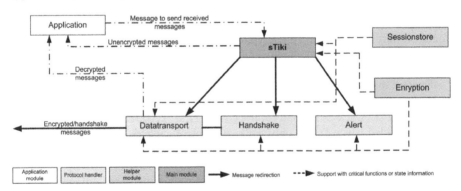

Figure 7.5. *sTiki's architecture (Siffert 2018). For a color version of this figure, see www.iste.co.uk/khatoun/cybersecurity.zip*

In order to establish session keys, the ANOR (AN Otway-Rees) (Abadi and Needham 1994) protocol is used, where each node has a key it uses to communicate and authenticate itself with the key server (see Figure 7.4). It is globally assumed that each participating node shares a unique key with the key server S in advance. From this key, two keys are derived during node startup (by encrypting separate hard-coded values), which are then used to communicate with the key server S. There is one key for computing the MAC, and another for message encryption. This shared key is called the *initial master key* (IMK) and, thus, S knows all IMKs of all nodes of the network, especially A's IMK, called K_{AS} and B's IMK, called K_{BS}. When performing the handshake to create the session key K_{AB}, the following steps are performed and four messages are sent between A, B, and S, as illustrated in Figure 7.4 (Siffert 2018; Schmitt 2019):

1) The handshake is initiated by node A, sending message M_1 to node B. This message includes A's identification ID_A, the destinations's identification ID_B, and is encrypted with K_{AS} a nonce N_A.

2) When node B receives M_1, it first verifies that ID_B in M_1 matches its own ID and ID_A matches the ID of the source node A.
- If this check fails, the handshake is aborted.
- Otherwise, B appends its own generated nonce N_B encrypted with K_{BS} to the message and sends the resulting message M_2 to the key server S.

3) S receives M_2 and checks if the IMKs of A and B are known.
- If not it aborts the handshake.
- Otherwise, S generates a random session key K_{AB} and two tokens T. Every T includes ID_A, ID_B, and the nonce of the appropriated node – either N_A or N_B – and K_{AB}. The resulting tokens T_A and T_B are generated as soon as S encrypts T with the IMK with A and B respectively.

4) S sends the message M_3 encrypted to B, including T_A and T_B.

5) B verifies M_3 (see Lowack (2013)) and if successfully verified it decrypts its token T_B, stores K_{AB}, and forwards T_A to A as message M_4.

6) A verifies M_4 (see Lowack (2013)) and if successfully verified it decrypts its token T_A and stores K_{AB}, completing the handshake.

By using B as an intermediate station to send the key to A, A only receives the session key after B has received the session key. This proves to A that the handshake was successfully completed and signals that buffered messages (e.g. template and data) can be sent securely, using the just established session key. As mentioned in Siffert (2018) using static keys to send the same data twice would result in the same encrypted message sent twice, allowing an attacker to draw a conclusion from repetition patterns. In order to overcome this problem, a counter mode is used for encryption with a changing initialization vector, resulting in a new key for each message (Lowack 2013). As sending large IVs would require a lot of space from the limited Message Transfer Unit (MTU) size, it was decided that only certain bytes of it acting as a Message Counter (MC) were sent along with the payload. This counter can also be used to prevent replay attacks, where an attacker captures a message and later sends it again. The reason for detection is that the counter is not increasing from one message to the next. To ensure that data has not been tampered with, a MAC (see Siffert (2018); Lowack (2013)) that was not mentioned in the handshake steps explicitly, is added to the messages.

7.5.1. *Design decisions taken*

The sTiki protocol implemented in Contiki version 3 shows four assumptions (Siffert 2018): first, the magic number is included in the header. Second, AES-128 was chosen for encryption. Third, only one ongoing handshake per node is allowed at a time, but several keying materials can be stored, meaning that a node can have several links to neighboring nodes at the same time. Since each handshake takes up to 50 B plus the overhead of searching through them during handling, this consumes too many resources on constrained devices at a time. And finally, a failed handshake step will not be retried, meaning the handshake itself has to be initiated again. With this, blocking the activity of a node is avoided due to trying to resend a message.

As the Contiki operating system is structured in a modular fashion, sTiki was also designed following this paradigm. Modules allow for a simple adaptation, if required, by switching out parts, such as the encryption algorithm, or making smaller changes for update purposes or extensions. A modular structure allows code to be kept local, simplifying maintenance and testing. Figure 7.5 illustrates the modular architecture of sTiki, where the **sTiki module** is the starting point. As soon as messages are received, the **sTiki module** checks whether the message is in sTiki format. If not, it is responsible for redirecting messages to the appropriate protocol(s). Thus, the **sTiki module** functions as a dispatcher delegating the handling to respective modules. Thus, it checks for handshake messages or data messages, delegating them as required. Besides the main module – **sTiki module** – and protocol handlers (**Datatransport module, Handshake module**, and **Alert module**), two helper modules – **Sessionstore module** and **Encryption module** – are included in the architecture. These modules perform critical functions or carry state information used throughout sTiki and are integrated in most files in the implementation. The final implementation of sTiki consists of a node (see section 7.5.2.1) and a key server part (see section 7.5.2.2).

Due to memory and power limitations, sTiki needs to be efficient here (Siffert 2018; Schmitt 2019):

> The limited RAM and ROM makes it necessary to keep in mind how much of these two resources is still available on the devices, as many decisions favor RAM, ROM or power savings at the cost of taking more of one or both of the other resources. For example, the fixed keys in each node: in sTiki, each node has a master key from which two keys are derived, in order to secure the communications with the key server. One is for encryption purposes, the other one is used to compute the MACs. It is possible to either store the master key in ROM and derive the two keys on startup, or precompute and store them in ROM so that the power to compute them can be saved on the expense of storing double the amount of keys. If the node has very little ROM left, it will probably be decided to spend the energy to recompute the keys.

7.5.2. *Implementation of sTiki's components*

As described above, the sTiki protocol requires a special implementation for nodes representing the collection point of data using TinyIPFIX as their payload, sending data to the gateway for further processing. This node specific implementation is presented below followed by the key server specific implementation. It is responsible for the key creation and the handling of the deployment in order to ensure a secure data connection from node to gateway, respecting the encryption properties.

7.5.2.1. *sTiki's node implementation*

For the node implementation part, the main code is integrated in a file called `stiki.h` using four methods. During startup, the `init_stiki()` method and the `set_stiki_packet_handler(packet_handler ph)` method are called. With these calls, the **Handshake module** resets the handshake status to IDLE, derives the keys for communicating with the server from the initial master key IMK and registers the connection the the key server S. Further, it is determined what should be done with incoming data, meaning which module they should be forwarded to. The `stiki_udp_sendto(...)` method encrypts the data before sending it, otherwise for uncrpted communication, the `stiki_udp_send_to(...)` method is selected. `stiki_receive(...)` is the function to be registered as a callback when setting up connections that will be used to send data.

The `stiki-main.c` and `stiki-main.h` files represent the core implementation of sTiki. Any action (e.g. sending, receiving) needs to pass through it. These two methods function as a dispatcher to the correct submodule (e.g. **Datatransport module** or **Alert module**). A receiving device automatically directs the packet received to the correct submodule. In case of a sender, a check for existing session or potential errors (e.g. lost IV or keying material) is required first before directing the packet to the corresponding submodule. In the two files structs and helper functions are also included for the configuration purposes of sTiki, such as encryption key length, nonce size, handshake timeout, and number of active sessions.

The designed handshake is included in the **Handshake module**. This module is responsible for initiating a new handshake and responding to handshake packets received. The `initiate_handshake(...)` and `handle_handshake(...)` functions are responsible for both. In order to track the status of an ongoing handshake, the `stiki_handshake_context` struct is used, holding the following information (Siffert 2018; Schmitt 2019):

– In `state` the process is tracked to ensure that no messages are skipped during the handshaking and to determine if a new handshake can be initiated, meaning no other handshake is running in parallel.

– `target_id` stores the identification (ID) of the handshake partner.

– `partner_conn` stores the (UDP) connection to the handshake partner.

– `target_ip` stores the IP address of the handshake partner, which is included in every message to the partner.

– `my_nonce` stores the current handshake's nonce, avoiding irritation to previous handshakes.

– `my_token` stores the secret part of the last handshake message.

– `timestamp` stores the corresponding timestamp for the last activity in the ongoing handshake.

– `stored_msg` and `stored_msg_len` stores the message and its length that was sent for handshake initiation.

When a handshake is queried to start, the `initiate_handshake` function is called from `stiki-main`. As defined in section 7.5.1, only one handshake is allowed at a time. Thus, the context attribute `state` is checked to see if it states IDLE and the `timestamp` attribute is checked for a timeout. If all of the checks are passed, there is no ongoing handshake, all context attributes are reset, and a new handshake is initiated by sending message M_1 and filling the context attributes accordingly. `handle_handshake` is filled as soon as handshake packets are received, which in turn feeds the message to the appropriate handler, creating messages M_1, M_3, and M_4. For message M_2 no handler exists, as this message should always be sent to key server S. As soon as the handshake is completed, the context attribute `state` is updated and the established session is added to the *Sessionstore*, where the session keys, IVs, and MCs are stored.

The **Datatransport module** is in charge of handling the data received or ready for sending using sTiki. The `datatransport_sendto(...)` method is activated when data should be sent, assuming that a valid session already exists. The corresponding session is fetched, and a corresponding packet including an IV (assuming it was already sent) is created and sent to the destination node. If a packet is received, the `handle_data_transport(...)` method is activated. It is checked if a valid session exists. If not, an alert (via the **Alert module**) is triggered and sent to key server S. In return S informs the sender of the missing session. In case the session exists, but the IV is missing, an alert (via the **Alert module**) is also triggered this time, causing a message to be sent to the sender requesting the IV in the next message. In case no alerts are triggered, everything is as required. The message is decrypted and the content is forwarded to the application (i.e. TinyIPFIX) using sTiki.

The **Sessionstore module** receives an entry as soon as two nodes successfully complete a handshake. The module stores a predefined amount of sessions and offers ways to access and manipulate them. The amount of valid session is set in a compiler flag determining the maximum number. An array called `sessions` stores pointers to the sessions, allowing interactions with specific sessions. Some examples include searching for a session, checking if an active session to a specific node exists, updating timestamps for a session, or creating a session. Sessions can also be deleted, for example when the message counter rolls over, which forces a new session to be established because key or IV renegotiation logic was skipped in favour of a smaller implementation. A session requires 80 B storage and includes the following information (Siffert 2018; Schmitt 2019):

- `node_id` stores the partner node's ID.
- `my_iv` stores the IV used for messages sent to the partner node.
- `remote_iv` stores the IV received from the partner node.
- `crypt_key` stores the encryption key for messaged.
- `mac_key` stores the key used for MAC computation.
- `last_event` stores the last message's timestamp between the two nodes, which is used to determine a session timeout.

The functions required for performing encryptions are integrated in the **Encryption module**. In the current implementation AES-128 is used, supported by the current version of Contiki. The `encrypt_message` function is responsible for encryption and decryption and requires a given key and the IV. The **Encryption module** itself applies bitwise XOR to the message for encryption. For decryption the bitwise XOR is applied again, delivering the original input per definition. The `encrypt_message` function also performs the integrity check, computing and verifying the MAC of a message according to Song *et al.* (2006). Additionally, this function is responsible for generating the random data used to generate nonces and IVs.

7.5.2.2. sTiki's key server implementation

The key server's implementation, consisting of a main dispatcher module and modules for each subprotocol (encryption and session handling), is programmed in Java and integrated into CoMaDa. Here, packet processing is done by stacking protocols on top of each other. Concretely, this means that when a packet is received it is parsed to the `WSNProtocolPacket` function and fed into the first protocol (here sTiki, see Listing 7.1). The output is used as the input for the next protocol and so on, until the last protocol has done its job. A packet is not forwarded to the next protocol if the current protocol returns `null`. An example is a control message. As line 20 shows, processing in sTiki is done by using a function called `process( )`. It manipulates session information and packet content according to the sTiki protocol and returns a new packet with decrypted content if it was a "datatransport packet". In order to select the correct processing function, the correct subclass of `STikiPacket( )` (see line 9) is determined by looking at the packet header when parsing the packet. Depending on the selection, the required manipulations are performed. For example, in case of handshake and alert packets, the session information gets updated. In case of datatransport packets, the content is additionally decrypted and returned in a new packet.

```
1   @Override
2   public WSNProtocolPacket process(WSNProtocolPacket
3       packet) throws WSNProtocolException {
4
5       if(!isSTikiPacket(packet)) {
6           return packet; //not an sTiki packet, do not touch
7       }
8
9       STikiPacket tikiPacket = STikiPacket.parse(packet);
10      if(tikiPacket.missesSession()) {
11          AlertPacket.sendInvalidSession(tikiPacket.
12              getSourceId(), 1/*Key server ID*/);
13          return null;
14      }
15
16      if(!tikiPacket.macIsValid()) {
17          return null;
18      }
19
20      return tikiPacket.process();
21  }
```

Listing 7.1. *sTiki's main processing function on CoMaDa (Siffert 2018)*

In order to have an efficient implementation in place the code was analysed concerning repetitions. It was recognized that this was the case for cryptographic functions and, thus, it was decided to locate the required classes in one package, called `Crypto`. It now includes the following classes: (1) `AES.java`, responsible for encrypting a single block with AES or an entire message in counter mode; (2) `AES_CMAC.java`, computing the checksum of messages or checking the MAC for correctness; (3) `CryptoUtils.java`, containing functions to generate random data, concerting byte arrays to strings and the other way around; (4) `KeyStore.java`, interacting with the file containing the initial keying material; (5) `STikiUtils.java`, containing functions converting IP addresses to node IDs and backwards, logging data and manipulating data (i.e. message header).

It is essential to complete the server side's implementation functions for storing nodes' IMKs, process the handshake message M_2 and relay the *missing_session* message to the right node, in order to initiate a new handshake.

7.6. sTiki's evaluation

As sTiki will run on constrained devices, special focus in the implementation was on resource usage, especially memory and energy consumption. The node's implementation requires an additional 4,538 B of ROM and 368 B of RAM for collectors, compared to the already existing TinyIPFIX implementation. For the aggregator device, an additional 4,556 B ROM and 368 B of RAM are required, compared to TinyIPFIX. The overhead is only caused by sTiki, the operating system's configuration stays the same as before. With this memory consumption measured, sTiki requires the OpenMote platform as a minimum, meaning it cannot run on TelosB. Thus, if a heterogenous network is in place, only parts of the communication can be secured with sTiki. Compared to TinySAM, sTiki is more memory efficient as only one handshake is allowed at a time. Savings in memory are also gained compared to MiniSec, but here especially in the time for encryptions, since MiniSec uses the Offset CodeBook mode to compute the ciphertext and the MAC in a single pass. Energy consumption measurements show that nodes in the standby-mode consume $29.5\ mA \pm 1.0\ mA$. When nodes send messages the current increases to $31.5\ mA \pm 0.2\ mA$. This was measured independent of the sTiki support as expected, because sending and computing data is the same process in both cases. Only the duration to perform the processes differed, due to MAC calculation, header creation, and session management.

7.6.1. *Secured communication between aggregator and server*

As a first step in sTiki, the aggregator with ID AEFD establishes a session with the key server that is at the same time the sink in the deployed network. Due to this special situation for the key server, the messages M_2 and M_3 of the handshake can happen internally at the sink and only the messages $M1$ and M_4 are required.

```
Frame 2: 58 bytes on wire (464 bits), 58 bytes captured (464 bits) on interface 0
Raw packet data
Internet Protocol Version 6, Src: fd00::212:4b00:615:aefd, Dst: fd00::1
User Datagram Protocol, Src Port: 1027, Dst Port: 1111
Data (10 bytes)

000   60 00 00 00 00 12 11 3f   fd 00 00 00 00 00 00 00   ......?  ........
010   02 12 4b 00 06 15 ae fd   fd 00 00 00 00 00 00 00   ..K.....  ........
020   00 00 00 00 00 00 00 01   04 03 04 57 00 12 e4 eb   ........  ...W....
030   ef 41 ae fd 00 01 f3 f9   84 22                     .A......  ."
```

Figure 7.6. *sTiki message M_1 captured with Wireshark (Siffert 2018). For a color version of this figure, see www.iste.co.uk/khatoun/cybersecurity.zip*

In order to initiate the handshake of sTiki, the aggregator (ID AEFD) sends message M_1 to the key server. As in this case, the aggregator is the initiator it matches, "Node A" in the protocol's description. The captured packet is shown in Figure 7.6, where the highlighted 10 byte represent sTiki's M_1 content. The bytes marked in red represent the header of sTiki including the magic number (here: EF), showing that the packet is in sTiki format and the respective protocol information (here: 41). The next four bytes marked in blue represent the node's ID (here: $AEFD$) and the destination's ID (here: key server with ID 0001). The last four bytes marked in pink build the random nonce, which will be sent back to the initiator node to determine which request the response belongs to.

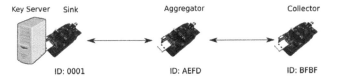

Figure 7.7. *Testing setup for sTiki (Siffert 2018)*

```
Frame 3: 105 bytes on wire (840 bits), 105 bytes captured (840 bits) on interface 0
Raw packet data
Internet Protocol Version 6, Src: fd00::1, Dst: fd00::212:4b00:615:aefd
User Datagram Protocol, Src Port: 1234, Dst Port: 1234
Data (57 bytes)

000  60 00 87 60 00 41 11 40  fd 00 00 00 00 00 00 00   .. .A.@ .......
010  00 00 00 00 00 00 00 01  fd 00 00 00 00 00 00 00   ....... ........
020  02 12 4b 00 06 15 ae fd  04 d2 04 d2 00 41 9b 6d   ..K..... .....A.m
030  ef 44 56 77 f2 99 f2 44  ed a0 ee 74 39 4a 0f 6e   .DVw...D ...t9J.n
040  e4 76 50 4f 9a f2 c1 85  30 31 6a ad 76 57 6d 2d   .vPO.... 01j.vWm-
050  d1 68 4d 4e 98 0b d0 75  7f e3 dc a5 d6 ce bb a9   .hMN...u ........
060  03 55 8c 9b c7 0d c3 ee  6e                        .U...... n
```

Figure 7.8. *sTiki message M_4 captured with Wireshark (Siffert 2018). For a color version of this figure, see www.iste.co.uk/khatoun/cybersecurity.zip*

As assumed due to the setup shown in Figure 7.7, the sink linked to the key server checks if the received message M_1 is a valid request. Listing 7.2 shows a debugging output captured in CoMaDa when message M_1 is received and the check was passed successfully. Lines 2–4 are responsible for the resolution of the received message M_1. In line 5, the MAC validation is done, which will always be successful as M_1 is not protected with a MAC. The token (see line 7) is the most important part of the response, because it consists of the following session details (Siffert 2018; Schmitt 2019):

– the involved nodes (here AEFD and 0001);

– following the nonce for matching, the response to the handshake's initiation;

– the last 16 B building the session key.

Line 6 shows the random IV, which is required together with the node's IMK to encrypt the entire token. In order to prove later that the packet has not been tampered with, a MAC is added to the message in line 9. Here, the MAC is calculated using the node's IMK. When everything is in place, message M_4 can be sent out by the sink as a response to the initiating node. Figure 7.8 shows the captured message in Wireshark, where the header is marked red (here 44 shows that it is handshake packet M_4), the IV is marked blue, the token is marked pink, and the MAC is marked green, resulting in a total length of 57 B.

```
Frame 4: 182 bytes on wire (1456 bits), 182 bytes captured (1456 bits) on interface 0
Raw packet data
Internet Protocol Version 6, Src: fd00::212:4b00:615:aefd, Dst: fd00::1
User Datagram Protocol, Src Port: 1234, Dst Port: 1234
Data (134 bytes)
```

```
00   60 00 00 00 00 8e 11 3f   fd 00 00 00 00 00 00 00   `......?  ........
10   02 12 4b 00 06 15 ae fd   fd 00 00 00 00 00 00 00   ..K.....  ........
20   00 00 00 00 00 00 00 01   04 d2 04 d2 00 8e 3c 4e   ........  ......<N
30   ef 21 e3 19 88 6a e6 2f   08 dc 06 59 c0 fa d0 32   .!...j./  ...Y...2
40   32 0e 11 7d 79 b1 ed 8e   1a cf 2c db ff 04 12 a0   2..}y...  ..,.....
50   69 cb ef ff 82 48 38 6a   32 a2 64 67 0f 9f 0b b4   i....H8j  2.dg....
60   fa 56 f4 cb f2 84 82 d2   ec 0f 14 43 49 a9 33 f6   .V......  ...CI.3.
70   fc 6e 86 89 66 ff 22 b1   66 f4 24 fc 20 51 93 2d   .n..f.".  f.$. Q.-
80   83 4e 0a 0d cf 3d ed 6d   7a 72 e0 92 13 eb 65 b7   .N..=.m  zr....e.
90   26 48 25 fa 00 d0 43 f4   b7 a5 ba 33 06 e0 78 da   &H%...C.  ...3..x.
a0   9b d9 2a cc 42 1e 46 42   10 02 1a fe 95 bd e9 c8   ..*.B.FB  ........
b0   68 79 2e ac b0 08                                   hy....
```

Figure 7.9. *Data Packet with an IV captured with Wireshark (Siffert 2018). For a color version of this figure, see www.iste.co.uk/khatoun/cybersecurity.zip*

```
 1  Starting tunnel
 2  [sTiki] Received data: EF41AEFD0001F3F98422
 3  [sTiki] Header details: Protocol 2, Subprotocol: 1
 4  [sTiki] [STiki.HandshakePacket$M_1$: IDa: 44797
 5          IDb: 1 nonce: F3F98422 ]
 6  [sTiki] MAC is valid!
 7  [sTiki] IV is 5677F299F244EDA0EE74394A0F6EE4
 8  [sTiki] token is
 9          AEFD0001F3F98422E8D1D612190E9E75590016E5DABC73AC
10  [sTiki] encrypted token is
11          76504F9AF2C18530316AAD76576D2DD1684D4E980BD0757F
12  [sTiki] MAC is E3DCA5D6CEBBA903558C9BC70DC3EE6E
13  [sTiki] sending EF445677F299F244EDA0EE74394A0F6EE476504
14          F9AF2C18530316AAD76576D2DD1684D4E980BD0757FE3DC
15          A5D6CEBBA903558C9BC70DC3EE6E to
16          /fd00:0:0:0:212:4b00:615:aefd
```

Listing 7.2. *Debugging output for message M_1 in CoMaDa (Siffert 2018)*

When the handshake is completed, the aggregator can send data. As no data was sent before, the first message includes an IV. Such a data message is illustrated in Figure 7.9. Here, a message is shown, including an IV that is obvious as the header is $EF21$ (marked in red). The upcoming 13 bytes describe the IV and are marked blue, followed by the data itself. The last 16 bytes of the message marked in pink build the MAC. When this packet is received, the just-received IV and the session key are used to decrypt the data packet. Once an IV was set, the upcoming messages include a MC (marked in blue) only, saving 11 bytes per message. Such messages are than indicated with a header $EF22$ (marked in red), as shown in Figure 7.10. Again, the MAC is marked in pink and represented by the last 16 bytes in the packet. Listing 7.3 illustrates the respective debugging output from CoMaDa. In line 3, the header details are checked, followed by a check to see if an active link exists to the source node (lines 4–5) and if the MAC is valid (line 6). If all of the checks are fine, the data is decrypted and uploaded (lines 7–9).

```
Frame 9: 97 bytes on wire (776 bits), 97 bytes captured (776 bits) on interface 0
Raw packet data
Internet Protocol Version 6, Src: fd00::212:4b00:615:aefd, Dst: fd00::1
User Datagram Protocol, Src Port: 1027, Dst Port: 1111
Data (49 bytes)
```

```
00   60 00 00 00 00 39 11 3f   fd 00 00 00 00 00 00 00   `....9.? ........
10   02 12 4b 00 06 15 ae fd   fd 00 00 00 00 00 00 00   ..K..... ........
20   00 00 00 00 00 00 00 01   04 03 04 57 00 39 a1 1f   ........ ...W.9..
30   ef 22 00 01 18 de d0 4e   6f 7b df 9a 38 0a 19 75   ."....N o{..8..u
40   75 20 a8 60 98 06 1e eb   8c 22 d9 11 f0 c5 e6 48   u .`.....".....H
50   ba a6 05 96 6d 58 70 31   85 99 a7 1c ae a6 d3 1a   ....mXp1 ........
60   84
```

Figure 7.10. *Data Packet with a MC captured with Wireshark (Siffert 2018). For a color version of this figure, see www.iste.co.uk/khatoun/cybersecurity.zip*

```
1    [sTiki]  Received  data:  EF22000118DED04E6F7BDF9A380A19
2             757520A86098061EEB8C22D911F0C5E648BAA605966D5
3             870318599A71CAEA6D31A84
4    [sTiki]  Header  details:  Protocol  1,  Subprotocol:  2
5    [sTiki]  [STiki.DataTransportPacket:
6             Source:  212:4b00:615:aefd:fd00:0:0:0
7             MAC:  A605966D5870318599A71CAEA6D31A84
8             subprotocol:  2  ]
9    [sTiki]  MAC  is  valid!
10   [sTiki]  decrypted  data  is  081D000BC50DE1E10D0000000FBF
11            BF000BC30DCBCB0D00000014BFBF00
12
13   Upload  response...
```

Listing 7.3. *Debugging output for Data Packet received with MC (Siffert 2018)*

```
Frame 6: 62 bytes on wire (496 bits), 62 bytes captured (496 bits) on interface 0
Raw packet data
Internet Protocol Version 6, Src: fd00::212:4b00:615:aefd, Dst: fd00::1
User Datagram Protocol, Src Port: 1026, Dst Port: 1234
Data (14 bytes)
```

```
000   60 00 00 00 00 16 11 3f   fd 00 00 00 00 00 00 00   `......? ........
010   02 12 4b 00 06 15 ae fd   fd 00 00 00 00 00 00 00   ..K..... ........
020   00 00 00 00 00 00 00 01   04 02 04 d2 00 16 12 41   ........ .......A
030   ef 42 bf bf ae fd 3b e7   51 aa 21 59 db 9a          .B....;. Q.!Y..
```

Figure 7.11. *sTiki message M_2 captured with Wireshark (Siffert 2018). For a color version of this figure, see www.iste.co.uk/khatoun/cybersecurity.zip*

```
Frame 7: 145 bytes on wire (1160 bits), 145 bytes captured (1160 bits) on interface 0
Raw packet data
Internet Protocol Version 6, Src: fd00::1, Dst: fd00::212:4b00:615:aefd
User Datagram Protocol, Src Port: 1234, Dst Port: 1234
Data (97 bytes)

000  60 00 87 60 00 69 11 40  fd 00 00 00 00 00 00 00   `..`.i.@ ........
010  00 00 00 00 00 00 00 01  fd 00 00 00 00 00 00 00   ........ ........
020  02 12 4b 00 06 15 ae fd  04 d2 04 d2 00 69 2c c2   ..K..... .....i,.
030  ef 43 f2 cf 7d 62 ee 6c  5c 26 4e 71 1d 33 a4 13   .C..}b.l \&Nq.3..
040  a8 9b c8 d1 82 ba e6 de  9c cb c1 0c 2b 09 50 6f   ........ ....+.Po
050  2b bf 11 2c 0f d0 7e 12  8a 18 a1 06 ef cc ec a8   +..,..~. ........
060  92 f6 8a b0 8a 52 40 6f  75 9b c8 d1 82 a0 58 54   .....R@o u.....XT
070  ac cb c1 0c 2b 09 50 6f  2b bf 11 2c 0f d0 7e 12   ....+.Po +..,..~.
080  8a fb 73 8c 30 84 fc 24  fd 7a 9e b0 51 5e 55 6d   ..s.0..$ .z..Q^Um
090  68                                                 h
```

Figure 7.12. *sTiki message M_3 captured with Wireshark (Siffert 2018). For a color version of this figure, see www.iste.co.uk/khatoun/cybersecurity.zip*

7.6.2. *Secured communication between collector and aggregator*

Communications between the collector and aggregator work similarily as described above with one difference, none of the participating nodes are a key server. Here, M_1 is sent from the collector to the aggregator and the aggregator sends message M_2 to the key server. Figure 7.11 illustrates the corresponding capturing of M_2, where the header is marked in pink, the node IDs (here $BFBF$ and $AEFD$) are marked in blue, and nonces are marked in pink. Based on the header (here: $EF42$), the key server is able to recognize that the received message is M_2 of sTiki's handshake and checks if the nodes are allowed to talk. This check is positive when the key server holds the IMK of each node, because per assumption they count to the same network. If the check is positive, the key server chooses a session key and calculates tokens (T_A and T_B) for both nodes, which include the IDs of the nodes ($BFBF$ and $AEFD$), respective nonces ($3BE751AA$ and $2159DB9A$), and the session key. Each token is encrypted with an IV and the node's IMK. Finally, the key server computes a MAC for M_4, because node B is not aware of node A's IMK. Putting everything together as described in the sTiki protocol results in message M_3 (see Figure 7.12, red = header, blue = IV, green = T_A, yellow = MAC for M_4, orange = T_B, pink = MAC), which is sent to node B, forwarding the token to node A, which in return can start with sending data.

sTiki also supports error recovery. The implemented recovery mechanism is activated as soon as (1) an IV or (2) a session is lost. Both result in sending alert messages in sTiki. Debugging examples are shown in Siffert (2018). For case (1) it is important to mention here that the not decryptable packet is lost, because the last received messages are not stored in the memory, and an alert packet is generated to send to the communication partner, indicating that the IV is missing, and including the following information: (a) the header $EF63$, (b) the IDs of the involved nodes (e.g. $AEFD$ for the aggregator and 0001 for the key server), and (c) the MAC computed with the session key, because an active session between the two nodes exists. For case (2) the receiving node would want to try to inform the sending node about the problem. As they do not have a shared session, the receiving node cannot do this in a secure manner. If the notification is possible in an unsecured manner, like sending a unsecured packet to initiate a new handshake, a DoS attack becomes possible by sending missing session packets to the complete network continuously. Thus, the message is relayed by the key server that can notify the sender node using its IMK to initiate a new handshake. In such a case, the key server recognizes the message as its header equals $EF65$. The packet includes the IDs of the involved nodes (e.g. $BFBF$ and $AEFD$) protected by a MAC, which is computed with the IMK of the sender node. The key server constructs a message with header $EF65$, including the two node IDs to the destination node. The message is protected by the IMK of the destination node. The destination node is able to decrypt the packet. Based on the included information, the destination node initiates a new handshake with the respective node.

	Collector		Aggregator	
	ROM	RAM	ROM	RAM
Operating System Contiki, TinyIPFIX	48,248	15,999	48,357	17,073
Operating System Contiki, TinyIPFIX, sTiki	52,796	16,367	52,913	17,441
sTiki only	4,548	368	4,556	368

Table 7.1. sTiki size according to `size` utility [Byte]

7.6.3. Communication costs

Power consumption was measured by connecting a multimeter in between one side of a battery and the power socket on the node. Multiple attempts were made and produced very similar results. During standby, the nodes had a power consumption of 29.5 mA $\pm$ 0.1 mA. When sending messages, the current increased to 31.5 mA $\pm$0.2 mA. This was the same on nodes with and without sTiki, which is to be expected because sending and computing data is the same process in both versions. The durations of those phases should be longer on the version with sTiki because the messages have some overhead because of the header and MAC, and the calculations should also take longer because the version with sTiki has to compute the MAC and manage sessions. On the nodes with sTiki the multimeter occasionally showed a lower current, flowing around 28 mA. It is unclear where this comes from, one possibility is that the hardware implementation of AES takes less power and the processor pauses calculations while the encryption is going on. However, the drops are not frequent enough to match with every encryption operation, but this may be caused by a low sampling rate of the multimeter, which misses short encryption sequences.

By analyzing the binary file generated by the `make` command with the utility `size`, it is possible to find out the ROM and RAM requirements of the code running on the nodes. Table 7.1 shows the measurements. It shows a RAM usage of 368 B (reported as `data` and `bss`) and a ROM usage of 4,548 and 4,556 B (reported as text) for sTiki. This difference in ROM usage most likely results from differing amounts of code that calls sTiki and/or differing compiler optimizations.

```
1   <?xml version ="1.0" encoding="UTF-8"?>
2   <configuration >
3    <match>
4     <field >
5      <name>Temperature (Sensiron SHT11)</name>
6      <fieldID >0x80A0</fieldID >
7      <enterpriseNumber >0xF0AA00AA</enterpriseNumber >
8      <type >Temperature </type >
9      <unit >Celsius </unit >
10     <expression ><![CDATA[ Math. round (
11               (-39.7+(0.01*x))*100)/100]] ></expression >
12    </field >
13    <field >
14     <name>Humidity (Sensiron SHT11)</name>
15     <fieldID >0x80A1</fieldID >
16     <enterpriseNumber >0xF0AA00AA</enterpriseNumber >
17     <type >Humidity </type >
18     <unit >%</unit >
19     <expression ><![CDATA[ Math. round ((-2.0468+(0.0367*x)
20               + (-0.0000015955 * (x * x))) * 100) / 100]]
21               ></expression >
22    </field >
23    ...
24
25   </match >
26  </configuration >
```

Listing 7.4. *XML example for sensors (Sgier 2017)*

7.6.4. *Integration into an existing system*

In order to configure and manage the deployed network using Contiki, the server component shown in Figure 7.3 was extended by the Contiki support including a user-friendly Graphical User Interface (GUI), called CoMaDa, offering **Co**nfiguration, **Ma**nagement, and **Da**ta handling functionality for the deployed network. The GUI works according to the "click buttons" principle. CoMaDa itself offers a panel to view received data after the network was deployed, the tunnel was activated, and the virtual network interface was created. In order to decode the received packets correctly, CoMaDa requires an XML (eXtended Marup Language) file, where all parameters for each sensor are stored together with the mathematical equation to calculate the correct value. An example is shown in Listing 7.4. A "field tag" is specified for each sensor of the device (e.g. lines 4–12 for a temperature sensor, lines 13–21 for a humidity sensor). The field tag for pull support is already included, but not yet activated in the implementation. Each enclosing field tag represents a Template Record from TinyIPFIX with additional information (Sgier 2017; Schmitt 2019):

1) `name` states the sensors name and indicates the sensor vendor (e.g. temperature (Sensiron SHT11) – line 5).

2) The `fieldID` and the `enterpriseNumber` are used to identify the data source uniquely (e.g. sensor from vendor X – lines 6–7).

3) `type` defines the type of the value measured (e.g. temperature – line 8).

4) `unit` defines the respective unit of the measured value (e.g. Celcius – line 9).

5) `expression` includes the mathematical equation translating the bit string received into a meaningful value, consistent with the `type` and `unit` information (e.g. lines 10–11)

As a result, the person sitting in-front of a device running CoMaDa can see the received data in a live stream, as shown in Figure 7.13. The data is sent to WebMaDa's backend to store it in WebMaDa-DB and make it accessible via WebMaDa's front-end, as described in Schmitt (2019) for a live-stream with $doa = 1$, meaning no aggregation is performed.

As can be seen in Figure 7.13, it is not visible in GUI CoMaDa if encrypted communication was activated or not. Thus, a proof of operability is performed by showing the captured messages in Wireshark, assuming the network setting shown in Figure 7.7 and that the aggregator performs message aggregation with $doa = 2$. Here, the aggregator waits until two messages are received from the collector with ID BFBF before it performs aggregation.

7.6.5. *Comparison to existing approaches*

The implementation of TinySAM on TinyOS in (Lowack 2013) uses almost 6.5 kB of ROM and about 1.5 kB of RAM with similar configurations, which makes sTiki 2 kB smaller in ROM and 1.1 kB smaller in RAM usage. The smaller size is mainly due to the limit of only one ongoing handshake at a time. Further reasons seem to point to the AES implementation, but such an evaluation was outside the scope of this work.

In comparison to TinyDTLS, sTiki requires about 15 times less ROM and 50 times less RAM. This large difference was expected, because DTLS requires three different encryption algorithms. Just the binding to RSA takes about the same amount of ROM as the entirety of sTiki (Kothmayr *et al.* 2013). The price for using such a small implementation is its non-compliance with the standard DTLS, which might be more important in some use cases.

sTiki's strength compared to MiniSec is size: it uses about half as much RAM and a little less than four times as much ROM as MiniSec uses. The important tradeoff during operation in comparison to MiniSec is in encryption speed, since MiniSec uses an Offset CodeBook mode to compute a ciphertext and MAC in a single pass. sTiki uses a separate algorithm for those two operations, thereby spending more time and energy to compute.

Comparing the power consumption in detail with these measurements collected is not feasible, since precise timings are not available for the Contiki implementation.

Figure 7.13. *CoMaDa's live stream showing the message aggregation*

7.7. Summary and conclusions

This book chapter detailed insights about the measurable paradigm change of the initial Internet toward the IoT. Due to this situation and the rising awareness of personal data's misuse, security concerns have been identified. As it was depicted, reasons for delivering these security measures in the IoT occur due to (a) constrained device characteristics and (b) communication protocols used (e.g. IEEE 802.15.4

or ZigBee). Thus, effective and efficient security protocols are demanded for IoT scenarios.

sTiki was designed as such a security protocol to face the aforementioned challenges to overcome the security concerns mentioned. sTiki was designed in a modular and efficient manner, mapping the resources of constrained devices to possble functionality. As seen in these evaluations, secure communication can be established in a constrained network, however, it remains invisible for the user, when only viewing data received in graphical user interfaces, such as CoMaDa and WebMaDa. A key server implementation is resource consuming and not intended to be implemented on constrained devices itself, but with sTiki the key server is implemented on a resource-full instance of CoMaDa, following the delegation manner and, thus, management work is performed there instead of within the nodes.

sTiki strengthens the constrained network deployed in its security: authentication and data integrity support is due to MAC usage, freshness support reached by counters and confidentiality via encryption using individual link-based session keys. Currently, symmetric encryption is used, but with a modification asymmetric encryption is feasible, too, if devices offer sufficient resources. Additionally, sTiki supports error recovery that can occur, (a) if a node has lost the initialization vector or has detected a packet with the wrong MC or (b) if a node has lost keying material, especially the session key. In the case of (a) the node causes the communication partner to send a new IV with the next message by sending a respective message. In case (b) the node will relay a command to have the other node initiate a new handshake via the key server. This message is sent via the key server, because the key server is the only node that operates with a key to communicate securely with the other node.

Overall, this chapter demonstrated that efficient security can be implemented in the IoT on constrained devices for smart home applications, collecting periodic data that addresses many security concerns from users. Furthermore, with sTiki's implementation and assuming OpenMote B as the node's platform, sufficient memory stays in place for further IoT applications on such constrained devices, such as data aggregation or collection. Due to the delegation of the main security operation of creating key material, the energy consumption for encrypting messages in the network is highly viable for IoT scenarios. In order to validate sTiki for industrial purposes, it is recommended to use an automated validation tool, such as Automated Validation of Internet Security Protocols and Applications (AVISPA).

7.8. Acknowledgements

The work was supported partially by the University of Zürich UZH, Switzerland, and the European Union's Horizon 2020 research and innovation program's project Concordia, under Grant Agreement No. 830927.

7.9. References

451 Research (2015). Explaining the Internet of Things ecosystem and taxonomy [Online]. Available at: https://451research.com/images/Marketing/IoT/IoT_Taxonomy_12.1.15.pdf [Accessed 19 July 2019].

Abadi, M. and Needham, R. (1994). Prudent engineering practice for cryptographic protocols. *Proceedings of 1994 IEEE Computer Society Symposium on Research in Security and Privacy*, 122–136 [Online]. Available at: http://ieeexplore.ieee.org/document/296587 [Accessed 14 August 2018].

Akyildiz, I.F., Su, W., Sankarasubramaniam, Y., Cayirci, E. (2002). A survey on sensor networks. *IEEE Communications Magazine*, 40(8), 102–114.

Andress, J. and Winterfeld, S. (2014). *The Basics of Information Security*, vol. 2. Syngress, Waltham, MA, USA.

Ashton, K. (2009). That "Internet of Things" thing. *RFiD Journal*, 22, 97–114 [Online]. Available at: http://www.rfidjournal.com/articles/view?4986 [Accessed 19 July 2019].

Badel, S., Dağtekin, N., Nakahara, J., Ouafi, K., Reffé, N., Sepehrdad, P., Sušil, P., Vaudenay, S. (2010). Armadillo: A multi-purpose cryptographic primitive dedicated to hardware. In *Cryptographic Hardware and Embedded Systems, CHES 2010*, Mangard, S. and Standaert, F. (eds). Springer, Berlin, Heidelberg, Germany.

Bechkit, W., Challal, Y., Bouabdallah, A. (2012). A new class of hash-chain based key pre-distribution schemes for WSN. *Computer Communications*, 36(3), 243–255.

Bhaiji, Y. (2008). Chapter 1: Overview of network security. Report, CISCO [Online]. Available at: https://www.networkworld.com/article/2274081/chapter-1--overview-of-network-security.html.

Bhatti, S., Carlson, J., Dai, H., Deng, J., Rose, J., Sheth, A., Shucker, B., Gruenwald, C., Torgerson, A., Han, R. (2005). MANTIS OS: An embedded multithreaded operating system for wireless micro sensor platforms. *Mobile Networks and Applications*, 10(4), 563–579.

Bormann, C., Ersue, M., Keranen, A. (2020). Terminology for constrained-node networks [Online]. Available at: https://www.ietf.org/archive/id/draft-bormann-lwig-7228bis-06.txt.

Bowen, P., Hash, J., Wilson, M. (2006). Information security. Technical report SP 800-100, National Institute of Standards and Technology, Gaithersburg, MD, USA.

Boyd, C. and Mathuria, A. (2010). *Protocols for Authentication and Key Establishment*. Springer, Heidelberg, Germany.

Cao, Q., Abdelzaher, T., Stankovic, J., He, T. (2008). The LiteOS operating system: Towards unix-like abstractions for wireless sensor networks. *2008 International Conference on Information Processing in Sensor Networks (IPSN 2008)*, IEEE, 233–244.

CISCO (2019). Cisco visual networking index: Global mobile data traffic forecast update, 2017–2022. Technical report C11-738429-01, CISCO, San Jose, CA, USA.

Çoban, M., Karakoç, F., Özen, M. (2017). Cryptanalysis of QTL block cipher. In *Lightweight Cryptography for Security and Privacy*, Bogdanov, A. (ed.). Springer International Publishing, Cham, Switzerland [Online]. Available at: https://link.springer.com/chapter/10.1007%2F978-3-319-55714-4_5 [Accessed 14 August 2018].

Cremers, C., Lafourcade, P., Nadeau, P. (2009). Comparing state spaces in automatic security protocol analysis. *Formal to Practical Security: Papers Issued from the 2005-2008 French-Japanese Collaboration*, Cortier, V., Kirchner, C., Okada, M., Sakurada, H. (eds). Springer, Cham, Switzerland.

Davis, R. (2016). The Internet of Things – Opportunities and challenges. *European Parliamentary Research Service* [Online]. Available at: http://www.europarl.europa.eu/RegData/etudes/BRIE/2015/557012/EPRS_BRI(2015)557012_EN.pdf [Accessed 19 July 2019].

Dolev, D. and Yao, A. (1983). On the security of public key protocols. *IEEE Transactions on Information Theory*, 29, 198–208.

Dunkels, A., Gronvall, B., Voigt, T. (2004). Contiki – A lightweight and flexible operating system for tiny networked sensors. *29th Annual IEEE International Conference on Local Computer Networks*, 455–462.

Eckert, C. (2014). *IT-Sicherheit: Konzepte – Verfahren – Protokolle*, vol. 9. Oldenbourg Wissenschaftsverlag GmbH, Munich, Germany.

Eisenbarth, T., Kumar, S., Paar, C., Poschmann, A., Uhsadel, L. (2007). A survey of lightweight-cryptography implementations. *IEEE Design Test of Computers*, 24(6), 522–533.

ETSI (2010). Machine-to-Machine communications (M2M), smart metering use cases. Technical report ETSI TR 102 691 V1.1.1, Valbonne, France.

European Parliament and Council of the European Union (2016). Regulation (EU) 2016/679 of the European Parliament and of the Council of 27 April 2016 on the protection of natural persons with regard to the processing of personal data and on the free movement of such data, and repealing Directive 95/46/EC (General Data Protection Regulation) [Online]. Available at: https://eur-lex.europa.eu/legal-content/EN/TXT/PDF/?uri=CELEX:32016R0679&from=DE.

Farooq, M.O. and Kunz, T. (2011). Operating systems for wireless sensor networks: A survey. *Sensors*, 11(6), 5900–5930.

Gerke, J., Hausheer, H., Mischke, J., Stiller, B. (2003). An architecture for a service oriented peer-to-peer system (SOPPS). *Praxis der Informationsverarbeitung und Kommunikation (PIK)*, 2, 90–95.

Hummen, R., Shafagh, H., Raza, S., Voig, T., Wehrle, K. (2014). Delegation-based authentication and authorization for the IP-based Internet of Things. *2014 Eleventh Annual IEEE International Conference on Sensing, Communication and Networking (SECON)*, 284–292.

International Data Corporation (2014). IDC's Internet of Things (IoT) Taxonomy Map [Online]. Available at: http://www.idc.com/downloads/IoT_Taxonomy_Map_V2_Nov2014.pdf [Accessed 19 July 2019].

ITU (2016). Overview of the Internet of Things [Online]. Available at: https://www.itu.int/rec/dologin_pub.asp?lang=e&id=T-REC-Y.2060-201206-I!!PDF-E&type=items [Accessed 19 July 2019].

Karl, H. and Willig, A. (2007). *Protocols and Architectures for Wireless Sensor Networks*. John Wiley & Sons, Hoboken, NJ, USA.

Khan, S.U., Pastrone, C., Lavagno, L., Spirito, M.A. (2012). An authentication and key establishment scheme for the IP-based wireless sensor networks. *Procedia Computer Science*, 10, 1039–1045.

Kothmayr, T., Schmitt, C., Hu, W., Brünig, M., Carle, G. (2013). DTLS based security and two-way authentication for the Internet of Things. *Ad Hoc Networks*, 11(8), 2710–2723.

Kurose, J. and Ross, K. (2016). *Computer Networks – A Top-Down Approach*, vol. 7. Prentice Hall, Upper Saddle River, NJ, USA.

Lee, G., Park, J., Kong, N., Crespi, N. (2010). The Internet of Things – Concept and Problem Statement, draft-lee-iot-problem-statement-05.txt 05. IETF, Fremont, CA, USA.

Leontiadis, I., Efstratiou, C., Mascolo, C., Crowcroft, J. (2012). SenShare: Transforming sensor networks into multi-application sensing infrastructures, wireless sensor networks. *9th European Conference on Wireless Sensor Networks*, LNCS, Springer, Heidelberg, Germany, 65–81.

Levis, P., Madden, S., Polastre, J., Szewczyk, R., Whitehouse, K., Woo, A., Gay, D., Hill, J., Welsh, M., Brewer, E., Culler, D. (2005). Tinyos: An operating system for sensor networks. *Ambient Intelligence*, Springer, Berlin, Heidelberg, Germany, 115–148.

Li, L., Liu, B., Wang, H. (2016). QTL: A new ultra-lightweight block cipher. *Microprocessors and Microsystems*, 45, 45–55.

Lowack, P. (2013). Key management in wireless sensor networks with support for aggregation nodes. Thesis, Technical University of Munich, Germany.

Luk, M., Mezzour, G., Perrig, A., Gligor, V. (2007). Minisec: A secure sensor network communication architecture. *Proceedings of the 6th International Conference on Information Processing in Sensor Networks, IPSN '07*. ACM, New York, NY, USA, 479–488.

Mischke, J. and Stiller, B. (2003). Rich and scalable peer-to-peer search with SHARK. *5th Annual and International Workshop on Active Middleware Services (AMS 2003)*. IEEE, 1–10.

Mohd, B.J., Hayajneh, T., Vasilakos, A.V. (2015). A survey on lightweight block ciphers for low-resource devices: Comparative study and open issues. *Journal of Network and Computer Applications*, 58, 73–93.

Otway, D. and Rees, O. (1987). Efficient and timely mutual authentication. *SIGOPS Operating Systems Review*, 21(1), 8–10.

OWASP (2014). Application Security Verification (ASVS) Standards Project [Online]. Available at: https://www.owasp.org/index.php/Category:OWASP_Application_Security_Assessment_Standards_Project [Accessed 19 July 2019].

Potlapally, N.R., Ravi, S., Raghunathan, A., Jha, N.K. (2003). Analyzing the energy consumption of security protocols. *Proceedings of the 2003 International Symposium on Low Power Electronics and Design.* ACM, 30–35.

Romeo, S. (2016). The rising adoption and complexity of the IoT vision. *Beecham Research* [Online]. Available at: http://iotconvivio.com/wp-content/uploads/2016/10/Beecham-Research_IoTConvivio.pdf.

Sadeghi, S., Bagheri, N., Abdelraheem, M.A. (2017). Cryptanalysis of reduced QTL block cipher. *Microprocessors and Microsystems*, 52, 34–48.

SAP (2014). SAP brings you the Internet of Things for business – Connect, transform, and reimagine business in a hyperconnected future. Technical report, SAP SE [Online]. Available at: http://cornerstoneconsultinginc.com/wpcontent/uploads/2015/11/SAP_The_Internet_of_Things_for_Business.pdf [Accessed 19 July 2019].

Scarfone, K., Souppaya, M., Cody, A., Orebaugh, A. (2008). Technical guide to information security testing and assessment. Technical report SP 800-115, National Institute of Standards and Technology, Gaithersburg, MD, USA.

Schmitt, C. (2019). Trust & security in IoT: Monitoring with constrained devices. Habilitation Thesis, University of Zurich, Switzerland.

Schmitt, C., Kothmayr, T., Ertl, B., Hu, W., Braun, L., Carle, G. (2016). Tinyipfix: An efficient application protocol for data exchange in cyber physical systems. *Computer Communications*, 74, 63–76.

Schmitt, C., Stiller, B., Trammell, B. (2017). TinyIPFIX for smart meters in constrained networks. RFC 8272, RFC Editor [Online]. Available at: https://www.rfc-editor.org/rfc/rfc8272.txt [Accessed 14 August 2018].

Sen, J. (2009). A survey on wireless sensor network security. *International Journal of Communication Networks and Information Security (IJCNIS)*, 1, 55–78 [Online]. Available at: https://arxiv.org/abs/1011.1529 [Accessed 14 August 2018].

Sgier, L. (2016). Optimization of TinyIPFIX implementation in Contiki and realtime visualization of data. Software project, Communication Systems Group, Department of Informatics, University of Zurich, Switzerland.

Sgier, L. (2017). TinyIPFIX aggregation in Contiki. Internship, University of Zurich, Switzerland.

Shelby, Z. and Bormann, C. (2011). *6LoWPAN: The Wireless Embedded Internet*, vol. 43. John Wiley & Sons, New York, USA.

Shi, E. and Perrig, A. (2004). Designing secure sensor networks. *Wireless Communications*, 11(6), 38–43.

Siffert, S. (2018). Secure data transmission in Contiki-based constrained networks offering mututal authentication. Bachelor Thesis, University of Zurich, Switzerland.

Song, J., Poovendran, R., Lee, J., Iwata, T. (2006). The AES-CMAC algorithm. RFC 4493, RFC Editor [Online]. Available at: https://tools.ietf.org/html/rfc4493 [Accessed 14 August 2018].

Summers, A. and Tickner, C. (n.d.). What is security analysis? [Online]. Available at: https://www.doc.ic.ac.uk/~ajs300/security/CIA.htm.

Sundmaeker, H., Guillemin, P., Friess, P., Woelffle, S. (2010). *Vision and Challenges for Realising the Internet of Things*. European Commission – Information Society and Media DG, Brussels, Belgium.

Tex (2012). CC2538 a powerful system-on-chip for 2.4-GHz IEEE 802.15.4-2006 and ZigBee applications [Online]. Available at: http://www.ti.com/product/CC2538 [Accessed 14 August 2018].

The Open Web Application Security Project (2019). OWASP Top Ten Project [Online]. Available at: https://www.owasp.org/index.php/Category:OWASP_Top_Ten_Project [Accessed 19 July 2019].

Vilajosana, X., Tuset, P., Watteyne, T., Pister, K. (2015). Openmote: Open-source prototyping platform for the industrial IoT. In *Ad Hoc Networks*, Mitton, N., Kantarci, M.E., Gallais, A., Papavassiliou, S. (eds). Springer International Publishing, Cham, Switzerland.

Wang, Y., Attebury, G., Ramamurthy, R. (2006). A survey of security issues in wireless sensor networks. *IEEE Communications Surveys and Tutorials*, 8(2), 2–23.

Web Application Security Consortium (2004). WASC threat classification [Online]. Available at: https://cwe.mitre.org/documents/sources/WASCThreatClassificationTaxonomyGraphic.pdf [Accessed 19 July 2019].

Yick, J., Mukherjee, B., Ghosal, D. (2008). Wireless sensor network survey. *Computer Networks*, 52(12), 2292–2330.

List of Authors

Mirna ATIEH
Computer Science Department
Lebanese University
Beirut
Lebanon

Fayez GEBALI
Department of Electrical and
Computer Engineering
University of Victoria
Canada

Rida KHATOUN
Télécom ParisTech
Paris
France

Adrian KOTELBA
VTT Technical Research
Centre of Finland Ltd
Espoo
Finland

Vikas KUMAR
Central University of Haryana
Mahendergarh
India

Manju LATA
Chaudhary Bansi Lal University
Bhiwani
India

Axel LEGAY
UCLouvain
Ottignies-Louvain-la-Neuve
Belgium

Jean Pierre LORRÉ
Linagora Grand Sud Ouest
Toulouse
France

Mohammad MAMUN
National Research Council
of Canada
Government of Canada
Canada

Melody MOH
Department of Computer Science
San Jose State University
USA

Omar MOHAMMAD
Department of Computer Science
Lebanese International University
Bekaa
Lebanon

Robinson RAJU
Department of Computer Science
San Jose State University
USA

Nehme RMAYTI
Computer Science Department
Varna Free University
Bulgaria

Ali SABRA
Computer Science Department
Varna Free University
Bulgaria

Ramin SADRE
UCLouvain
Ottignies-Louvain-la-Neuve
Belgium

Corinna SCHMITT
Research Institute CODE
Universität der Bundeswehr
München
Neubiberg
Germany

Severin SIFFERT
Communication Systems Group
(CSG)
Department of Informatics IfI
University of Zürich UZH
Switzerland

Burkhard STILLER
Communication Systems Group
(CSG)
Department of Informatics IfI
University of Zürich UZH
Switzerland

Branislav TODOROVIC
Institute for National and
International Security (INIS)
Belgrade
Serbia

Darko TRIFUNOVIC
Institute for National and
International Security (INIS)
Belgrade
Serbia

Marvin WEBER
MNM-Team
Ludwig Maximilians Universität
München
Munich
Germany

Sava ZXIVANOVICH
Technology Partnership
Belgrade
Serbia

Index

Printed and bound by CPI Group (UK) Ltd, Croydon, CR0 4YY

27/10/2024

14580249-0003